THE POWER WITHIN!

TAP YOUR INNER FORCE AND PROGRAM YOURSELF FOR SUCCESS

James K. Van Fleet

PRENTICE HALL
Englewood Cliffs, New Jersey 07632

Prentice-Hall International (UK) Limited, *London*
Prentice-Hall of Australia Pty. Limited, *Sydney*
Prentice-Hall Canada, Inc., *Toronto*
Prentice-Hall Hispanoamericana, S.A., *Mexico*
Prentice-Hall of India Private Limited, *New Delhi*
Prentice-Hall of Japan, Inc., *Tokyo*
Simon & Schuster Asia Pte. Ltd., *Singapore*
Editora Prentice-Hall do Brasil, Ltda., *Rio de Janeiro*

© 1994 by

PRENTICE HALL

Englewood Cliffs, NJ

10 9 8 7 6 5 4 3 2 1

Library of Congress Cataloging-in-Publication Data

Van Fleet, James K.
 The power within! : tap your inner force and program yourself for
success / by James K. Van Fleet.
  p. cm.
 Includes index.
 ISBN 0-13-042946-5 (case). — ISBN 0-13-042995-3 (pbk.)
 1. Self-perception. 2. Success—Psychological aspects. 3. Self
-actualization (Psychology) I. Title.
BF697.5.S43V36 1994
158'.1—dc20   93-39089
                                                                                      CIP

ISBN 0-13-042995-3 (pbk.)

ISBN 0-13-042946-5

PRENTICE HALL
Career & Personal Development
Englewood Cliffs, NJ 07632

Simon & Schuster, A Paramount Communications Company

Printed in the United States of America

To my beloved sister, Marjorie Van Fleet Seymour,
and her husband, Ted, who brought love back into her life
when she thought it was impossible ever to love again.

OTHER BOOKS BY JAMES K. VAN FLEET

What This Book Will Do for You

This book—*THE POWER WITHIN: Tap Your Inner Force and Program Yourself for Success*—will enable you to turn your life around completely. It will help you develop the ability to achieve remarkable and spectacular successes instead of accepting average or even mediocre results.

This book is about a discovery I made that has brought me more than a satisfactory share of the good things in life. I know that when you follow the methods and techniques I outline in this book, that you, too, can gain a greater abundance of whatever it is that you most deeply desire.

For example, I know that you will be able to gain the love and respect you desire from others as well as fame, fortune, power, and vibrant good health. And you won't have to use the trial-and-error methods I did, for I carefully outline the exact route for you to follow, so you can more quickly and easily reach your goals.

Let me briefly tell you what this book is all about and exactly what it can do for you. You see, within each and every human being there is an infinite, unlimited, and powerful force that works even better than the most sophisticated computer you could ever imagine. That infinite and unlimited force within every person is the subconscious mind, *The Power Within!*

But do not think for one moment that you can compare your subconscious mind—that power within—with a man-made computer, for you cannot. The difference between the two is much too great. The man-made computer that can come anywhere near the capabilities of the power within—your subconscious mind—does not, and never will, exist.

Unfortunately, many people go through life without ever realizing that this tremendously powerful force even exists or understanding how to use it properly to get whatever they want. Only a small percentage of people ever discover that power within, understand it, and then learn how to use it to achieve complete success in whatever they set out to do.

Helping you develop your ability, not only to contact, but also to communicate with your inner power so that you can use it to become successful in everything you do is my specific purpose in writing this book. And you can become successful in all your endeavors when you understand exactly what your power within is and how you can use it for your own benefit.

Let me tell you about just a few of the good things that can be yours when you know how to use your power within properly to get what you want out of life. These few examples do not by any means constitute a complete list of all the many benefits that can be yours. They are only a small sampling of the good things that you can achieve.

- You'll discover how you can use the power within to create a positive self-image, which is so necessary for your success in whatever you choose to do.
- You'll learn how to deactivate and defuse your failure attitudes and ideas and replace them with positive thoughts and ideas that will help you gain personal power, prestige, respect, and recognition from others.
- You'll acquire techniques that will help you set goals for yourself. Without goals to achieve, you cannot succeed. It's a proven fact that people with goals in life succeed; those without goals fail.

- You'll learn how to program yourself for financial success by using two great principles. You'll also meet some people who succeeded by following these methods, including Bert Bartingale, whose small company that he founded in 1912 is still alive and well today, more than eighty years later, a remarkable record for a small business venture.

- You'll also learn how you can become highly successful in your own business. You'll see how to visualize yourself as a successful business entrepreneur and you'll meet three highly successful people who did exactly that.

- And if owning your own business doesn't interest you, you'll learn the procedures you can use to get to the top of the executive ladder in a big corporation.

- You'll learn how to use the power of your imagination to achieve success in everything that you do. You'll also discover how to work smarter—not harder! And you'll meet a man who used his creative imagination to become a highly successful speaker and author.

- You'll learn how to be a winner in everything you do. You'll be given the twenty-four specific hallmarks that mark winners as leaders and set them apart from losers.

- You'll discover that you can have a good memory even if you don't have one now. You'll find that a good memory will help you succeed in business, especially when you learn the knack of remembering people's names.

- You'll learn the primary cause of fear and worry and the techniques you can use to rid yourself of those fears and worries permanently.

- You'll acquire the techniques necessary to get rid of any undesirable habit that you have, whether it's excessive drinking, smoking, overeating, even anger and resentment toward others. You'll also learn why you can't break a bad habit with willpower, but only with imagination.

- You'll learn thirty-three self-starters you can use to stop wasting time and putting things off until tomorrow.
- You'll discover the techniques you can use to improve your health and cure emotionally induced illness, which is a real physical disease, not a mental one.
- You'll acquire the one major technique you can use to win friends and improve your personal relationships. I'll also give you lots of examples that will show how to put that technique to work for yourself.
- Lastly, in one of the most interesting chapters of this book, you'll discover how you can improve your family relationships. I'll give you the twelve secrets of lasting love that happy couples use to have a successful marriage.

Your power within—the subconscious mind—is lying there dormant, just waiting for you to use it. It is a source of energy stronger than electricity, more powerful than high explosives. Your subconscious mind is unlimited, infinite, and inexhaustible. It never rests, it keeps right on working for you even when you're asleep. You need only to activate it and put its power to work in your life so that all these marvelous benefits—and more—can be yours.

Contents

1

A Positive Self-Image: Your Key to the Power Within

All of us start out in the beginning with the same basic raw materials to create if not a perfect life for ourselves, at least a highly satisfactory one. Unfortunately, as a result of negative mental programming from our parents, teachers, preachers, and other authority figures while we are young, things go wrong and most of us end up with low self-esteem and such negative attitudes and ideas as "I can't do this," "I'm not smart enough," "I don't have enough education," and the like. Let me give you a couple of quick examples to show you exactly what I mean.

> I have a nephew in his mid thirties who cannot to this very day balance his checkbook or do a simple problem of addition or subtraction and get the right answer. When he was in elementary school, Danny's father used to bawl him out when he got a poor grade on his arithmetic paper. His father used such derogatory words and phrases as "I can't believe you're my son," "You're stupid, dumb, a real idiot," "You'll never learn," "You're a dud, a complete failure," "You'll never amount to anything." And the more his father yelled, the worse Danny's grades became.
>
> To make it even worse, the teacher used the same sort of unkind words with Danny. As a result of this criticism,

1

Danny became convinced that he just wasn't smart enough to learn arithmetic. He programmed his subconscious mind with the negative concept that he was a complete failure in math, and he has maintained that negative belief about himself for his entire life.

A couple I know have twin daughters in their teens. The one named Susan is outgoing and extremely confident. She brings home good grades in her schoolwork, gets along well with people, and is popular and welcome everywhere. There's always a long list of young boys wanting to date her. Susan has an extremely good, positive self-image.

But the other sister, Carol, is withdrawn and shy. She brings home poor grades in her schoolwork, and although she could be as attractive as her sister is, she has no interest in her appearance or the clothes she wears. As a result, never once has a boy shown any interest in her or asked her for a date. All in all, she has a completely negative attitude about herself, low self-esteem, and a poor self-image.

Why is there such a difference in these twin sisters? On numerous occasions, they overheard their parents talking about them—praising Susan to high heaven but criticizing Carol, cutting her to pieces, and putting her down.

The result of these overheard conversations was that Carol felt she was no good, that she had no abilities at all, that no one liked her, that she would probably never have a husband, and that she would be a complete failure in life. Carol is a perfect example, although in a negative sense, of the old adage, "As you believe, so shall it be done unto you." Unfortunately, this is the kind of negative self-image that far too many people develop in their lives.

Now let me give you another example that will show you how a negative attitude about one's self and a poor self-image carried over from childhood can be changed almost overnight into a positive self-image, creating almost miraculous results for the individual.

You see, a great many people are handicapped by a poverty complex that has been programmed into their subconscious minds by events and circumstances from their childhood. This alone can prevent them from achieving financial success and enjoying a full, happy, and prosperous life.

For instance, I know a very capable young doctor of veterinary medicine, Martin F., who was struggling to make ends meet in his practice. The cause of his problem was rooted deep in his childhood.

> Martin's parents had been dirt poor. There'd been many times when there wasn't enough food to eat and Martin had been forced to go to bed hungry. He wore patched hand-me-downs and clothes bought at a secondhand store.
>
> Martin did odd jobs after school to help supplement the meager family income. Whenever he wanted something extra, the answer from his parents was always the same: "We can't afford it," "We don't have the money," "We're too poor."
>
> But Martin was determined to get ahead in life and succeed. With the help of a sympathetic veterinarian for whom he had worked, who saw how much Martin loved animals and recognized Martin's potential, and with a scholarship and a job as a night watchman at the college, Martin was able to get his degree as doctor of veterinary medicine and open his own small-animal clinic.
>
> Unfortunately, Martin still thought in terms of his own childhood. His subconscious mind had been programmed by the poverty complex all those years while he was growing up. As a result, he charged only a pittance for his services, believing that people could not afford to pay him even a reasonable fee.

Finally, I was able to convince Martin that just because he'd been raised in poverty that did not mean that all his clients were poverty-stricken, too. As I told Martin, I too had worn patched clothes when I was young, and there never had been money for anything except the bare necessities. I was fortunate, though, in that I had never been forced to go to bed hungry, for my parents lived on a farm and there was always plenty of food to eat.

Martin finally realized that I was right and that his fees were entirely out of line with what his services were actually worth. After he rid himself of the poverty complex that had plagued him since his childhood, he raised them substantially. His income rose to a proper level after he learned to reprogram his subconscious mind with the proper success ideas and with a positive self-concept of his own worth.

I've told the story of Martin F. in great detail because I felt it was extremely important for you to see how changing a negative self-image to a positive one can make such a tremendous change in a person's life, sometimes almost overnight.

So if you, yourself, are troubled by a poverty problem that is a hangover from your childhood, remember that even if your parents were as poor as Martin's and mine were, that does not mean that you have to remain poor, too. All you have to do is reprogram your subconscious mind with ideas of material success and adopt a new and positive self-concept of your own worth, just as Martin did, and you can become financially independent and enjoy life to the fullest yourself.

I could give you dozens of other examples—of how F students became straight-A students, how shy and withdrawn salesclerks became positive-minded and confident of their abilities, and others that would show you how and why a positive self-image is your first key to a successful and happy life—but I am sure that these are enough to illustrate my point.

If you are having a problem with low self-esteem and a negative attitude about your self-worth and capabilities, then this chapter will help you immensely.

BENEFITS YOU WILL GAIN

- You'll learn how to create a positive self-image for yourself.
- You'll learn how to get rid of your negative attitudes and self-concepts.
- You'll gain confidence in yourself to succeed in whatever you choose to do.
- You'll learn how to make your attitude your ally instead of your enemy.
- You'll become a positive, outgoing person in control of yourself and your own life.

HOW YOUR SUBCONSCIOUS MIND CAN HELP YOU ACHIEVE A POSITIVE SELF-IMAGE

First, let me explain briefly exactly what the meaning of self-image is. The term *self-image* seems to have had its origin in the book, *Psycho-Cybernetics*, by Maxwell Maltz.*

My *Webster's Unabridged International Dictionary of the English Language,* which was published before *Psycho-Cybernetics,* does not contain the word *self-image.* However, my *Webster's New World Dictionary,* which was published after *Psycho-Cybernetics,* contains this definition: "A person's self-image is his concept of himself and his own identity, abilities, worth, etc." (Of course, this definition is applicable to both men and women, although it uses only the masculine pronoun.)

---

*Maxwell Maltz, *Psycho-Cybernetics* (Englewood Cliffs, NJ: Prentice Hall, 1960).

Whatever the origin of the term, simply said, *self-image* means what you consider yourself to be: positive or negative, extroverted and outgoing or shy and withdrawn, intelligent or dumb, handsome or ugly, a success or a failure.

Your attitudes about yourself are primarily the result of what has been programmed into your subconscious mind by your conscious mind, and also by the words and actions of your parents, teachers, friends, boss—by everyone with whom you come in contact.

It is up to you to ward off and prevent the negative comments of others from being absorbed into your subconscious mind, causing you to create a negative image of yourself that will cause you all sorts of troubles in both the present and the future. Let me explain that more fully to you now.

You see, you have two separate minds, the *conscious one* and the *subconscious one*, sometimes called the unconscious mind. Your conscious mind uses logic, deduction, and reason to reach its conclusions and make its decisions. Your choices in life, your decisions regarding what you will or will not do, are made by your conscious mind, not by your subconscious mind. However, those conscious decisions are influenced by the memories stored in your subconscious mind. I will explain the memory storage function of your subconscious mind in more detail a bit later.

But for now, let me say that, in essence, your conscious mind is the mind of your *head*, while your subconscious mind is the mind of your *heart*. Your conscious mind *thinks*; your subconscious mind *feels*.

Your conscious mind also acts as the guardian at the gate to prevent negative thoughts and ideas from reaching the subconscious mind, where they are held in permanent storage in its memory bank. But you must *actively cause* your conscious mind to act in this way. If your conscious mind allows your subconscious mind to be programmed with negative ideas, then you will develop a negative self-image and get negative results or failure in your life. But if you program your subconscious mind with positive thoughts and ideas from your conscious mind so that you create a positive self-image, then you will achieve positive results and always succeed in whatever you choose to do. Let me show you exactly how that works.

You see, your subconscious mind makes no moral judgments. It accepts whatever you send it from your conscious mind, be that positive or negative, good or bad, moral or immoral. Your subconscious mind follows the bidding of your conscious mind. If you send your subconscious mind thoughts of health and strength from your conscious mind, it will bring health and strength to your body. But if you let suggestions of disease and sickness penetrate through to your subconscious mind, either from your conscious mind or from the ideas and suggestions of others around you, then you can easily become sick yourself.

Let me give you a quick example of how susceptible your subconscious mind is to suggestions from those around you. In this case, fortunately, the subconscious mind is allowed to absorb and accept a good suggestion from another person.

Dr. Z. is one of the finest clinicians in the state of Georgia. He has served as chairman of the Department of Internal Medicine at a famous Atlanta hospital for nearly twenty years.

The hospital administrator told me that from the moment Dr. Z. enters the sickroom, the patient begins to improve. "The art of healing seems to surround his physical body like an aura," she said. "It is often not his treatment but his physical presence that actually cures the patient."

How is it possible for a sick person to get better just because of the doctor's presence? Because the sick person's subconscious mind believes that healing has happened. And as you believe, so shall it be. Remember?

Let me give you another quick example, this time of creating the wrong self-image for yourself by giving your subconscious mind improper orders or negative suggestions that will cause you to fail. For instance, if your conscious mind tells your subconscious mind that you are poor and can never afford a big house or a new car, you can rest assured that you will never have either of them, or anything else worthwhile for that matter, for you will have given your subconscious mind the wrong goals to reach. (I will tell you in complete detail how you can give your subconscious mind the right goals and the proper objectives in Chapter Three.)

Program Your Subconscious Mind with Positive Thoughts and Ideas

The reason it is so important to program your subconscious mind with positive success thoughts and ideas rather than negative failure ones is that your subconscious mind *is your permanent memory bank.* Your subconscious mind never forgets anything. Information that has been fed into your subconscious mind is kept stored in it forever, even though there are times when your conscious mind cannot seem to recall that information immediately.

But even if your conscious mind may not be able to remember some name, event, or incident, that does not mean the item has been forgotten. The information stored in your subconscious mind is never lost unless you take active steps to erase it. Sometimes a bit more effort is required for your conscious mind to bring it up to the surface, that's all.

This does not mean that improper information stored in your subconscious cannot be changed. It can, but only when you override that negative idea with new and positive concepts to take its place. You literally must tell your subconscious mind that certain information in it is improper and then give it the order to erase it permanently. Only then will it be erased from your memory or at least controlled—in the case of Martin F., his poverty complex from childhood was not forgotten, but it was pushed down and overridden by his new ideas of successful achievement. It no longer held any power to influence his actions.

YOUR SELF-IMAGE DETERMINES YOUR SUCCESS OR FAILURE

As I am sure you can see, if you have a negative self-image programmed into the memory storage of your subconscious mind, you are bound to fail. However, if you have a positive self-image programmed into the memory storage of your subconscious mind, you are bound to succeed. In fact, you cannot fail, for it is literally impossible for you to have a positive self-image and fail. The two are absolutely incompatible.

Let me give you this simple example here: You may not be a farmer or even have a small garden in your backyard, but I'm sure you realize that you cannot plant corn and get a crop other than corn. This is simply saying that nothing can come from corn but corn, and nothing from weeds but weeds.

The same is true of your subconscious mind. You cannot plant negative ideas of failure in it and expect to become successful. If you want to be successful in life, then you must plant positive ideas and concepts in your subconscious mind. Only then will you be able to develop a positive self-image that will ensure your success.

Most people understand this law in the physical world, even if they are not farmers or have never raised a single vegetable in their entire lives, but few persons really understand it in the mental world, although its operation there is just as exact and undeviating as it is in the physical world. Therefore, they do not cooperate with it in the mental world.

Once you realize that *humans are the only ones of God's creatures who is allowed to finish the act of their own creation*, you will understand how you are responsible for what you become. Let me now give you six small words that will open the door to success for you if you use them constantly:

YOU BECOME WHAT YOU THINK ABOUT

That is how you finish the act of your own creation. To help you better understand that concept, let me point out the differences between a negative self-image and a positive one. First I want to give you . . .

The Six Characteristics of a Negative Self-Image

1. Low Self-esteem. That is to say, you regard yourself as worthless or of no value either to yourself or to anyone else. This attitude can easily lead to suicidal tendencies or even actual suicide, especially in discouraged teen- agers. I have personally known three boys in their late teens who took their own lives.

2. Lack of Drive and Enthusiasm. This often happens when a person is given a job to do for which he lacks the basic abilities. It can also occur if the job is far below the indi- vidual's capabilities, resulting in boredom.

3. Tendency to Procrastinate. This can come from many sources: laziness, inability to do the job, lack of interest in the work, failure to establish priorities, and so on.

4. Negative Attitudes and Emotions. These program your subconscious mind improperly with pessimistic ideas of failure instead of optimistic and positive ideas of success. You cannot possibly succeed when you harbor negative ideas and emotions in your mind. Remember always that *you become what you think about.*

5. Shy and Withdrawn Behavior. This type of behavior can result from hurt feelings in childhood, criticism from parents, and insults and ridicule from peers, teachers, employers, and so on.

6. Self-indulgent Actions. These include smoking, overeat- ing, drinking to excess, gambling, promiscuity, and the like.

The end result of these six negative characteristics is a completely negative self-image. But do not despair. Even if you find yourself in this dismal category, all is not lost. I'm going to give you the basic tools you can use to wipe the slate clean, to free yourself from the negative influences of your past, and to take full control of yourself and your new life in the days ahead.

To help you program your subconscious mind with positive thoughts and ideas so that you can replace the negative concepts that you have allowed to infiltrate it, I'm going to give you now . . .

The Six Characteristics of a Positive Self-Image

1. **High Self-esteem.** This can be developed by learning to like yourself. Many people thoroughly dislike themselves and will never develop a positive self-image until they change that negative attitude about themselves and learn not only to like themselves but also to love themselves. In Matthew 12:31, we are told by Jesus that you shall love your neighbor as yourself. So a bit later on I'm going to give you some techniques that you will find invaluable in learning not only to like but also to love yourself.

2. **Ambition and Goal Orientation.** You'll become ambitious and set goals for yourself when you adopt a positive self-image. Establishing a goal gives you a mission to achieve and an objective to reach. People without goals merely drift along in life and get nowhere. But when you have a concrete goal to reach, your daily work becomes meaningful and worthwhile instead of being just a monotonous, humdrum job.

3. **Organization and Efficiency.** No longer will you drift aimlessly through the day and procrastinate, putting things off. A good habit to develop to keep yourself from procrastinating and wasting time is to have your in- and out-boxes completely empty at the end of your working day. But don't wait until four o'clock to unload your out-box on some poor subordinate. Keep your desk cleared throughout the day.

4. **A "Can-Do" Attitude.** This attitude will be automatic when you adopt a positive self-image. And "can-do" people are highly sought after as managers in both business and industry, for they are rare indeed.

5. **Outgoing Personality.** Instead of being shy, withdrawn, and backward, when you program your subconscious mind with a positive self-image, you'll reach out to the world.

6. **Self-control.** You'll be in control of your entire life when you rid yourself of self-indulgent habits such as smoking, overeating, drinking to excess, and the like. Instead of being controlled by your bad habits, you can be free of them completely.

Whether they realize it or not, all high achievers program their subconscious minds with these six major characteristics of a positive self-image. If you yourself practice them faithfully, you can achieve whatever you really want in life. You can improve your health, increase your energy, heighten your physical and mental well-being, and, yes, you can even lose weight, quit smoking, stop excessive drinking, and get rid of any other of your undesirable habits. You can also improve your personality and become a kinder, more patient, more loving—and more lovable—person.

LIKING YOURSELF IS ESSENTIAL TO SUCCESS

If you don't like yourself, then no one else will like you either. But if you do like yourself, so will everyone else. A positive self-image will lead you to be an optimistic, outgoing person with an excellent attitude toward others and a healthy outlook on life.

Now there is a marked difference between liking yourself and being an arrogant, conceited person, and there is an easy way to tell the difference between the two. If you like yourself without being conceited or arrogant about it, you will not consider yourself better than others. If you look down on people with the attitude that they are not as good as you are, then it's a cinch that you will be a conceited, arrogant, overbearing person whom no one likes.

If you want to like yourself but not become conceited or arrogant about it, then I would recommend that you should never compare yourself with others. This is extremely dangerous ground and you'll take a big fall if you compare yourself with others, because no matter how much money you make, how smart you are, or how good-looking you are, comparing yourself with other people is one of the quickest ways to program your subconscious mind with failure attitudes and negative ideas.

When you compare yourself with others, you will be constantly programming your subconscious mind with negative thoughts like these: "She's more beautiful than I am," "He's a lot smarter than I am," "She makes a lot more money than I do." Such ideas eventually lead to even more negative concepts such as, "I'm ugly," "I'm dumb," "I'm poor," "I'm a failure."

How can you stop this from happening to you? Easy. Never, and I do repeat *never*, compare yourself with other people. Compete only with yourself. For example, if you're a salesperson, don't worry about being the top one in your company. Strive only to improve your previous week's performance by increasing your own sales. If you're on the company bowling team, don't concern yourself about being the best bowler. Just work to improve your last week's score. Do that, and sooner or later, you'll become the top salesperson, or the best bowler, or whatever else it is you're trying to do.

Now let me give you some specific techniques.

Nine Steps Toward Liking Yourself

1. **Never, and I Repeat, Never Criticize Yourself.** Criticism never changes a single thing for the better. So refuse to criticize yourself for any of your past mistakes. Accept yourself exactly as you are. Everybody changes, either

for the better or for the worse. When you criticize your-self, your changes in attitude and behavior will be nega-tive. But when you approve of yourself, the changes will be positive.

2. **Don't Frighten Yourself with Thoughts of the Future.** Stop scaring yourself with thoughts of what the future might hold for you. What you're imagining may never come true. Worrying about the future is a horrible way to live. So think of something that gives you pleasure in the present and immediately change your scary future thought to a pleasant present thought. As an old man on his deathbed once told me, "My entire life has been filled with terrible troubles, most of which never happened to me."

3. **Be Gentle and Patient with Yourself.** Be gentle with your-self, and be patient as you learn these new ideas and ways of thinking about how to like yourself. Treat yourself as you would someone whom you really love deeply.

4. **Be Kind to Yourself.** Self-hatred is only hating your own thoughts about yourself or what you have done wrong in the past. Don't hate yourself for having those negative thoughts. Gently change your negative thoughts and atti-tudes to positive ones.

5. **Praise Yourself.** Criticism breaks down the inner spirit; praise builds it up. Praise yourself as much and as often as you can. Tell yourself how well you are doing with every little thing that you accomplish.

6. **Support Yourself.** Find ways to support yourself and build up your morale. Reach out to friends and allow them to help you, too. You are being strong and showing courage when you ask for help when you need it.

7. **Be Loving to Your Negative Thoughts.** Acknowledge that you are the one who created those negative ideas and atti-tudes to fill a need. You must find new and positive ways to fulfill your needs. Let go of those old negative patterns that are hurting you now.

8. **Take Care of Your Body.** To really love yourself, you must take care of your body. Learn about nutrition. What kind of fuel does your body need to have optimum energy and vitality? Learn about exercise. What kind of exercise can you do and really enjoy it? Cherish and revere the temple that God gave you to live in.

9. **Really Love Yourself and Do It Right Now.** Don't wait until you get well, lose weight, get that new job you want, or find that new relationship. Begin right now and do the best you can.

Learn to Love Yourself With the Mirror Technique

Practicing mirror work is another way you can learn not only to like but also to love yourself. Look into your eyes often in the mirror throughout the day and say out loud, "I love you; I really do love you." Do this the first thing in the morning and the last thing at night. Do it often during the day. If uncomfortable feelings come up, let them pass through.

While looking in the mirror, forgive yourself for your mistakes. Forgive your parents, your spouse, your children, too. When you look in the mirror, say, "I love you; I really do love you." If these affirmations feel strange to you at first, do them anyway. *Act as if it were true and it will become true.*

If something happens that is unpleasant for you, immediately go to your mirror, look at yourself, and say, "It's all right. Don't worry; I really do love you." Look into your eyes in the mirror when you've made a mistake and say, "I forgive you and I still love you."

If something wonderful happens, go to your mirror and say to your reflection, "That's terrific; thank you!" Acknowledge yourself and give yourself credit for the good things that happen in your life.

You can use the mirror to talk to other people, too. Tell them the things you are afraid to tell them in person. Tell them you want their love and approval. If you have a problem with what they have done to you, tell them that in the mirror, too. Get it off your chest. Don't hold it inside of you to fester and grow. Get it out of your system.

I know these new procedures of liking yourself and using mirror work will seem strange and uncomfortable to you, perhaps even silly, at first. But when you practice these techniques consistently, you will find you can make great changes in yourself and in your personality in a very short time.

TEN SIMPLE RULES FOR A PERFECT DAY

To develop a positive and outgoing self-image, you must learn not only to like yourself but also to expect a good day rather than a rotten one. I don't care if it's cloudy and gloomy, raining or snowing, if you will follow these rules for a perfect day, it will be exactly that for you. As my father used to say, "When it starts raining inside the house, I'll start worrying, but not until then." He lived a long and productive life without worrying about things, for it never did start raining inside the house.

Before I give you the specific techniques for how to have a perfect day, let me give you these tips about how to get rid of the worries of yesterday and tomorrow:

> There are two days in every week about which you should not worry, two days that should be kept free from fear and apprehension. One of these days is yesterday, with its mistakes and cares, its faults and blunders, its aches and pains. Yesterday has passed forever beyond your control. All the money in the world cannot buy back yesterday. You cannot undo a single act you performed. You cannot erase a single word that you said. Yesterday is gone forever, beyond recall.
>
> The other day you should not worry about is tomorrow, with its possible adversities, its burdens, its large promise, and perhaps its poor performance. Tomorrow is also

beyond your immediate control. Tomorrow's sun will rise, either in splendor or behind a mask of clouds, but it will rise. Until it does, you have no stake in tomorrow, for it is yet unborn.

This leaves only one day for you to worry about— *today.* Anyone can fight the battles of just one day. It is only when you and I add the burden of those two awful eternities, yesterday and tomorrow, that we break down in despair.

It is not the experience of today that drives people mad. It is the remorse or the bitterness for something that happened yesterday or the dread of what tomorrow might bring. Therefore, do your best to *live only one day at a time.*

I am sure you can see from this that it is impossible for you to develop a positive self-image if you waste your time worrying about yesterday's mistakes or tomorrow's possible errors. The only time you can ever improve yourself and develop that positive self-image that you need to succeed is right now, today, the *ever present now,* so do exactly that.

And to make sure you do exactly that, follow these rules for a perfect day:

1. Just for Today, live through this day only, and don't tackle your whole life's challenges at once.

2. Just for Today, choose to be happy. You can be as happy as you make up your mind to be; remember that happiness comes from within, not from outside yourself.

3. Just for Today, adjust yourself to what is. Don't try to adjust everything to your own desires.

4. Just for Today, take care of your body. Exercise it, care for it, nourish it. Do not abuse or neglect it, so it will be in perfect harmony with your will.

5. Just for Today, exercise your spirit in four ways: (1) Do someone a good turn and not be recognized for it. (2) Do at least two challenging things to help develop your

willpower. (3) Don't harbor negative feelings toward anyone. (4) Work on developing your positive self-image.

6. Just for Today, strengthen your mind. Study to learn something new and useful. Read something worthwhile that requires effort, thought, and concern.

7. Just for Today, be agreeable. Look as good as you can, dress becomingly, talk low, act courteously, and be liberal with your praise toward everyone.

8. Just for Today, have a program to follow. Set goals for yourself to achieve. This will save you from two pests: indecision and hurry. Remember that old saying, "The hurrier I go, the behinder I get."

9. Just for Today, take a half hour all by yourself to reflect upon God in whatever form you understand that to be so that you can get a better understanding of your own life.

10. Just for Today, be happy. Enjoy what is beautiful. Be willing to love and to be loved by others.

Here are a few final tips on how to achieve a positive self-image.

1. **Feel Important and Look Important.** Your appearance tells others what you think of yourself. If you look important and have a good appearance, you will project a positive self-image. Your subordinates will view you as an important person who is intelligent, capable, and dependable. Their attitudes toward you will reflect back to you and cause your positive self-image to grow.

2. **Think That Your Work Is Important.** Remember that as you think, so shall you believe; you become what you think about. When you think that your work is important, you will receive mental signals from your subconscious mind on how to do your work even better. If you think that your work is important that way, then your subordinates

will think that their work is important, too, and they'll do a better job for you.

3. **Give Yourself a Pep Talk.** Do this several times a day. Think up some sort of a "sell-yourself-to-yourself" commercial. Remind yourself at every chance you get that you really are a first-class person.

4. **Remember That You Become What You Think About.** Ask yourself, "Is this the way an important person with a positive self-image thinks?" If you can't answer "yes" to that question, then change your way of thinking so that you can.

If you remember nothing else from this chapter, then please do remember that *you become what you think about.* If you keep that stored in your memory, then you will be able to develop a positive self-image.

2

How to Program
Yourself for Success
with the Psychology of
Self-Achievement

Strange as it might seem, the majority of people fail to achieve anything really worthwhile in their lives. Why is that? Well, there are two major reasons: First of all, many people have programmed themselves with failure concepts and ideas or allowed themselves to be programmed by the negative ideas of others so that failure, not success, becomes inevitable for them. Second, some people just coast along not living up to their potential simply because they act as lazy as they dare to and still get by.

In this chapter, then, I want to give you the steps you can take to deactivate those failure concepts and ideas that are embedded so deeply in the memory storage banks of your subconscious mind. After that, I'll show you how to program yourself for success once you've been able to deactivate your subconscious mind's failure mechanism. Then, in Chapter Three, you'll see how establishing concrete goals with the psychology of self-achievement will help you become successful in whatever you set out to do.

But before we go any further, I think I should give you my definitions of *success* and *failure.* It could well be that our definitions of these two words are not quite the same.

Most people in these United States think that if you have a lot of money, you are successful. But that is really putting the cart before the horse, as the old saying goes. In other words, you must first be successful in your chosen profession before you can realize great financial rewards.

Let me quickly add that a person does not have to be rich to be considered to be successful. Actually, the best definition of success is this: *Success is the progressive realization of a worthy ideal.*

For example, if a person is working toward a specific goal that she has picked out for herself, then she is a success. A success is that individual who is a plumber, a mechanic, musician, salesperson, whatever, not because she has to be that but because that's what she wants to be. She is a success because that is the profession or occupation that she really wanted to be in and that she has chosen for herself.

For example, I have a son-in-law who is a schoolteacher because that is what he always wanted to be. He loves children and loves the opportunity he has to help them grow and become worthwhile citizens. Is he rich as a result of his profession? No, at least not in dollars and cents. Is he successful? Yes, he most certainly is, because he is doing what he wants to do and he excels at what he is doing. He is in the profession that he chose and he is a real professional at it, no doubt about that.

A success is also the housewife and mother who wanted to be a housewife and mother and who is doing an outstanding job of doing exactly that. In other words, then, the successful person is the one who is deliberately doing whatever he or she really wanted to do, and not what someone else—a father or mother, for instance—wanted him or her to do.

You can be successful financially, but a miserable failure in life because you are not doing what you want to do. For example, I know a medical doctor who is a doctor not because he wanted to be one but because his father insisted that he become one. Why? Because his father was a frustrated person who wanted to become an M.D., but he lacked the money necessary to get through medical school. So he became a pharmacist instead.

And what is the son's attitude? Here's what he told me: Frankly, Jim, I don't enjoy medicine at all, for I can't stand the sight of blood. I let my nurse draw blood and give shots. All I do is talk to the patient and write prescriptions. Now that my dad is gone, I'm going back to college so I can get my Ph.D. in biochemistry. I won't be satisfied until I do. I've always wanted to teach in college, so that's exactly what I'm going to do.

So even though Doctor Jeff has plenty of money, he is not really successful. He's a failure because he's not doing what he really wants to do in life.

A failure is also someone who has the talent and the ability to accomplish much more than he has. But he's just plain lazy, merely drifting along, not living up to his fullest potential. Therefore, he is a failure, no matter how high his position is or what his income might be.

Now if you are an *unwilling* victim of that failure syndrome because of past negative programming of your subconscious mind by others, and you want to make a change for the better, then this chapter will most certainly do wonders for you.

BENEFITS YOU WILL GAIN

- When you deactivate and defuse the failure attitudes and negative ideas that have been programmed into your subconscious mind's memory banks, you'll be able to replace them with positive thoughts and ideas. Then you can channel your energy and your efforts in the right direction so that you can become successful in everything you do.

- When you learn how to reprogram your subconscious mind with positive thoughts and ideas, you'll be able to concentrate on worthwhile goals instead of wasting your time on objectives of secondary or negligible importance.

- Your self-esteem will soar and you'll develop a positive self-image as you find out that you can succeed at whatever task you undertake to do, no matter how difficult it might seem to you at first.

- Personal power, prestige, respect, and recognition from others, along with financial rewards, will all be yours as you establish a positive self-image and rid yourself of those failure attitudes and negative ideas that previously held you captive.

HOW TO DEPROGRAM YOUR MIND OF FAILURE IDEAS AND NEGATIVE ATTITUDES

As I told you in the first chapter, whatever is programmed into your subconscious mind will never completely be forgotten. It will always be retained for recall by your conscious mind. This means, then, that if you (or someone else, if you have allowed them to) have been feeding failure ideas and negative concepts into your subconscious mind, you are going to get back negative thoughts of fear and failure, for output always equals input.

Just as is true in the physical world, *you will reap what you sow.* You cannot plant negative ideas in your subconscious mind and expect to get positive results any more than you could expect to plant corn in your garden and get peas. As I have said already, *you become what you think about.*

Or if you have been just coasting along, taking it easy, being as lazy as you dare to be and still get by, completely unwilling to make the extra effort required for successful achievement, then your subconscious mind will coast along, too. Don't expect any brilliant ideas or inspiration to strike when you have that sort of attitude. Success usually consists of 2 percent inspiration and 98 percent perspiration.

You can, however, override those negative concepts that you have stored in your subconscious mind when you start programming it with success ideas instead of failure ideas. The moment you do that, your subconscious mind realizes that you are no longer interested in failure, so it begins to bury those attitudes and ideas deeper and deeper into your memory banks. Even though those memories will always be retained, they will never surface to bother you again *unless your conscious mind allows them to do so.* For all practical purposes, they will have been completely forgotten by your subconscious mind.

How, then, can you accomplish such an important change in your subconscious mind? Remembering that you become what you think about, *you must think about how you can be successful instead of being a failure.* Here is a very simple concept you can use to do that. Simply said, that rule to success is this:

ACT AS IF IT WERE IMPOSSIBLE TO FAIL

Once you realize that you do become what you think about, this simple formula is precisely what you need to make a complete about face from a dismal failure to an outstanding success.

This does not mean that you will not encounter some temporary defeats along the way; you no doubt will. But that doesn't mean that you have lost the war; it only means that you have lost one little battle. Every time you try a method that does not work, you will know to cross that one off your list and try again. That's exactly what Edison did, and the end result was the electric light.

So if you feel blue because your boss didn't like the suggestion you gave him, or if you have the blahs because you feel everyone has rejected you and your ideas, you're in good company.

Beethoven, Rembrandt, James Joyce, Abraham Lincoln, yes, and especially, the Father of Our Country, George Washington, went through the same low valleys of despair before they finally succeeded—but succeed they did, because they wouldn't give up.

In addition to those people, let me now tell you about some others who practiced the technique of acting as if it were impossible to fail, all of whom became highly successful in spite of temporary defeat and rejection.

Grace Metalius, author of *Peyton Place*, a highly successful novel and television series, saw her novel turned down fourteen times before it was finally published.

Irving Stone's first book was about van Gogh. He took it to the prestigious publishing firm of Alfred Knopf. "They never even opened it," he said. "The package containing the manuscript got home before I did!" Then he took it to Doubleday. Everyone liked it except the marketing division. The salespeople there said, "There's no way we can sell a book about an *unknown* Dutch painter." After fifteen more rejections, the book, *Lust for Life*, was finally accepted and published in 1934. It has now sold more than twenty-five million copies!

Dr. Seuss, the creator of a whole menagerie of lovable floppy creatures, many of whom have strayed into radio and TV, survived initial rejection by two dozen publishers.

Gone With the Wind suffered thirty-eight rejections by various publishers. But finally, a conscientious editor at Macmillan saw the manuscript and went to Atlanta, Georgia, to encourage the author, Margaret Mitchell, not to give up. After that, no other publisher ever had an opportunity to see the book again.

James M. Cain's novel *The Postman Always Rings Twice* was not about the postal service at all. It was about sex. When asked about the title, Cain explained that he had given his book its odd name because before it was accepted for publication, it was rejected over and over. Each day the postman brought another letter of rejection, he always rang the doorbell twice.

A Grammy Award went to Joe Brooks, who wrote the words and music for the phenomenally successful song "You Light Up My Life." At the presentation ceremony, he said, "As

I look out there tonight, I can't help but think that just about every company in this audience turned this song down. As a matter of fact, about ten of you turned it down twice, so I must admit that this award tastes oh-so-sweet."

The Muppet Show, created by the late Jim Henson and his wife, is perhaps the best-loved contemporary television program in the entire world, yet for nearly two decades it was initially rejected by every network that it was offered to!

So never give up. When you act as if it were impossible to fail and program your subconscious mind with that positive idea, you, too, can survive temporary defeats and succeed in life, just as these people did.

Let me also point out here that it is ever so important to use positive words in reprogramming your subconscious mind for success instead of failure. For instance, you should never make such statements as "I am not a failure." *Defeat* is the picture going into your subconscious mind when you use negative words such as *not, never,* and *failure.*

Negative words and thoughts will not reprogram your subconscious mind properly even though you try to use them in a positive manner. You should always use positive words to program your subconscious mind for successful achievement. Instead of saying, "I am not a failure," say instead, "I am an outstanding success!"

I have gone through some temporary defeats, too. Although I had already had a successful career as a management consultant before I decided to become a writer, that did not mean my manuscripts were automatically going to be accepted. To tell you the truth, I have had my share of rejections by publishers, too.

I realized that I would have to do some additional study and research into this new field. So I searched for various books by famous authors to study. I found one that was supposed to contain practical advice for budding writers by about forty well-known and world-famous authors. However, I soon found that most of their advice seemed to be that a beginning writer ought to take up some other profession to earn his living!

One chapter by a prominent New York publishing company's editor-in-chief said that out of every ten books published, only one makes money, two break even, and seven lose money!

"So don't become a writer," he said, "unless you have some other means of support." Then about a third of the way through this dismal book, I read these words by one of the most prominent and well-known authors of the last forty years: "The odds against the beginning writer being published are about 50,000 to 1," he wrote. I threw the book away, for it was far too depressing. I just don't see any sense in reading books that tell people how to fail. I can do that well enough on my own without any outside help!

But I stuck with it and eventually I was published. That was more than a dozen books ago and I haven't quit yet, for I, too, use the principle of *acting as if it were impossible to fail.*

I wanted to tell you this because I especially want to suggest that you not read books on how to fail. Read instead books like this one that tell you how you can succeed.

HOW TO AVOID THE FEAR OF FAILURE

Psychologists have found that the *fear of failure* is a businessperson's biggest stumbling block and his greatest obstacle to successful achievement. And the fear of failure is not limited to businesspeople. From my observations after many years of studying why people say and do the things they say and do, I know that the fear of failure is the biggest psychological stumbling block of every single living person.

A person fears failure because she fears that she'll be ridiculed; she fears the possibility of being laughed at. That's why an amateur writer will finish a manuscript, put it in the desk drawer to gather mold and mildew, and never mail it off to a publisher. When she does this, she's not running the risk of rejection and humiliation. As long as her manuscript is safe in the desk drawer, she can dream and pretend all day long.

I personally know an aspiring writer who has been working on a travel book for more than ten years now. He is constantly revising it and bringing it up to date. Since he is retired, his entire day is occupied with doing that. He attends annual writers' conferences, listens to talks by editors and published writers, and enjoys rubbing elbows with them. Will he ever have his manuscript published and made into a book? Not a chance, at least according to his lovely and patient wife. "Keeps him busy and out of mischief," she told me. "He's happy with his daydreams, and I am, too. As long as he's working on that book, he doesn't have time to worry about his heart, his blood pressure, his stomach, or any other possible ailment for that matter."

The fear of failure is the reason unsuccessful salespeople spend so much time at coffee call or just sitting in the office reading the newspaper or shooting the breeze. They don't want to get out and make a call on a prospect because they're so deathly afraid of failing and not making a sale.

But to do something is far better than to do nothing, even if it's wrong. Remember, all you need do is act as if it were impossible to fail. If you do stumble once in a while, just remember that a single fall doesn't mean that you're awkward or clumsy.

For instance, if your son flunks a math test, that doesn't mean he's a failure at math. Or if your daughter fails one spelling test, that doesn't mean that she's incompetent at her schoolwork. Or if I get a writing proposal back from the publisher with a letter of rejection, that doesn't mean that I'm a failure as a writer. It only means that one particular manuscript didn't sell at that one specific moment in time. That's all it means: that, and nothing more.

The Importance of Doing the Thing You Fear

Let's examine now this technique at some length. If you do the thing you fear to do, then you will have the power to do it. But if you do not do the thing you fear to do, then you will never gain the power to do it. It is just that simple. For instance, if you want to be a painter, you must first paint. Daydreaming won't make you a famous and successful artist. Until you actually pick up the brush and start painting, you will never gain the power to do it.

If you want to be a successful writer, then you must write. If you want to be an expert swimmer, then you must swim. The same statement can be made about golf, baseball, skiing, sales, science, medicine, music, management, and on and on. Whatever it is that you want to gain the power to do and become proficient at, you must make the first move yourself. Until you do that, you'll never gain the power to do anything.

For instance, speaking to an audience strikes fear in the heart of nearly everyone at first. I know that I nearly panicked the first time I stood up in front of a large group of people to speak to them. My throat was dry, my voice was hoarse and raspy, my palms were sweaty, and my heart pounded.

But as soon as I spoke the first sentence, I felt better. And as I continued to speak, my fears began to fade away. Confidence came back to me, for as soon as I did the thing I feared to do, I gained the power to do it. Now I'm able to speak to audiences of fifteen hundred and more without the slightest bit of fear.

I know you can be helped to do the thing you fear to do because I have been able to help so many other people do exactly that. Let me give you just two quick examples.

Henry J., a Jacksonville, Florida, salesman, wrote me to say:

> After I heard your talk on how to get rid of the fear of people, I felt I could take on anyone. Last week I walked into the office of a really tough purchasing agent—a man I'd always feared and who'd never once given me an order. Before he could tell me to get out, I had my samples spread out on his desk. First time I'd ever had the courage to open my case in his office. Well, he gave me one of the biggest orders I've ever received. Why? Because my attitude was

positive and confident. I was no longer afraid of him, and he knew it.

Jennifer S., a shy Orlando salesclerk, wrote me this:

I was so afraid of customers I gave them the idea that I was apologizing to them for waiting on them. I was even afraid to come hear you talk. I was afraid someone I knew might see me there and laugh at me. Then I was scared to death to try your idea of doing the thing I was afraid of doing so I would have the power to do it, but I finally managed to scrape up the courage to do it. Amazingly, it worked!

Now I'm confident of myself. My self-image is positive, and I feel I could whip the world if I had to. The sales manager has been so impressed by my performance that she told me to start thinking about taking over the management of one of the departments.

Now doing the thing you fear to do so you can have the power to do it is not really humankind's idea alone. It is actually a law of nature. For instance, when you see birds fly, you would think that it is automatic for them to do so. But that is not true at all. Let me tell you how I discovered that.

One year a robin built a nest just outside my study window. I watched the growth of this robin's family, from the eggs in the nest until the day when four little heads popped up demanding to be fed. And then, one by one, the mother robin nudged her babies off into the air when the right moment came.

But one little fellow was so afraid he couldn't fly that he cringed in terror in the nest and refused to even look over its edge. It took him nearly a week longer than the others until finally the mother had to force him out of the nest into the air.

And when she did, he suddenly flapped his tiny wings and flew awkwardly away. Now no one had taught him to fly;

nature had put that instinct in him. But still, he had to fly before he had the power to do so, for that is the law of nature. It is nature's way of doing things.

The same principle applies to you and me. We must do the thing we fear before we can gain the power to do it. And that's the truth, strange though it might sound at first.

Never Listen to Other People's Negative Ideas

An extremely important point that you should remember about your subconscious mind is that it will accept suggestions and take orders not only from your own conscious mind but also from outside sources *when your conscious mind is bypassed*; that is, if you allow that to happen. Let me show you now by a very simple example exactly how this can work.

Let's imagine that you're on a luxurious vacation cruise to the Bahamas. You go up to a timid-looking passenger and say something like this: "You look very ill. Your face is terribly pale. You're evidently getting seasick. If you would like, I'll help you to your cabin."

This person, who has been deathly afraid all the time about getting seasick, now becomes extremely ill, all as a result of the negative suggestion you've planted in his subconscious mind.

But if you made that same suggestion to a seasoned seagoing traveler or to a sailor, she would probably laugh at you. After many voyages, she knows she has nothing at all to worry about. Therefore, her conscious mind rejects your negative suggestion, and she does not allow it to enter her subconscious mind.

I have traveled across the ocean many times, both the Atlantic and Pacific, and I have never gotten sick once, not even in the roughest seas. My wife, however, always gets seasick as soon as she gets on board, even before the ship leaves port. She spends her entire trip in our cabin eating soda crackers.

Why the difference? Well, her parents, who were adamantly opposed to her taking an ocean voyage, constantly programmed her subconscious mind with the idea that she would be seasick all the time, that being out on the ocean out of sight of land would be extremely dangerous, and on and on. So her subconscious mind absorbed all those negative suggestions from her parents as well as from her midwestern friends in Iowa, who had never seen an ocean and didn't even know what seasickness really is. As a result, she gets seasick the moment she sees an ocean, even if she isn't on a ship. I have often kidded her, saying: it's surprising that she doesn't get seasick in a bathtub.

But I have never accepted such negative ideas—not even when the ship sailed up the western coast of Canada from Seattle to Alaska and rolled from side to side, as well as from stem to stern, and the dining room was always empty because all of the passengers were seasick. I had been warned that even seasoned sailors get seasick on this part of the voyage, but I continued to eat like a horse, three full meals a day with snacks in the afternoon and evening, and I never once had even the slightest hint of sickness. My only problem with sailing is that I usually gain ten pounds and then have to diet like mad when I'm back home again.

Now I want to give you a classic example of a person who knew how to play upon people's fears and program their subconscious minds successfully for his own benefit.

I used this example of John Wesley, the founder of the Methodist faith, in one of my previous books,* but it is such a classic example of programming the subconscious mind that it is appropriate here, too. If you have read it before in my previous book, please bear with me and read it again. The repetition will be most valuable to you.

John Wesley enjoyed enormous success as an English evangelist. He had a shrewd and intuitive understanding of the inner workings of both the conscious and subconscious minds.

---

*James K. Van Fleet, *Hidden Power: How to Unleash the Power of Your Subconscious Mind* (West Nyack, NY: Parker, 1987).

He would open his sermon with a long and vivid description of the agonies and torture that his listeners would suffer for all eternity unless they became converted to the faith. Then, after a sense of terror, guilt, and extreme anxiety had brought his audience to the brink of a complete nervous breakdown, he would offer eternal salvation to those who accepted Christ and repented of their sins.

By this kind of "hellfire and damnation" preaching, Wesley converted hundreds and thousands of people. Intense, prolonged fear exhausted their nervous systems and produced a state of greatly intensified suggestibility. In this vulnerable condition people accepted his theological message without question. They emerged from this religious ordeal with new behavior patterns firmly planted in their subconscious minds.

So let me conclude this section by saying that you'll get all kinds of negative advice from people. You'll constantly hear comments like these: "It'll never work," "You can't do it," "That's impossible," "Don't waste your time trying it." Don't listen to trash like this. Don't let negative-minded people clutter up your subconscious mind. Let it go in one ear and out the other, or better yet, plug both ears so you'll never hear their negative comments at all.

Never Place Artificial Limits on Yourself

This is another way of programming your subconscious mind with negative thoughts and ideas. You can place artificial limits on yourself in many ways that will prevent you from attaining the results you really want. One of the most common ways is to give yourself a goal that is below your capabilities. Another is to be too easily satisfied and to accept the minimum instead of going for the maximum. Let me give you a quick example of that.

Robert Pierce, a business management and sales consultant, told me this story from his own personal experience. Although the amount of money mentioned in Robert's story has long ago been made obsolete by the passage of time and inflation, the principle involved still holds true today.

I had been called in as a sales consultant to a particular company. The sales manager called my attention to a most remarkable case. One of their salespeople always managed to make almost exactly $20,000 a year, regardless of the territory to which he was assigned or the amount of commissions that he was paid.

Because this salesman had done well in a small territory, we gave him a larger and more lucrative one. But the next year his commissions amounted to almost the same amount that he had made in the previous territory— $20,000.

The following year we increased the commissions we paid to all our salespeople, but this man still made exactly $20,000. He was then assigned to one of our poorest sales territories, and guess what. He again made his usual $20,000!

Well, I had a talk with him and found out that the trouble was not in his assigned territory but in his own evaluation of himself. He had always thought of himself as being a $20,000-a-year man, and as long as he held that self-image in his subconscious mind, outside conditions didn't seem to make any difference to him at all.

When he was given a poor territory, he worked hard to make his $20,000. When he was assigned a good territory, he found all sorts of excuses to coast when his goal of $20,000 was in sight. Once, when his goal had been reached too early in the year, he got sick and was unable to work any more, although doctors could find nothing physically wrong with him. Amazingly, he recovered completely by the first of the next year.

Upon my suggestion, he received some counseling from our company psychologist, who helped him figure out what his problem was. It seems that in his salesmanship class in college, the instructor had always used the figure of $20,000 as representing ultimate success. His subconscious mind accepted that figure as the top of his ability, so he was always satisfied with that.

Today, he has reprogrammed himself to establish higher monetary goals, and his commissions are now over $70,000 a year—all because he gave himself a new and more positive self-image.

You can see from this example that *we really do become what we think about!*

WHY NOTHING SUCCEEDS LIKE SUCCESS!

Programming yourself for success is important in deactivating and defusing your subconscious mind's failure attitudes and ideas. In addition, an actual goal to reach is required. To reach a goal, some action is necessary. You must do more than just think about it. You must actually do something; you must take action of some sort.

I can well remember to this day—and it has been more years than I care to think about—when I went through the United States Army's advanced infantry officers course at Fort Benning, Georgia. In our tactical exercises, we were faced time and again with the requirement to make rapid decisions.

As our instructors always told us, "Do something, even if it's wrong. Don't just stand there doing nothing because of fear. Remember that a poor plan carried out with vigor and enthusiasm can succeed where the best plan in the world that is never executed has absolutely no chance of success. Action of some sort is always required if you want to succeed."

So please remember this if you will. If you are faced with a problem, the longer you put it off, the bigger it becomes and the more fearful you will become of your ability to solve it.

Learn to trust the inner guidance from your subconscious mind. Make decisions and take action, for if you do not, you will invite total failure simply by your inaction.

You see, it is the fear of doing the wrong thing that paralyzes a person and creates the wrong results. So make your decision and act upon it. In so doing chances are that your troubles will fade away into thin air—whether you make a mistake or not.

All great people are persons of quick decision, which comes from their intuition, their accumulated knowledge, and their past experience. So learn from them. Trust your inner guidance from your subconscious mind so that you, too, can be quick in making your decisions and audacious in your actions.

To quickly summarize, please remember and use the three main concepts I have given you in the first two chapters:

1. You become what you think about.
2. Act as if it were impossible to fail.
3. Do the thing you fear to do and you'll gain the power to do it.

When you use these three techniques, you will always succeed. And take it from me, nothing succeeds like success!

3

How to Use the Power
Within to Establish Goals

POINT YOURSELF TOWARD
SUCCESS—SET GOALS

Setting a goal is the most vital and important step you can take toward achieving both personal and financial success. Scientific studies have shown that every successful person must set goals before he can succeed. It is also a proven fact that even if a person has failed many times before, he can still become successful if he establishes a goal for himself to achieve.

The moment a person begins setting goals, the subconscious mind goes to work to bring those goals into reality. Since the subconscious mind is a goal-seeking mechanism, the moment you give it an objective to reach or a target to shoot for, it will go into action for you.

You will become more alert to and aware of opportunities you can use to achieve your goals. You do not have to be concerned about the methods that your subconscious mind will use. If you simply concentrate on the goals you want to attain, the methods will always take care of themselves. When you have a goal to reach, life always becomes more worthwhile, for you will have something to look forward to and accomplish.

37

WHY PEOPLE WITHOUT GOALS TEND TO FAIL

If you do not give your subconscious mind a goal to reach, it will not work for you. If you just coast along with no purpose or objective in life, then your subconscious mind will coast or float along, too. When people have no personal goals in which they are interested, they feel lost, and they go around aimlessly in circles. That is why they feel their lives are without any important purpose. I have personally found that those who say that life is meaningless are people who have no really worthwhile goals in life.

I have read statistics that show that only five out of every one hundred people become financially successful. By the retirement age of sixty-five, only one of these five people is truly wealthy. Four are financially independent but not rich enough to do everything they would like to do. Of the remaining ninety-five, fifteen are still working, twenty-six have already died, and fifty-four are completely broke and dependent upon either welfare or their children for their support.

Why is it that only five out of every hundred become successful? Because those five have given themselves goals to reach. They know where they want to go, and they have planned on how to get there. Why do ninety-five out of every hundred fail financially? Because they have not established any goals to reach or objectives to attain.

If you were to go on a long trip, I'm sure you would determine your route, the roads you would use, how long it would take, and your exact destination. A person's life should be planned the same way. After all, your life should be much more important than a single trip.

Of course, as I said in the last chapter, there are other ways of measuring successful achievement, but a certain amount of financial success is necessary for complete happiness. I have never been convinced that a person can come up with sound ideas for successful achievement on an empty stomach. All he can think about is how hungry he is, or how hungry, how cold, and how miserable his wife and children are.

I do know that failure sours people and gives them a bitter attitude about life. People will be kind or hostile in their feelings and actions toward others in the proportion that they feel their lives are either highly successful or a dismal failure.

The idea that success spoils people by making them vain and egotistical is not true. It is sometimes true that inherited wealth does cause people to be spoiled and egotistical, but, after all, they themselves have not been successful. Their parents or grandparents are the ones who have succeeded.

For the most part, success makes the person who has earned it humble, tolerant, and kind. There are always exceptions, of course. But it is failure that makes people bitter and cruel. As one of the cofounders of Amway, Rich De Vos, who built his financial empire from scratch, once said, "It is not a sin to be successful."

Let me give you now the results of a university study that show why people without goals fail in life. In 1970, a questionnaire was given to graduating seniors of a large California university. They were asked if they had written down their life goals along with the necessary steps or plans to reach their goals. *Only 3 percent had done so—97 percent had not.* In 1990, twenty years later, another survey of that class revealed that *the 3 percent who had set goals for themselves were worth more financially than the other 97 percent put together!*

If you, too, will set goals for yourself to attain, just as the 3 percent of those graduating college students did:

YOU'LL GAIN THESE VALUABLE BENEFITS

- The first huge benefit you'll gain is the successful accomplishment of whatever goal you set. Your goal may be financial success or improved personal relationships with your family, your friends, and associates. It could be the development of a more vibrant personality, a higher level of health, more stamina and endurance, or improvement of your innate natural talents and abilities. Whatever goals you've given your subconscious mind to achieve for you can be attained.

- The second huge benefit you will gain is personal happiness from achieving your goals. This will give you a deep feeling of self-satisfaction. You will never be truly happy in life unless you are working to reach a worthwhile and challenging goal. If you desire little, you most certainly will achieve little, for you will not be required to use your true talents and natural abilities to their maximum. But if you desire much, you can achieve much, for you will have programmed your subconscious mind for great success when you give it challenging and worthwhile goals to reach.

THE IMPORTANCE OF DEVELOPING YOUR NATURAL TALENTS AND ABILITIES

First of all, let me say that *you cannot become completely successful in your chosen field unless you love what you are doing.* If you do not look forward with eager anticipation and enthusiasm to going to work each morning, if you do not truly love what you are doing for a living, then you can forget about setting any goals, for you are in the wrong profession or occupation. The best thing you can do is to change your line of work as quickly as you can.

Each and every one of us has certain natural abilities and talents that are far above the average. But we also have certain areas in which we are not as talented or as capable as other people are. It is a waste of time and effort to try and work in an area or a field for which you have no natural talent or ability.

For instance, my Uncle Harrison was an expert carpenter and cabinetmaker. But I am all thumbs when it comes to manual work and would have been a complete failure doing the kind of work he did. If I so much as pick up a hammer, a wrench, or a screwdriver in a vain attempt to repair something around the house, my wife heads for the farthest bedroom, closes the door, and covers her ears.

My two sons, Bob and Larry, are both talented musicians. They have excellent singing voices, as does my daughter, Teresa. But I have the voice of a bullfrog and could not carry a tune if I were given a bucket to put it in!

Now by the same token, each one of us is endowed by nature with the ability to achieve excellence or outstanding accomplishment in at least one specific area. All of us have something valuable and special to contribute to the human race. Each one of us can be outstanding in at least one area.

I consider my field of excellence to be writing. I have been able to help hundreds of thousands of people, not only in the United States, but throughout the world, with the books I have written. Most of my applied psychology and management books have been bestsellers in such countries as Canada, Mexico, Brazil, Japan, England, and Indonesia.

Andrew Carnegie, the famous steel magnate, once said, "No man becomes rich unless he enriches others." That is how he made his immense fortune of $500 million! By lowering the price of steel from $160 a ton to $20 a ton he benefited all Americans and himself as well.

One of the most rewarding feelings you can have is the joy you experience from serving or helping others. I certainly have not made as much money from my profession as Andrew Carnegie did from his, but I have been rewarded greatly, both financially and psychologically, by helping others get ahead in their own chosen fields.

The first thing, then, is to determine your own area of excellence so that you can channel all your energies and abilities into becoming superior in that field. To set your goals in a field for which you have no talent or do not like and are not enthusiastic about is a complete waste of time and effort and invites only failure.

Let me give you a specific example. A friend of mine, I'll just call him John, has worked on the assembly line of a washing-machine factory for more than thirty years and hated every minute of it. John loves to paint, and when an opening came along in that department, he applied for the job and was accepted. But he lasted only two days there, for he didn't like to get his work clothes all spattered with paint. So back he went to his hated job on the assembly line. Then, because of his years of seniority with the company, John was offered the position of supervisor, but he turned it down, saying, "I don't want to be an SOB and lord it over everyone else. I just want to be one of the boys."

So John goes on his unhappy way of life, hating his job, fighting his ulcers with antacids, taking out his frustrations on his helpless wife, and looking forward only to his retirement in two more years. But I know that John will never enjoy his retirement years for he never learned how to be happy, no matter what he does, in his entire life.

Fortunately, his son, Fred, is much wiser than his father. Fred learned to be a tool-and-die maker, but after six months on that job he realized that it was not what he really wanted to do for the rest of his life. So he went into the insurance business, and in only a few short years he was one of the top sales producers in the state of Iowa. Then Fred looked for greater fields to conquer, and is now a highly successful banker whose specialty is investment counseling.

Of course, Fred's father thought that Fred never should have left the occupation he studied for: "Wasted his time and money going to school to train for a job he didn't use," John says. What John failed to realize is that his son is much wiser than he is, for Fred saw very soon that he would never be satisfied as a tool-and-die maker and was smart enough to make a change before it was too late to do so.

So I urge you, too, to make sure you are in the right field where you can use all your native talents and innate abilities to become highly successful. And I will say this to you one more time: *You must love what you're doing.* If you don't, do as Fred did. Get out before you're too old and it's too late to change.

HOW TO PROGRAM YOUR SUBCONSCIOUS MIND

Step One: Visualize Your Goal

First, of course, you should give yourself a goal worth working for. Find out what you really want to do in life. Visualize your goal in your mind. Picture what you want to be, the kind of person you want to become.

Your subconscious mind can work in only one way. Since it is a goal-seeking mechanism, it must be given a specific target to shoot for, an exact objective to attain. The more clearly you can see in your conscious mind the exact picture of what you want, the more your subconscious mind can work for you to help you attain your desired goal.

Let me show you how top professional athletes visualize their goals to succeed in sports. Take the best batters in baseball, for example. Top hitters always visualize their bat hitting the ball even before the pitcher has thrown the pitch. They always have a mental picture of making a hit. Never once do they see themsevles striking out.

The best pitchers in the game also use mental pictures to throw the ball exactly where they want it to go. Before the pitch is ever thrown, they see the ball going into the catcher's mitt exactly where he is holding it.

Professional basketball players visualize the ball going through the hoop as they shoot for the basket. Football quarterbacks see the football being caught by the receiver even before it has left the quarterback's hand. The receiver imagines catching the ball before it has been thrown by the quarterback. The top professionals in any sport have learned to relax and let their subconscious minds do all the work for them.

Top professional golfers always mentally rehearse each shot, just before making it. They make the shot perfectly in their imagination. They mentally visualize the club head striking the ball exactly as it should. They see themselves performing a perfect follow-through, and then they imagine the ball falling into the cup.

I've been told by some of my professional golf friends that I could cut ten to twelve strokes off of my score if I would visualize every shot before I make it. In fact, one of them told me that the mental side of golf represents 90 percent of the game; the physical side, 8 percent; and the mechanical side, only 2 percent. This alone indicates how important visualization is in reaching your desired goals.

Even if your ball playing consists only of playing catch in the backyard with your son, I know you don't have to look at your glove to catch the ball. Even if it's way over your head where you cannot see it, you catch the ball instinctively because your subconscious mind tells you exactly where to hold your glove based on past experience.

Step Two: Get All the Facts About Your Goal

Your next step in setting a goal and attaining it is to gather up all the facts you can about it. Read everything that is available on the subject from your library. Ask friends of yours who are experienced in this specific field how they succeeded and what they did. And then, most important of all, listen to what they say.

You do not have to limit your inquiries to successful people whom you personally know. You can do as Paul J. Meyer, the president and founder of Success Motivation Institute of Waco, Texas, did before he became successful in the field of motivation. Before Mr. Meyer founded SMI, he sold insurance in Florida. In fact, he made his first million doing that before he was twenty-seven years old! And it was while he was in Florida, at a yacht basin, that the flash of inspiration came to him. It was this sudden insight that was to grow into a brand-new and different idea: selling success—and SMI.

Mr. Meyer reasoned that anyone who owned a yacht must have some good ideas about how to become successful. Jotting down the license numbers of those yacht-club Cadillacs, Lincolns, and Mercedes, he traced the owners and then asked each of them, honestly and sincerely, to what they attributed their success.

These people were so impressed by Mr. Meyer's sincere approach that they answered his questions without hesitation. And Mr. Meyer learned what he needed to know about how to achieve his first goal: financial success.

I'm sure you've heard of Napoleon Hill. But did you know he used the same procedures to gain the information for his world-famous book *Think and Grow Rich*? He interviewed most of the leading successes of early twentieth-century America, men like Thomas Edison, Alexander Graham Bell, Henry Ford, Andrew Carnegie, and more than five hundred others to gain the answers to questions he had about their secrets of success.

When you've researched your field and learned all that you can about it, then you are in a position to analyze, discuss, and test those facts. You can use all the information that you have gained to help you determine exactly what you have to do to reach your goal.

Step Three: Concentrate on Your Goal

Don't allow anything or anyone to divert your attention or distract you in any way from your goal. Stay on the straight road that leads to your goal without any detours.

The best way to do this is to become a "one-eyed man." By that I mean, give your subconscious mind only one goal at a time so that it can work at its maximum potential for you. Concentrate only on a single point; don't scatter your fire all over the place.

That is what Jesus meant when He said, "When your eye is single, your whole body also is full of light." So do as Jesus said. Become a one-eyed man. Have only one single purpose in mind that you want to achieve. Then you can exert all your efforts and energies on that one specific goal. When you do that, you will become highly successful.

You should sincerely believe in your heart of hearts that you can reach your goal. Don't allow negative thoughts—either yours or others—of defeat or failure to enter your mind. As Paul Meyer once said, "What you ardently desire, sincerely believe in, vividly imagine, and enthusiastically act on must inevitably come to pass."

THREE CHARACTERISTICS EVERY GOAL MUST HAVE

If your goal lacks any one of these three characteristics, it will usually be unobtainable.

1. Your Goal Must Be Concrete and Specific.

You must know exactly what it is you want to attain. Just to say, "I want to be wealthy," is not enough. It is only wishful thinking. *Just exactly how rich do you want to be?*

If you want an income of $50,000 or $100,000 or more a year, then give that exact figure to your subconscious mind to attain for you. Do you want to own a $250,000 home? Then tell your subconscious mind exactly what you want. Burn the exact picture of that house into your mind. Then leave it up to your subconscious mind to furnish you with the ideas you need to make that deep desire of yours come true.

Intangible and nonspecific goals are almost impossible to mentally visualize, for they are too vague and abstract for the mind to grasp. They will not inspire or stir your subconscious into action. If you are not sure in your conscious mind exactly what it is that you want to accomplish, then you are in no position to properly program your subconscious mind for successful achievement of a goal. So if you want to reach your goal successfully, make sure that it is specific and concrete.

2. Your Goal Must Be Measurable.

By that I mean you should be able to judge your progress toward your attainment of that goal. Your goal may be quantifiable—how much do you intend to do or how far do you want to go?

For example, your goal might be to become president of the company you work for, no matter what your present position is. A certain man I know did exactly that. Henry rose from the position of a night-shift supervisor in a tire-and-rubber factory to president of the company in just fifteen years, for that was the specific goal that he wanted to acheive.

He visualized the exact goal that he wanted to attain, as I've already shown you how to do, by picturing himself as president of the company. Exactly how did he do that?

Well, since he was in charge of the plant during his shift as night supervisor, he had the keys to every office. So he had a picture taken of himself sitting in the president's chair behind the president's desk and with his nameplate bearing the title of "President" in front of him on the desk.

Then he had copies of that photograph made. He put a small one in his wallet, where he would see it every time he opened it. He placed one on the windshield visor of his car. Another one went on the refrigerator door. Still another was placed on the mirror in the bathroom, where he would see it every time he shaved. There was one on the dresser in his bedroom, and one on his desk in his study. Wherever he looked throughout the day, he would see the picture of himself as president of the company.

Of course, he had to use some intermediate goals along the way before he reached his final objective. He went from night-shift supervisor to department foreman and then to production superintendent in charge of all departments in the plant. Then he became the vice-president in charge of manufacturing and marketing. From there he was promoted to the position of executive vice-president, directly under the president of the company. And when the president of the company retired, Henry became the president and chief executive officer of a company that employed fifteen hundred people.

As Henry rose from one position to another, he never took his eye off his final goal, that of president of the company. In his subconscious mind he was already the president and chief executive officer of the company, even while he was still the night-shift supervisor. He was determined to get to the top and he did. As Henry once told me, "The important thing to keep in mind is not where you were or where you are, but where you are going."

3. Your Goal Must Be Achievable in a Definite Time Period.

When you make your plans to reach your final goal, you should give yourself a definite and reasonable time period in which to attain that final objective. If you do not, you will find it is all too easy to procrastinate, to daydream, and to put things off.

For instance, if you want to become president of your company, just as Henry did, you're not going to be able to do that overnight, that is, unless your father is the owner and you are going to inherit his position. But that is not true for the majority of us. Most of us have to work our way to the top.

So if reaching your final objective is years away, then you'll have to give yourself some intermediate goals so that you can pace yourself for the long haul, or you might not be able to make it.

Take a student starting out on the long, slow grind to become a doctor of medicine, for instance. First, she'll need to make her initial goal a bachelor's degree. From there, on to medical school; after that, her internship; and finally, her own private practice. But if she wants to specialize in a particular field, it will take still more education and time to reach that goal.

No matter what a person's final goal is, cutting it up into intermediate steps will make it more attainable. Most worthwhile goals cannot be reached overnight. If you want to make a million dollars, you're going to need a definite time period in which to accomplish that.

So plan your progress carefully, year by year, month by month, day by day, even hour by hour if necessary. If you happen to miss one of the dates on your timetable, don't become discouraged and give up. You may need only to readjust your schedule a bit. Perhaps you were a little unrealistic and too much in a hurry when you drew up your original timetable. It's more important that you are still moving in the right direction and in an unswerving straight line toward your final goal.

My college roommate took eight years to get his bachelor of science degree in business administration at the University of Iowa. Why did it take him eight years to get a degree that normally would take only four? It took that long because Gus was an orphan and had to earn his own way through college. He would work in the Princess Cafe in Iowa City to save enough money to go to school for a year. When he completed that year of his college education, he would go back to work in the cafe for another year.

But Gus was one of the most patient people I've ever known. He knew what his goal was and he achieved it. He never gave up. As the Chinese proverb goes, "Patience is power; with time and patience the mulberry leaf becomes silk." Gus wasn't Chinese; he was Greek, but he knew that proverb by heart, and he often quoted either that one or some other old saying about patience to me when I wanted everything done yesterday instead of today. When I was in college, patience was not one of my better virtues. With age, my attitude about not being patient enough has changed for the better.

PUT YOUR GOAL IN WRITING

Before you force yourself to become realistic and put a specific goal on paper, it's all too easy to think only in generalities, like this one: "I want to be rich by middle age." But this is not a goal; it is not even a plan. It is only daydreaming or wishful thinking. First of all, how much money does it take to be rich? And exactly how many years have to pass before a person is truly middle-aged?

You must force yourself to write down the exact amount of money you want, right down to the penny, by a certain and specific date. For example, if you say, "I want to have $150,000 in sound investments by the time I'm thirty-five," or "I want to own a $250,000 house free and clear when I'm forty," you now have real goals that you want to reach.

I'm sure you've heard someone say, "I know what I mean, but I can't seem to get it down on paper in the right words." If you yourself have ever been guilty of saying that, it means you were not completely sure of what you wanted or precisely sure of what you meant. If you couldn't get your goal down in writing, then you didn't really have a specific and concrete objective yet with which to program your subconscious mind. You were still indulging in wishful thinking or idle daydreaming.

MAKE YOUR GOAL EXCITING AND WORTHWHILE BY FOCUSING ON THE BENEFITS

If you want to get out of the rut of boredom and complacency then you must make your goal exciting and worthwhile. One of the best ways to do this is to visualize all the benefits you're going to gain when you reach your goal.

For instance, let's say you want to stop smoking. Instead of trying to use willpower or thinking to yourself how hard it's going to be, motivate yourself to quit by listing all the good things that will happen to you when you stop.

That's just what I did when I quit in 1965. I had been smoking since I was nineteen. I had tried, unsuccessfully, to quit many times before by using willpower. In fact, once when we were living in Baltimore I said I was going to quit and I threw a full pack of cigarettes out into the street in the middle of a snowstorm. An hour later I was out there digging in the snow trying to find them! So much for willpower.

Finally, a friend who had been a heavy smoker told me bluntly that I'd never be able to quit simply by using willpower: "If you think you can stop smoking by using willpower, Jim, try using willpower the next time you have diarrhea and see how far you get! You'll never quit until you convince yourself of all the benefits you'll gain when you do."

So I finally quit at the age of forty-five after I made up that list of benefits. It has now been more than twenty-seven years since I've had a cigarette.

A little over a year ago, my family doctor was trying to quit smoking and was going through hell with all kinds of withdrawal symptoms. He was about to give up and go back to smoking when I asked him if he had made a list of all the good things that would happen to him when he quit.

"Hell, no!" Antonio said. "I've been too damned miserable to even think about that."

"Well, let me give you the list of benefits I dreamed up for myself when I quit," I said. "They helped me quit; I'm sure they'll help you, too."

Here, then, is the list I gave my doctor. It helped him tremendously. He's not had a cigarette for more than a year now. If you're trying to kick the habit, the following list of benefits will help you, too.

When you quit smoking:

1. You'll no longer have that hacking smoker's cough.

2. Your food will taste better and smell better, too, for you'll not only regain your sense of taste but also your sense of smell.

3. You won't run the risk of offending others with smoker's breath.

4. You'll no longer run the risk of bronchitis, emphysema, asthma, or, worst of all, lung cancer. It is a proven fact that your lungs begin to heal within only twelve hours of your last cigarette, although it will take several months before they return to completely normal health.

5. You'll lessen the risk of cardiovascular disease and reduce the chance of heart attack as well as stroke from high blood pressure.

6. Your digestion will improve dramatically. You'll run less risk of gastritis as well as duodenal ulcers. Even your heartburn can become a thing of the past.

7. You'll no longer run the risk of premature aging and facial wrinkles. It is a proven scientific fact that smokers have more facial wrinkles at fifty than nonsmokers do at seventy.

8. You'll save a small fortune in a year, enough to go on a luxurious vacation. A two-pack-a-day habit at $1.50 a pack costs you annually more than $1,000, and that is a lot of money, at least to me.

Now that's a carload of benefits you can gain when you reach your goal of not smoking anymore. And that makes your goal exciting and worthwhile to achieve. You can use the same sort of system of setting goals for losing weight, controlling your temper, making more money, whatever. The more exciting and worthwhile you make your goal, the more ambitious you will become to reach it, and the better your subconscious mind will work for you.

CREATE YOUR OWN PLAN FOR SUCCESSFUL ACHIEVEMENT

Over the years, I have read any number of plans made for successful achievement. But the best one I have ever seen was compiled by Paul Meyer. An expert in inspiring people to give it their all, Mr. Meyer calls his formula for success the . . .

*MILLION-DOLLAR PERSONAL SUCCESS PLAN**

1. *Crystallize Your Thinking.* Determine what specific goal you want to achieve. Then dedicate yourself to its attainment with unswerving singleness of purpose, the trenchant zeal of a crusader.

**Reprinted by permission of Paul J. Meyer, Chairman of the Board, SMI International, Inc., Waco, Texas. All rights reserved. Copyright 1962.

2. *Develop a Plan for Achieving Your Goal and a Deadline for Its Attainment.* Plan your progress carefully, hour by hour, day by day, month by month. Organized activity and maintained enthusiasm are the wellsprings of your power.

3. *Develop a Sincere Desire for the Things You Want in Life.* A burning desire is the greatest motivator of every human action. The desire for success implants "success consciousness," which in turn creates a vigorous and ever-increasing "habit of success."

4. *Develop Supreme Confidence in Yourself and Your Own Abilities.* Enter every activity without giving mental recognition to the possibility of defeat. Concentrate on your strengths instead of your weaknesses—on your powers instead of your problems.

5. *Develop a Dogged Determination to Follow-through on Your Plan.* Do this regardless of the obstacles, criticism, or circumstances, or what other people say, think, or do. Construct your determination with sustained effort, controlled attention, and concentrated energy. Opportunities never come to those who wait—they are captured by those who dare to attack.

▽ ▽ ▽

Here are some things you should remember as you set your goals:

1. *Pinpoint Your Specific Goal and Dedicate Yourself to Achieving It.* Set only one goal at a time—the one that is most meaningful to you at this particular moment.

2. *Make a Specific Plan to Reach Your Goal.* Write down your goal along with your plan to reach it in simple, clear, concise, and concrete language.

3. *Keep the Payoff Constantly in Mind.* Think about it all the time. Build mental pictures of yourself achieving your

goal. If possible, use all five of your senses to bring your total personality to bear upon it.

4. *Drive Your Goal Deep into Your Subconscious Mind.* Remember that your subconscious mind is fantastically creative. It never rests. Your subconscious mind continues to work even when you are sound asleep. It will bring to fruition whatever desire or goal you have programmed into it to do.

5. *Don't Let Thoughts of Defeat or Fear of Failure Slow You Down or, Worse Yet, Stop You Completely.* Develop a fierce satisfaction and pride in your ability to surmount any difficulty. Always maintain the attitude of "I will win. It is impossible for me to fail!"

4

How to Achieve Financial Success with the Psychology of Self-Achievement

In Chapter Two, I said that *success is the progressive realization of a worthy ideal,* and that some people who are successful in their chosen field are not necessarily immensely rich or financially well-to-do. But that does not mean they are not successful.

I specifically mentioned my son-in-law, who is a highly successful high school teacher because that is exactly what he always wanted to be. Arch taught for several years after he graduated from college, but he became dissatisfied with the comparatively low pay of a teacher, so he left the teaching profession for a while to go into the insurance business with Mutual of Omaha.

There he made more money than he did as a schoolteacher, but it would not be fair to say that he was successful, since he was not nearly as happy as he had been teaching school. He loves children and he missed the opportunity he had to help them grow into worthwhile citizens, so he went back to his original profession.

As I said, Arch is not wealthy in dollars and cents as a schoolteacher, but he is successful because he is doing what he wants to do—help others—and he excels at what he is doing. I am extremely proud of him and his dedication to youth. It is unfortunate that we do not pay a teacher what he or she is really worth for what they do.

In this chapter, however, I want to discuss success primarily from the point of view of financial success.

BENEFITS YOU WILL GAIN

1. Recognition. People who are successful financially always receive far more recognition than those who are unsuccessful. When people need a doctor or a lawyer, or even a mechanic, they always look for those who are successful and who are recognized for their skills and abilities.

When a person moves to a new community, he always looks for a knowledgeable and capable doctor and an honest and dependable mechanic. I have never yet known anyone to look for an unsuccessful doctor or a "shade-tree" mechanic when he wants to find someone on whom he can really depend.

2. Self-Esteem. This comes not only from recognition by others, but it also comes from the knowledge that you are in control of your own life and that it is proceeding along the planned route in the proper time.

3. Enjoyment. Successful people enjoy not only investing their money, but spending it. If you want to earn more money just for the sake of having more money to stash away in your wall safe at home or in the safe deposit box in your bank, that is not a good enough reason. Money is useful only when you use it for all the good things that it will do for you, which means both investing and spending. Idle money is of no use to anyone. Money must be kept in circulation and used before it can become valuable.

For the most part, successful people know how to use the money they have earned. They have learned to enjoy life more than unsuccessful people. They live in better homes and drive more expensive cars. Some even fly their own private planes, as did a highly successful chiropractor I met in

Wisconsin. They travel more and meet more interesting people. They have infinitely more options in life that they can exercise for themselves.

Successful people are not forced to spend the final years of their lives in limited or unfortunate circumstances. They enjoy life more and tend to enjoy more years of life than do people who are not successful.

4. Change and New Experiences. The stimulation of change and new experiences is of great importance. Change keeps us alert and makes life much more worthwhile. It prevents boredom and monotony. Some psychologists feel that the stimulation of change and new experiences is the third most important desire on the part of people everywhere, right after recognition and ego gratification.

Successful people experience much more change and stimulation in their lives than do unsuccessful people. They can go to more new places, do more new and different things, and meet many more interesting people. They are not stuck in one place. They can travel and go wherever they want to go.

5. Service. Successful people do a far better job of serving others than do unsuccessful people; otherwise they would not be successful. Service is one of the most important keys to successful financial achievement. (I will discuss this later in this chapter, when I tell you about Bert Bartingale.)

Financially successful people have many more options and the freedom to be of special service to society through foundations, grants, libraries, hospitals, universities, and the arts. The successful people of this country serve without fanfare or publicity through their donations to charitable organizations of all sorts.

But the successful person's greatest service to the community is through the means by which that success was achieved—as a doctor, a banker, a lawyer, a judge, or a retail merchant of any sort. Whatever created that person's success did so by also serving the community in one way or another.

6. Freedom. Financial success gives a person the freedom
to do what he wants to do when he wants to do it.

A SOUND ECONOMIC PLAN: THE BASIS OF YOUR FINANCIAL SUCCESS

Sound economics is at the bottom of everything that is desir-
able in your life. A sound economic plan is the foundation of
your financial success. There has to be a satisfactory financial
basis for your life if you want to grow, to accomplish more,
and to experience more.

Money is very important. Ever since the Phoenicians in-
vented money several thousand years ago, the primary aim of
every person has been to earn as much of it as possible. You
should be no exception to this rule. Without money, nothing
happens. With it, everything becomes possible.

The old excuse that it takes money to make money is
nothing more than that: an excuse. I could give you the names
of hundreds of successful people who started with absolutely
nothing and made it clear to the top.

When you find the business or profession that you want
to be in and in which you feel confident of succeeding because
of your inborn talents and abilities, there are any number of
ways to obtain the necessary financing. Let me tell you about
my first experience in getting a business loan from a bank.

Now two things are usually important to a bank when
you're asking for a business loan: your credit rating and collateral. But not all banks demand the same amount of collateral,
nor do they all think the same way when it comes to credit rat-
ings. Some banks are easier to do business with than others.
Don't pick a tough adversary if you can deal with an easier one.

When I was starting out on my first business venture
many years ago, I needed $5,000, of which I had only $1,000.
My father-in-law, who was also a businessman in the same
small town, tried to pave the way for me, so he took me to his
bank and introduced me to its president.

But I could tell from the moment I walked in that my chances of getting the loan I needed were minimal. The bank had the atmosphere of a morgue. People spoke only in whispers. The place had cold tile floors, clammy marble walls, and dim lights. Not even a chair to sit on could be found in the lobby. And sure enough, I didn't get the loan.

So without the aid of my father-in-law, I went on my own to another bank. This one was modern and progressive. The atmosphere was warm and comfortable, with wall-to-wall carpeting, good lighting, and comfortable easy chairs for its customers to sit on. Soft, pleasant background music could be heard. The cashiers were all warm and friendly—and so were the bank's loan officers. All in all, it was a completely different kind of bank. And I got the loan.

So choose your bank as carefully as you do your friends. Chances are, you'll be dealing with that bank all your life.

How to Build an Excellent Credit Rating

If you want to borrow money from a bank to start your own business, then you must have established your reputation as a person with a good track record of honesty and responsibility with no slip-ups in the credit department about paying your bills on time.

Let me tell you now about Karen G. and how she did it. Karen wanted to establish a credit rating for herself. Eventually she expected to open her own women's clothing store, since she didn't want to spend the rest of her life working for someone else. So while she was still working as a salesclerk in a dress shop, she first borrowed $100 from the bank's small-loan department. She did not use the money at all; she wanted only to build her reputation as a reliable person who was a good credit risk.

She then borrowed $200, next $500, then $1,000, and finally, $2,000, all on signature loans without any collateral whatever. Each loan was paid off promptly. The bank officials in the loan department got used to seeing Karen come in to make her monthly payments, and they looked at her as a responsible person who kept her word and paid her debts.

Karen told me that she never mailed in any of her monthly payments. She always went to the bank to make them in person so she could establish cordial and friendly relationships with the people in the bank's loan department. That way she was much more than just a name on paper to the bank. She was a real, live person whom they came to know and like.

The day came for Karen to make her big move. The store she wanted to buy became available, and she needed $5,000 for a downpayment. But she had managed to save only a few hundred dollars herself.

When she went to the bank, the chief loan officer was on his way to lunch—as Karen knew full well that he would be—so on his way out he told his assistant, "Take care of Karen—don't wait for me to come back—give her whatever she wants. She's one of our most reliable customers."

Twenty minutes later, Karen walked out of the bank with a certified check for $5,000 in her hand, borrowed without any collateral whatever except her signature. It was the biggest loan Karen had ever taken from the bank. By prior planning and using her head, Karen was able to accomplish what a lot of people would never have had the courage to do.

The final chapter of Karen's story has not been written yet, for she is still in business. I can tell you, though, that she now owns one of the largest, most-successful women's clothing stores in her city as well as the building she had constructed for her business.

Incidentally, the bank from which she borrowed her money is the same bank that gave me my first business loan many years before. Many of the personnel whom I knew are gone, either retired or deceased, but the bank's policies of making loans has not changed one bit.

I've included this section to give you some ideas about what you can do to be successful in acquiring the financing that you need. This is not to say that you should use Karen's system. All you need do is use your imagination and do some creative thinking of your own so that you can come up with your own plan.

What Becoming Rich *Really* Means to You

Wealth indicates that you are making a significant contribution to your community and that you are serving it well. This does wonders for your self-esteem. Had you not made a significant contribution to your community, you would not be successful and well-to-do. You can measure the good you have done for your city or your community by what the residents there have paid you over the years that you have been in business. A person can judge very well what he has been worth by what he has received.

I've heard many a person say, "You can't make any money in this town anymore. If you want to make money and become rich, you'll have to go to a city bigger than this one." My answer to that is that that person simply doesn't know what he's talking about. If he would talk to people and find out what they wanted, and then figure up the profits he could make by giving them what they wanted, he would soon discover untold wealth right within the range of his own voice. Is a huge city the only place where you can become rich? No way. No matter how small the town, you can become rich if you serve its residents by giving them what they want.

For instance, I lived in a small town of 9,500 people in the Midwest for a great many years, and I could name at least fifty people who were extremely wealthy as a result of their business efforts in that small town over the years. Those businesses in which they were engaged included men's clothing stores, women's dress shops, shoe stores, supermarkets, garages, restaurants, dairies, drugstores, and on and on. The secret to their success was giving people what they wanted and giving them the best service possible, a subject that I will discuss shortly.

WHY YOU MUST BECOME A "PEOPLE PERSON" TO SUCCEED

If you want to succeed in business, you must become a people person, whether you like that idea or not. You have two audiences that must like you and feel that you have their special interests at heart: your customers and your employees. Even as a writer working at home in a solitary study by myself, I have to be a people person and a people pleaser if I want to succeed, even though I may never come in personal contact with either my reader or my publisher.

People will make all the difference in the world for you just as they have for me. If they're not with you, you'll fail and go out of business. It's people you're serving and it's people you depend on for the money that you earn every week and every month of the year. They will happily pay you whatever you ask—within reason, of course—if you offer them good service, and if you make them feel important in your place of business, or when they are using your product or your service.

People will make you rich or keep you broke depending upon the way you treat them. You must make up your mind when you go into business that people are going to be your special concern above all else. How you treat them will make the difference between your success or your failure. That principle should be taught in business administration courses in college; unfortunately it usually is not. Too many people learn that lesson the hard way by failing in their business ventures. Businesspeople who fail usually do so because they haven't yet learned how to be a "people person" before they start out.

How can *you* become a people person? Ask yourself how you would like to be treated if the situation were reversed and you were the customer. Then treat that person as you would like to be treated. You'll never lose money on a customer, and you'll never lose a customer if you treat him that way. To love your neighbor as yourself is the philosophy that Jesus Christ taught humankind nearly two thousand years ago, and it is still an excellent principle for you to follow in business.

Let me tell you about Marshall Field, who built the largest department store in the world (for that time) in Chicago, Illinois. Since he died in 1906, his name might not be as familiar to you as that of Sam Walton, the founder of Wal-Mart stores, and one of the richest men in the United States when he died in 1992. But I think you ought to know that Marshall Field was a pioneer in many modern retailing practices that are still being used today.

Field's business philosophy must have been good, because in his lifetime he built one of the largest private fortunes in the United States. His large philanthropies included the Art Institute of Chicago, the University of Chicago, and the Field Museum of Natural History.

Now Marshall Field used to take a lot of ribbing because of his policy of letting the buyer return merchandise if she was not completely satisfied with it. This was a major innovation in the retail business, for Field was the first businessperson ever to do that. In other stores, when you walked out of the store, you'd bought the item. No business before Marshall Field had ever offered such a radical policy.

Friends used to tell him that his customers took advantage of him and his return policy. For instance, women used to buy expensive fur coats, wear them for only one night to some important social or business occasion, and then return them the next day for full credit.

When he was kidded about such things, Field would ask that the woman's account be sent up to his office to show to his criticizing friend. Without fail, the woman would turn out to be a good regular customer who bought many other items of clothing on her account. She was a good customer, and if she wanted to "borrow" a mink coat for one evening to make her feel more important, then "So what?," Field would say. She was still an excellent customer and an important person to him.

It was Field's fine treatment of his customers that was largely responsible for his outstanding success in business. As he said, a woman who was not a regular customer would never have the courage to charge an expensive fur coat on a nonexistent account and then return it the next day.

Marshall Field's innovative policy of complete satisfaction guaranteed or your money back without question has carried over into today's business world. It is the policy of every successful retailer, from Neiman Marcus, Macy's, Sears Roebuck, and Wal-Mart to smaller businesses that you might name right in your hometown.

Now if you're going to be a people person, you must also learn to be courteous and polite to your customers. There is absolutely no excuse for mistreating or insulting a customer in any way. To do so simply shows a lack of employee training—one of the major problems of unsuccessful businesses today.

Not giving proper recognition to the customer and making him feel important is the greatest offense in business anyone can commit. Remember that recognition and feeling important are the greatest desires that every person has. No customer should ever be allowed to leave a place of business without receiving a big, cheerful smile and a special thank you from the cashier and the owner, too, if he or she is there.

Let me tell you right now that I am no exception to this rule. I, too, like to feel important and appreciated. Only a few blocks from my house is a large, modern supermarket. But I never go there to buy anything, for the clerks and cashiers are all grumpy and sour-faced. If they ever do say thank you, which is seldom, they look only at the cash register. Never once do they look at the customer. Not only that, they are usually too busy chatting with each other about their personal affairs to pay any attention to the customer. And lack of attention is simply another way of insulting the customer.

So instead of shopping for my groceries there, I drive almost two miles in heavy traffic to another supermarket, where everyone is pleasant and cheerful. When you pay the cashier there, she looks straight at you with a big smile and says, "Thanks a lot, sir. Please come back and have a real good day." I ask you now; where would you go for your groceries?

About four months ago, Larry, a friend of mine, opened a small restaurant that seats sixty people. He felt that he should be doing a better business than he was and knowing that I was a business and management consultant asked me to look his place over.

I spent a few days in his restaurant and then made these recommendations. First of all, I told him what I just told you about giving the customer recognition and making him feel important. Then I told him that even if his place was packed and every waiter or waitress was busy, he himself should be sure that the new customer gets a menu, a glass of water, and the assurance that he will be taken care of just as soon as possible. And I told him not to make the person wait to be seated. He is a customer, not a waiter, and seating him immediately is another way of making him feel important.

I also told him to be sure to give his customers their checks in a timely fashion, that he should never make a customer wait for his check. It is an insult to make a person wait, since the customer's time is important, too. Then I said he should greet customers with a big smile at the cash register. Thank them, really thank them, I said, and be sure to look at them when they pay their bill. That makes them feel important to the owner of the restaurant, and of course they are important to him. If they don't feel that they are, they will not be back.

Of course, it goes without saying that the customer will not come back to Larry's restaurant if the food is not good. In his case, however, the food was excellent and, actually, so was the service. He was just being a little impatient and expected a little too much too soon. As I told him in my final report, just keep doing what you're doing and you'll make it.

If you are in business, no matter what it is, if you don't give your customers the service, the importance, and the recognition that they want, they'll take their business elsewhere. Never underestimate the value of your customer; there are no unimportant ones.

HOW TO BECOME THE "GREATEST" IN YOUR CHOSEN FIELD

It might come as a great surprise to learn that if you want to be the greatest in your field, you must be the servant of all. But that is precisely what Jesus told His Apostles when James and John asked Him for the two highest places in the kingdom, and the other ten were displeased at their request. But Jesus said to all of them, "Whosoever will be great among you, shall be your minister. And whosoever will be the chiefest, shall be servant of all" (Mark 10:43–44). Or in other words, "He who would be the greatest of all must be the servant of all."

Now I know that some people might say that the Bible is out of date and that we have progressed too far to follow those old-fashioned ideas today. Well, I have news for you. Actually, the statement seemed even more foolish to the businesspeople of His time than it does today. You see, businesspeople in the time of Jesus followed the policy of *caveat emptor*—that is, "let the buyer beware!" And they were not at all ashamed of that policy. It was not until the 1800s that the notion of *caveat emptor* changed. A. T. Stewart, a young merchant in New York, and Marshall Field in Chicago were the first businesspeople who believed that service to the customer was a far better policy for winning business than that of letting the buyer beware.

"Do you want to become the greatest lawyer in this state?" I once asked a young law student. "You can be. Just prepare yourself to render greater service to your clients than any other lawyer in the state does. If you get to where you are giving greater service to your clients than any other lawyer is, then you will become the greatest lawyer in the state."

And this principle applies to any profession or occupation you can think of. In the summer of 1992 I visited my sister, Marjorie, and her husband, Ted, in La Crosse, Wisconsin. While there, I met their charming next-door neighbor, a beautiful widow named Marion McLean. When Marion learned that I was a writer and that I was interested in stories about successful people, she told me about her father, Robert O. Bartingale.

Now Robert Bartingale, better known to his friends as Bert, had only a fifth-grade education. But he was determined to better himself, so he took a correspondence course in plumbing and heating. During this time he worked for a plumbing company so that he could learn the trade firsthand while he studied.

But Bert was not content to work for someone else all of his life. He longed to become an independent businessman so that he could put his own ideas into practice in a company of his own. And that is exactly what he did.

A deeply religious man, Bert vowed that when he had his own plumbing business, he would operate it strictly on the principle, "He who would be the greatest of all must be the servant of all," which his father had taught him. Bert also was determined to follow the principle of "The customer is always right," which he had learned from the owner of the plumbing company for whom he worked while he was taking his correspondence course.

Finally, the day came when Bert got his diploma from the correspondence school, and, shortly afterward, after passing a rigorous examination, he received his license as a state-certified plumber.

He then founded the Bartingale Plumbing and Heating Company in Eau Claire, Wisconsin, in 1912. Bert was much admired and well thought of by his fellows in the plumbing profession, primarily because he never cut down a competitor or criticized one in any way. He always had a good word to say about his competition. He was so well liked that he became known as the "dean of plumbers" in northwestern Wisconsin.

Bert always set aside part of his company's income in a "trust fund" to be used in case of a rainy day. And rain it did, during the Great Depression of the 1930s, when company after company went bankrupt and formerly successful business-people were selling apples on street corners to survive.

"My father, bless him, cared deeply about his employees," Marion said, "so much so that during that Great Depression he used that company trust fund to retain a core of his best employees. He paid them week after week while his savings slowly melted away. But he honestly cared for those men and their families, and he carried them on the payroll until the depression was over and the company started to make money again."

Bert died at the age of ninety in 1967, but the company that he founded is still alive today, more than eighty years later, an amazing record for a small business. His son, R. W., better known as "Wes" to all his friends, took over the company until he, too, died, and passed the business on to his son, Jack.

Today there are six co-owners of the Bartingale Company, including Bert's grandson, Jack. All of them are making an excellent living because the company still practices the two great principles that Bert founded the company on: *"He who would be the greatest of all must be the servant of all"* and *"The customer is always right."*

Bert Bartingale, I salute you. I wish I could have known you. And Marion, I thank you for telling me about your father and for letting me use both his name and yours in my book.

HOW YOUR ATTITUDE INFLUENCES YOUR SUCCESS

Let me explain to you now the role of attitude in achieving success. You see, whatever you expect to happen usually will come true for you. Your attitude will set the stage for whatever you expect to take place.

If you expect or anticipate failure, then that will happen to you over and over again. That sort of attitude sets the stage for failure. When you expect failure, you think of failing, and then, as a result of your negative thinking, you fail. Remember always that you really do become what you think about. Even if you have an excellent education and a college degree, you will fail if you have a negative attitude and an expectation of failure.

But if you have great expectations of success, you are bound to succeed and attain high levels of achievement. Even if you have a limited education, as Bert Bartingale had, you will succeed if you constantly believe and think that you will. I cannot say it too often: You do become what you think about, and if you think about being successful, then most assuredly you will succeed.

The attitude of "that's good enough" will not do if you want to be an outstanding success in your profession. I've often heard the expression, and I'm sure you have, too, "That's good enough for government work." Is there any wonder why one can't understand government directives, rules, and regulations? Even the people who wrote them don't know what they really mean.

Sir Henry Royce used to roam around the old Rolls-Royce factory every single day. One day he heard one of his engineers say to a worker, "That's good enough." Sir Henry immediately jumped into the conversation to say, "It's never good enough. That's why we're all here, to make it better today, and then to make it even better tomorrow, and even better than that the day after tomorrow. I never want to hear you say, 'That's good enough,' for it isn't!"

That's what the goal of excellence is all about. It demands an attitude of great expectations. Today, the name of Rolls-Royce remains synonymous with all that is fine and worthwhile about a product. It's a symbol of quality.

An expectant attitude, an attitude that expects great things to happen, that expects complete success, seems to have an uncanny way of shaping future events in a positive way for successful achievement.

An American woman vacationing in Europe was impressed by the spaghetti sauce at a fine Italian restaurant in Rome. She asked the chef if he would give her the recipe. Since she was a tourist and would not be in competition with him in a local restaurant, he agreed to do so.

A few years later this same woman was in the restaurant again, and she scolded the chef for not giving her the complete recipe. "My spaghetti sauce didn't taste as good as yours did," she complained. "What ingredient did you leave out?"

The chef went over the recipe again and assured her that he had not left anything out. But she insisted that he must have done so, for she said she had followed his instructions to the letter, and still her sauce was not as good as his. Upon hearing this, the chef said, "Perhaps you left out the most important ingredient of all, Madam. You didn't put yourself into it."

That's the difference an attitude can make in the end result. She didn't expect her spaghetti sauce to taste as good as his did, and therefore, it didn't.

One of the greatest professional quarterbacks of all time told me about his role in leading his team to victory. Here is exactly what he said, word for word: "A winning attitude on the part of the quarterback that is displayed in his posture, his facial expression, his voice, the plays he calls, his entire attitude can do more than anything else to lift the spirits of the entire team for the extra effort that is required to win. So much of sports is a mental game."

HOW YOU CAN USE CREATIVE THINKING TO SUCCEED

Let me explain how creative thinking can help program your subconscious for success. All you need is one good idea to succeed.

For example, let me tell you about the man who was in the auto-rebuilding and -resale business. He rebuilt car engines, but in doing so, he got his hands so greasy, it was impossible to clean them thoroughly without at the same time destroying his skin.

He began to experiment with various skin softeners and conditioners with which he and his wife mixed cleansing agents. It was his hands they were trying to save, but in the process of experimentation they produced a skin-cleansing and -protecting agent that has since made them millionaires many times over.

His original occupation was rebuilding cars, but, as a result, the problem of how to clean his hands had to be solved. And in solving this problem, a great opportunity was created to become rich.

Now when someone succeeds in solving a problem, as this man and his wife did, he usually becomes rich, and many more people benefit. Thousands and thousands of mechanics and laborers now use this cleansing cream to take care of their hands.

Federal Express is another example of creative thinking. You don't have to have a brilliant idea to be a creative thinker. All you need to do is find a need and fill it. The founder of Federal Express revolutionized package and mail service by offering overnight delivery, not just to the post office, but right to a person's front door. I have at times had to get out of bed to answer the front door for the Federal Express delivery person. Sometimes it seems that they are almost too efficient!

Please remember that creative thinking at times requires you to take a risk. But there is no success without some risk. Unsuccessful people don't like to take risks; they prefer to make their lifestyles fit their income. But successful people will not accept that idea. They make their incomes fit their lifestyles, and that's why they must be creative.

At times it is true that successful people go broke as a result of taking risks. But being broke is only a temporary situation. Being poor is a state of mind that belongs to unsuccessful people. You will never succeed with the attitude that you are poor. I have been broke many times myself, but I have never been poor.

REPETITION IS ESSENTIAL FOR SUCCESS

If you are in sales, you know that repetition is necessary to wear down your prospect's resistance. As Job once said, "The water wears down the stones." And so it is with repetition. You will eventually succeed if, like a pile driver, you continue to pound away just a fraction of an inch at a time.

"How many times do you call on a person before you finally give up on him?" I once asked Craig Lambert, a top-notch hardware salesman out of Atlanta, Georgia.

"It depends on which one of us dies first," Craig replied.

Craig then went on to tell me that if he is convinced that a prospect is worth calling on, he will keep calling as long as that person is there.

"I once made forty calls on one man before he gave me an order," Craig said. "Finally he told me that he could not keep from buying from me. When I asked him why, he replied, 'Your persistence has paralyzed my resistance!'"

You can use the same sort of persistence to succeed.

ARE YOU WILLING TO PAY THE PRICE OF SUCCESS?

After her brilliant concert, a great violinist was being entertained by her hostess, when one of the guests remarked, "I'd give anything to be able to play the violin the way you do."

"No you wouldn't," the violinist said.

"Yes I most certainly would," responded the guest, who was greatly surprised by the violinist's response, as were the rest of the guests.

"No you wouldn't," the violinist said again. "You mean you'd love to play the violin as I do today. But you wouldn't be willing to spend six hours a day seven days a week for twenty years as I have to be able to play that way. If you were willing to do that, you would have already done it, and then you and I could have played a duet together."

Many unsuccessful people see a successful person and say, "Oh, look at that. Man, would I love to have what he or she has. How lucky can you get!"

Lucky? Luck is what happens when preparedness meets opportunity. Unsuccessful people don't know about the planning, the study, the long hours of preparation, the hard work. All they see is the end result, and they call that luck.

QUESTIONS TO ASK YOURSELF

1. Have you really programmed yourself for success?
2. Do you always expect the best from yourself?
3. Do you act like the person that you want to be?
4. Do you have the self-discipline necessary to become the person that you want to be?
5. Do you use a "mental rehearsal" to program your subconscious mind before an important event?
6. Are you constantly changing and growing toward the full development of your potential?
7. Do you use visualization to program your subconscious mind?

If you can answer these seven final questions with a positive yes, then you are well on your way to programming yourself for success with the psychology of self-achievement in everything you do.

Before we move on to the next chapter, I would like to add this one final sentence:

Remember that service is more important than status, and you'll never go wrong.

5

How to Use the Power Within to Become a Successful Entrepreneur

This chapter is a natural sequel to the preceding one, *How to Achieve Financial Success with the Psychology of Self-Achievement.* In this chapter, I want to get right down to the nuts and bolts of the techniques you can use to succeed in your own business.

BENEFITS YOU WILL GAIN

- A great deal of pride and prestige is associated with being in your own business or in fulfilling the role of entrepreneur.

- You can be your own person. You don't have to take orders, orders with which you may not fully agree, from someone higher up on the totem pole as you would in a big company or corporation. When you are in business for yourself, you are the boss—except for the customer, of course—and you can make your own decisions.

- The sky is the limit. The only limitation on your success is you, yourself, and you alone. You can go as high as you want to go, dependent only upon your own talents, abilities, and your creative imagination. You don't have to wait for someone to die or retire to be promoted as you often have to do in the big company or corporation.

- To succeed in your own business will bring you one of the greatest feelings of achievement that you will ever know. It is a truly fantastic feeling to start your own business and to become highly successful in it.

USE YOUR TALENTS TO DO WHAT YOU ARE MEANT TO DO

Why is it that a man like Frank Bettger could be a topnotch salesman and ninety-nine others are complete duds as salespeople? How could Conrad Hilton build a string of successful hotels when many a lesser person would have fallen flat on her financial face? How could Paul J. Meyer become a millionaire selling insurance before he was twenty-seven and then go on to found the world-famous Success Motivation Institute? How could Earl Nightingale and Vic Conant establish the largest and most successful motivational cassette-tape business in the entire world? How could Mary Kay become so wealthy in a cosmetics business that she started from scratch? Or Rich De Vos become a millionaire with Amway, the company he founded?

Or take the entertainment field: What makes certain musicians and singers the best in their field? Why was Jack Benny tops in his profession for so many years? Why do singers like Barbra Streisand and Neil Diamond, just to name two, become so successful? What made Jackie Gleason the "Great Gleason"? Why is one person a brilliant success, while a hundred other would-be entertainers are abject failures? What makes the difference?

Each and every one of these people became successful because they were using their talents and abilities to do what they were meant to do. Now I'm not suggesting that fate or destiny controls your future. Not at all. But I am saying that it is absolutely impossible for you to become the greatest in your chosen work unless you are in the right field to begin with. You must be doing work that will utilize your talents to their fullest. How can you become the greatest at what you're doing unless you are doing what you really want to do, unless you're doing what you're best suited to do? If Jackie Gleason had not become an entertainer, for instance, he would probably have been the character he portrayed on TV: a disgruntled, frustrated, dissatisfied bus driver!

Let me sum up by saying that one of the most important steps you can ever take is to find out what you are best suited to do in the first place. And the earlier in your life that you find that out, the better.

Don't try to make yourself into something for which you have no inborn talents. And don't accept something that's second best. Go for broke; go all the way. And, if you discover that you're in the wrong field, then change no matter how old you are or how many years you have invested in your career. You'll never be happy doing something you don't like to do or that you're not at all fitted for. Use your talents to do what you were meant to do. When you do that, you can become the greatest in your chosen field.

HOW TO PICTURE YOUR WAY TO SUCCESS

Once you have decided what business or profession you're going into, based on your natural talents and abilities, then it's time to put your subconscious mind to work to help you become highly successful.

Remember, your subconscious mind cannot tell the difference between a real experience and one that you vividly imagine. For this reason, your subconscious mind accepts the emotional fantasies that you program into it as being real, and, as a result, it will make them a reality for you!

For instance, if you picture yourself as a famous and highly successful restaurateur with scores, even hundreds, of profitable restaurants, then it can happen for you. Why do you think McDonald's, Wendy's, Burger King, Long John Silver, and others like them are so successful? They surely didn't become that way by accident or pure luck.

Or if you see yourself as a great businessperson with contracts totaling thousands or even millions of dollars annually, you are programming your subconscious mind for success. And its mighty power will give you thoughts and ideas for how to make your fantasy come true.

You can visualize yourself driving that new, expensive car. Or imagine yourself owning that big, beautiful house complete with swimming pool and tennis court. You can actually fantasize sitting in the living room or the family room, being surrounded by comfortable furniture and expensive paintings; walking across thick, luxurious carpets; warming yourself by a magnificent fireplace; sitting in your own Jacuzzi like a Roman emperor; swimming in your own pool; or playing tennis on your own private court. You can even see the deed to your gorgeous home locked up in your bank's safe-deposit box. What a wonderful and comfortable feeling that is.

You can make this programming of your subconscious mind even more realistic by following through on all your imagined activities. By that I mean you can go to a new-car agency and test-drive the kind of automobile you want. You can visit a real-estate broker and have the agent show you through the kind of house you have your heart set on.

You should invest energy and action into this fantasy picture as you program it into your subconscious. The more you reinforce the picture with concrete action, the more real it will become. Soon you won't have to imagine yourself being a successful businessperson. You will actually become one when you use the mighty powers of your subconscious mind to get everything that you want for yourself.

THE FIRST REQUIREMENT FOR A SUCCESSFUL BUSINESS

Have you ever wondered why some businesspeople are so successful while others fail so miserably? Or why so many small business ventures fold only a year or so after starting? The answer is really quite simple. Those who failed didn't find out what people wanted and needed before they started.

The successful businesspeople didn't guess. They found out what their customers wanted and needed before they ever opened for business.

So if you want to go into business for yourself and become successful, you ought to do the same thing. Only by talking to people and asking them questions can you find out what they want. That is the only way you can get the answers you need.

Even medical doctors, who are usually successful, or so it seems at any rate, must get information from their patients if they want to succeed in helping each person get well—because, if people do not get well, the doctor's practice will not flourish. As my own family doctor told me, "There is one cardinal rule that you must follow if you want to be successful in practicing medicine. You must always listen to the patient."

As Frank Bettger, one of America's all-time top life-insurance salesmen and author said: "When you show a person what he wants, he'll move heaven and earth to get it. This universal law is of such paramount importance that it takes precedence over all other laws of human relations. It always has been and always will be the most important. Yes, it looms up as the Number One Rule over all others in civilization."*

If a person will move heaven and earth to get what he wants, and if you can offer him what he wants, then you can't help but become financially successful, can you? When he gets what he wants, you'll automatically get what you want, too.

The late Sam Walton, founder of the Wal-Mart stores and one of the richest men in the whole world, said that the secret of a successful retail business is to *give your customers what they want.*

---

*Frank Bettger, *How I Raised Myself from Failure to Success in Selling* (Englewood Cliffs, NJ: Prentice Hall, 1958).

And what do they want? Well, if you're carrying a variety of merchandise, as the Wal-Mart stores do, you'll find that they want a wide assortment of excellent quality products. They want the lowest possible prices. Your customers also want satisfaction guaranteed or their money back. They ask for friendly and knowledgeable service. They want convenient hours, free parking, and, all in all, a pleasant shopping experience. Customers love it when they visit a store that exceeds all their expectations. But if the store inconveniences them, gives them a hard time, or pretends they are invisible, they will not be back.

How Rachel Brown Used This Formula and Achieved Success in Real Estate

Now I want to tell you how Rachel Brown used this technique—finding out what the prospect wants—to become successful in her profession. But before I tell you that, let me say that the real-estate business is one of the hardest professions in the world in which to become successful. Why? Because it is a business where you have to find both the buyer and the seller. And then you have to satisfy both of them before you can ever close the sale.

Dave Evans, a friend whom I knew when I lived in Springfield, Missouri, told me the following story about his experience with Rachel Brown.

> A few years ago, I decided to sell our house in Springfield so I could buy one out in the country. So I called the Landmark Real Estate Company, and they sent a saleslady, Rachel Brown, out to see me. We talked for a while. Or I should say that I talked. Actually, Rachel just asked me questions and I answered them.
>
> "You have a beautiful house here, Dave," she said. "Good part of town, excellent location, conveniently close, yet not too close, to a new shopping center with lots of good stores. Why on earth do you want to sell your house and buy another home?

"Is it too small for your present needs? I understood you to say that your children are all grown and gone. Or is your house too large for you now that they're gone? Does the room arrangement or space utilization dissatisfy you? Why don't you like your present house, Dave? Tell me what's wrong with it so I'll be better able to know exactly how I can help you."

"Rachel, I'll tell you the straight truth," I said. "There is absolutely nothing wrong with our house. I like it a great deal. If I could just pick it up and move it somewhere else, I'd keep it.

"You see, when we first moved in here, we had a beautiful view of the valley out the front-room window: green fields and beautiful large oak trees. Now all I can see is that new two-story house across the street from me. And the same thing is true in my backyard. All I can look at are my neighbor's garbage cans, his doghouse, the tool storage shed, and a messy barbecue pit. I want a home with a decent view that I can really enjoy like we used to have."

"Good. Now I know exactly what you want and I have just the home you're looking for, Dave," Rachel said. "Twenty miles out south of town. A beautiful home built on top of a hill. You can see for miles around. It has a gorgeous, breathtaking overlook of the James River valley from the front porch. Nothing but green trees and miles of rolling pastureland with the river winding gently through it. You'll love it, Dave. It's exactly what you're looking for from what you've told me."

So we drove out to see the place. Rachel was right. It was everything that I wanted, but the price was really high. "You're asking too much, Rachel," I said. "My house is a newer one, and you know full well I can't begin to get that kind of a price for it."

Rachel didn't argue with me. "Could be, Dave," she said. "But just look at that view of the valley below with its trees, its green pastureland, and the James River winding through it. No one will ever be able to build anything that will destroy that for you. That view belongs to you from now on. No one will ever be able to take it away from you."

"But I don't think I can afford it, Rachel," I said. "I don't have that kind of money lying around loose, and besides . . ."

"Financing is no problem, Dave," Rachel said, interrupting me. "I know of no less than five lending institutions that would loan you the money today without a single question. Your credit rating is tops. I checked that before I ever left the office. Not only that, you don't have to finance the entire cost of your new home. Your present house will handle the majority of the cost for you. .

"And just look at that view from the front-room window here, Dave. Isn't that absolutely spectacular? No house across the street to block your view of the beautiful James River valley. And there never will be. The way the hill drops off, you don't need to worry about anyone ever building a house on it. That's impossible. This is exactly what you asked for, Dave. This is precisely what you said that you wanted."

Each time I talked price or money or financing, Rachel talked about scenery and the beautiful view of the James River and the valley through which it flowed, for she knew full well that was what I was primarily interested in: the scenic view. I'd already told her that back at my house. By asking questions and by listening carefully to my answers, Rachel had found my main interest. She had found my most vulnerable point, and she concentrated on that.

So I bought the house. Or I should say that I bought the view, for that is what Rachel actually sold me. She sold me the view and the scenery . . . the rolling green pastureland of the valley below . . . the James River and the big oak trees. She threw in the house as an extra bonus; it was an additional dividend.

Now I had never met Rachel Brown before that day. She and I were complete strangers until I bought my new home from her. But as soon as Rachel found out exactly what I wanted and then showed me how to get it, she took charge of the situation. She held me in the palm of her hand, for she was in complete control, much as I hate to say that!

You can use the same techniques Rachel Brown used with Dave Evans to get what you want from your prospective customer, too. When you find out precisely what your prospect wants and then show him how to get it, when you discover a person's most vulnerable point and then concentrate on that, and on that alone, you'll be able to succeed in your business, too, no matter what it is. There's absolutely no doubt in my mind about that.

After hearing Dave's story, I wanted to meet Rachel Brown myself, so I called her for a personal interview, which she was kind enough to grant to me. I soon found out that Rachel is one of the smartest businesspeople I have ever met. She knew full well that before she could ever sell a house to a prospect, she had to find out exactly what that prospective buyer wanted. Only then would she ever be able to close the sale.

Rachel also gave me a few more tips about the real-estate business, tips that could be extremely valuable to you even if you're not a real-estate salesperson. For instance, Rachel said that she always tells the owner that she will be glad to sell his *house*. She said she never uses the word *home* when talking to the owner. Home is an emotional word, and the seller can become reluctant to part with his *home* even though he is perfectly willing to get rid of his *house*. By the same token, she says she never sells the buyer just a *house*. She always offers him a *home*.

These two words represent two entirely different ideas for the same object, Rachel said. A house is not a home; it's only a house. It's make of bricks, wood, and concrete. It's a very nonemotional idea. But a home is where your heart is, where your family lives, where your children grow up.

So if you're in sales, and almost everybody in business is in one way or another, please remember that *emotional words are power words,* and that people are always ruled more by emotion than by logic and reason. Smart salespeople always use emotional words because those words cause people to buy. A top salesperson will never ask a person what she *thinks* about a product. Instead, he will always ask the prospect how she *feels* about it.

Think is a nonemotional word that requires the person to use logic and reason. But *feel* is an emotional word that goes right to the listener's heart. If I haven't told you this before, I want to do so right now: *The head never hears 'til the heart has listened.* That one statement will tell you more about how to understand the human psyche than all the psychology books in the world ever will, and it will help you climb clear to the top in the business world.

How Bill Wilson Became a Resoundingly Successful Entrepreneur

In my last book, *21 Days to Unlimited Power with People,** I discussed Bill Wilson's success story as a "small" businessman. But Bill is such an extremely successful young businessperson, I felt it was well worthwhile to tell you about him here, too, just in case you haven't read *21 Days to Unlimited Power.*

So in December 1992, I visited Bill again, so that I could bring myself up to date on his activities since I last

---

*James K. Van Fleet, *21 Days to Unlimited Power with People* (Englewood Cliffs, NJ: Prentice Hall, 1992).

interviewed him. Bill bought R & S Soft Water Services in January 1973 for less than $17,000, mainly for accounts receivable, one truck, and used office furniture. The outlay for parts, equipment, and supplies was only $1,287.35. Bill knew the amount right down to the last penny.

Today, the building he is in, which he had built in October 1978, and with the addition of another building of 6,000 square feet in January 1983, is worth more than half a million dollars, not including supplies and equipment contained therein.

This is amazing growth when you consider that when I interviewed Bill in December 1992 it was just one month short of his being in the business for twenty years.

"Bill, I want to ask you, and don't answer me if you don't care to, are you a millionaire yet?" I said.

Laughing at my question, Bill said, "Not quite, Jim. After all, I did have to put two kids through college, and that's an expensive proposition, as you yourself know only too well. But I'm getting there. Another hundred thousand or so and I'll have made it."

That is quite an impressive record. When Bill started his business, he was the only employee. R & S Soft Water Services was his only business. Today there are thirty-six employees and three subsidiary companies: Water Queen of Florida, Eagle Drilling Company, and Pennington Well Drilling Company. Bill also opened up a new branch location in 1991 so that he could better serve all his customers.

What is the key to Bill's astounding success? Well, let him tell you himself: *"Total service is the real key to business success—the customer must come first, last, and always.* Whatever a customer needs regarding water—whether it is a well, water purifier, irrigation system, or a pump—we provide it. We never send our customers anywhere else."

How did Bill make the decision to go into the water business? Well, Bill was tired of working for someone else. He wanted to go into business for himself. But he was not exactly sure of what kind of business to go into.

So, before he made this crucial decision, he wisely decided to make a survey of the area so that he could find out what people wanted or what essential service they were lacking. He went from house to house, knocked on dozens of doors, and talked to a tremendous number of people to get his answer.

And Bill found out that the majority of people complained about the high cost of using city water to keep their yards beautiful and green. You see, in spite of its lakes and water on three sides, Florida never has enough rainfall. Grass must be watered constantly throughout the year or lawns will die out and become nothing more than barren weed patches.

Based on his survey, Bill decided to go into the lawn-sprinkling business. He digs a deep well so that the homeowner has a source of free water for his lawn. Then he puts in a yard-watering system complete with pump, underground pipes, and lawn sprinklers.

Another major complaint that people had was the extremely hard city water that corroded plumbing fixtures, ruined washing machines and dishwashers, made clothes take on a dirty gray and grimy look, and left a filthy ring that could never be completely removed from the tub after a bath. So Bill installs water-conditioning units that eliminate these problems.

At R & S we take a personal interest in our customers. I, or any one of my irrigation people, can tell you the name of the homeowner for whom we installed our first irrigation system and how many sprinkler heads it took.

Some of our customers who are retired and living on a fixed income get special consideration on pricing. Hopefully, someone is treating my mother and father like we treat their's.

R & S is open six days a week. We pride ourselves on same-day service. We do very little advertising; the majority of our new irrigation business comes from personal referrals like you, Jim.

Another example of Bill's commitment to personal service to the customer is his firm's reaction to the December 1989 freeze that killed citrus trees by the thousands, broke water mains and water pipes everywhere, and paralyzed Florida as far south as Miami.

The weekend before Christmas the temperature dropped to 28 degrees, and the calls started coming in. Pipes were freezing, leaving homeowners and businesses without water.

I called my people in from their Christmas vacation, and we stayed open during the entire crisis. We were even open on Christmas Eve and Christmas Day until 9 P.M. We helped people get their water back and saved them some expensive repair bills. Many homeowners found out they could depend upon us in a pinch. So who do you think they'll call when they decide to put in an irrigation system or install a water conditioner?

The Palm Bay community has learned that Bill Wilson is also generous with both his personal time and his money. "I believe in putting back into the community what I take out of it," Bill said, and he does exactly that, for he sponsors Little League baseball, soccer, and bowling teams.

Bill has set an outstanding example for you to follow if you want to be successful in your own business. If you follow his methods of finding out what people want and need so you can help them get it as he has done, and if you practice his philosophy of total dedication and service to the customer just as Bert Bartingale, the plumber I told you about previously also did, then you cannot help but succeed no matter what business you decide to go into. It will be absolutely impossible for you to fail.

What Made Dale Carter Successful

When you move from one place to another, two people that you want to find immediately are a good doctor and an honest and reliable mechanic.

After I moved to Florida, I found the good doctor almost at once. But it took me several years to locate the garage with the honest and capable mechanic whom I could trust. Here's how that happened.

One morning my neighbor was having trouble with her car. "I can't get it out of second," she told me. "I suppose I'll end up paying several hundred dollars for a new transmission," she said as she drove off to the garage in second gear.

But less than an hour later she was back home and her car was in the driveway again. "Marcia, what happened?" I asked her. "Is your car fixed already?"

"Oh yes," she replied, laughing happily. "It was only a missing cotter pin. Dale fixed it for only three dollars."

I could hardly believe what I had just heard. "Where is this place?" I asked. "I've been looking for a good garage and an honest mechanic ever since we moved down here."

"Well, take your car to Carter's Garage down on Palm Bay Road," Marcia said. "They know what they're doing, and they won't cheat you either."

Now I had driven past Carter's Garage many times, but it was back off the street quite a way all by itself, and I hadn't been impressed by its appearance. All I could think of was "shade-tree mechanic" when I looked at the garage so far back off the main road.

But Marcia was right. I've had my car worked on at Dale Carter's Garage for nearly twenty years now. In fact, I now live in Orlando, and I still drive seventy-five miles over there to have Dale service my car. That's how much I think of his work and how much I trust him and his mechanics.

Dale is so honest he'll let you watch his mechanics work as long as you don't get in the way. No other garage will ever let you do that. Most of them will tell you it's because of insurance regulations, but don't let them kid you for one moment. They don't want you to see what they're doing, period.

Dale told me about the elderly gentleman who brought his car in one day. "'Do you mind if I watch your work?' he asked me," Dale said. "When I said it was all right to do so, he went back to his trunk, got out a three-legged stool, brought it to the front of the car, sat down on it, and then said, 'Go right ahead; I'm ready.' When he said *watch*, he really meant it," Dale laughed.

Dale has never lost a customer in all the time he has been in business. Everyone recommends him without any reservation whatever. His customers all support him 100 percent and back him to the hilt.

His business philosophy is quite simple and like a breath of fresh air in a cynical business world. "If I can't earn an honest living working on cars, I'll do something else," Dale says. "I don't have to cheat anyone to make money."

I must say that I agree with Dale's business philosophy wholeheartedly. It's no wonder that his parking lot is always packed full with customers' cars. It's also no wonder that he is so successful in what he does for a living.

HOW TO MAKE SURE YOUR CUSTOMER COMES BACK

Before you part company with your customer, be sure to stress again all the benefits she has gained by doing business with you. Always leave her with a good feeling toward you. Remember that the best business is repeat business. The one-time sale where you have to make a new customer every time is a tough business to be in.

Let me ask you this now: After you've bought a new car, how many salesmen have ever contacted you again to see if everything was okay with your car or just to thank you for your purchase? I've bought a number of new cars in my life, and of all those salesmen, only one ever bothered to get in touch with me afterward.

In fact, when I'd take my car to be serviced by the agency I'd bought it from, most salesmen would run and hide to avoid hearing me complain.

So let me give you a little tip here about doing business with people. *Never forget a customer; never let a customer forget you.* Another way of saying this is *the best way to get new customers is to take care of the old ones.*

So always leave the person with a good taste in her mouth. Make her glad that she did business with you. Remember, you may have to come back to the same well more than once for a drink of water.

NINE WAYS TO LET YOUR BUSINESS DO YOUR TALKING FOR YOU

Here are nine methods you can use to let your business talk for you even when you are home and sound asleep in bed.

1. Have a Big Sign—a Gigantic One.

Make your sign the biggest one in the whole town, one that can be seen and read twenty-four hours a day. People should be able to read it plainly in daylight, and it should flame your name and business in big neon letters at night.

Let it work for you twenty-four hours a day. This is the most effective and inexpensive advertising you can use. As one highly successful businessman told me, "I want people to remember the name of my business, and advertising with a big outdoor neon sign is the best and least expensive way I can do that. After the initial cost of installation, maintenance is negligible."

2. Always Use Your Windows as Silent Salesmen.

Your window displays can easily pay for 25 percent of your overhead if you use them as silent salesmen. Keep the lights on in your store windows and let them work for you twenty-four hours a day, just as your big outdoor sign does.

3. Let Your Store Shelves Sell for You, Too.

Well-displayed goods are already half sold. Letting people wait on themselves and pick their purchases off the shelves is the key to success in the supermarket. Items behind the counter don't sell nearly as well as those on the shelves in the aisles. If people can't see what you have to sell, then they can't buy it.

4. Let Friendly and Cheerful Employees Sell for You.

Remember what I told you before, about how I drive nearly two miles to a supermarket because the one only two blocks from me has such surly, sour-faced, discourteous employees. If I would do that, so would other people. A cheerful and friendly face attracts customers. A sour face drives people away. A smile is one of the biggest assets your employees can have, so make sure they always wear one.

Tell them to leave their troubles at home. Bob Gannon, a business friend of mine, told me that he was once congratulated by one of his employees for coming to work every day with a big smile on his face and for never carrying his personal problems to the office with him.

"What he didn't know was that some mornings I had to stand outside the door and screw that smile on my face before I went into the office, but evidently it was worth my doing that," Bob said with a laugh.

5. Tie an Easily Remembered Slogan to Your Business.

Give people something specific to remember you by. For instance, people always remember the slogan, "You're in good hands with ALLSTATE."

So make up your own slogan. A successful furniture store in a small Iowa farm town has a huge sign that says "Brin's Furniture Store Around the Corner on Seneca." That's not an earthshaking slogan by any means, but it is unique enough for people to remember, so they come from miles around to buy their furniture at Brin's rather than go somewhere else.

6. Use Color to Promote Sales.

Bright colors are cheerful and attract customers. Paint the door red and let people know you're alive and kicking! For instance, if you have a paint-and-wallpaper store, color is what you're selling above all else. Use color on your trucks, in your store, on your stationery, and on your wrapping paper. That's a natural for you to do.

7. Advertise, Advertise, Advertise.

Advertise, even if it's only a few lines in a newspaper, on a billboard, or mail promotion. Doing business without advertising is like winking at a girl in the dark. You know what you're doing, but no one else does. Maybe that sounds old-fashioned to you, but it's still true.

You must do something to reach that person out there who gets to town only once in a while, and believe it or not, there are still a lot of people like that, especially in the Midwest in farm country.

You need to let those people know that you have shoes and suits or dresses and blouses or paint and brushes or whatever it is you have in your store. If you don't let them know, then some company or store down the street will be telling them, and that store will end up with the business. Every potential customer is important to you, so go after him or her.

8. When Something New Comes Out, Get It for Your Customers.

New is the greatest word of all in merchandising. People always want the very latest thing, so give it to them. The two most used words in television advertising are *new and improved,* but they must work, for advertisers use them over and over again.

9. Get All the Free Publicity You Can.

If you can do it, get your company's name in your local newspaper without using advertising to do so. A great many people, especially in a small town, are interested in news of local importance, for they can see all the latest world news on television.

So if you can, get the name of your business in the newspaper when you have a wedding or an anniversary in your store or your company. Tell the reporters about it. Have a photographer take pictures. This will give you free space in the news column where people can see your name. Publicity like this can't be bought for any price. What could be cheaper than that?

TWENTY-TWO FINAL TIPS ON HOW TO SUCCEED IN YOUR OWN BUSINESS

The fear of failure is always the greatest fear a businessperson can have, so I want to give you twenty-two final tips on how to succeed in your own business, so you can avoid that fear.

Perhaps even more than money, pride is on the line with a new business venture. The threat of failure will almost drive a person to do the unthinkable to make the business a resounding success.

The wife of a young man going into the restaurant business told me this: "We have to succeed in this venture. Everything we have is in it, our savings, our home, the whole works. We just can't go down the tubes. I swear that death would be only slightly worse than our failure!"

To help her gain confidence, I said this to her: "Never let the fear of failure enter your mind. If you think for just one moment that you are going to fail, then you surely will, for as you think so shall you become. But if you think that you will succeed, then you most certainly will, for you will be programming your subconscious mind with the proper thoughts, and again, the same concept is true, you always become what you think about."

That conversation took place more than a year ago. Did it help them? Of course it did. Their business is booming today in spite of competition from a cafeteria, a Chinese restaurant, a bagel shop, and a McDonald's all in the same shopping center.

Some people don't understand how programming the subconscious mind with positive success thoughts will help them succeed. The reason it works is because the subconscious mind is creative and will feed you fresh ideas that you can use to become successful in your business, whatever it is.

That is exactly what happened for the young couple with the restaurant business. Thinking positive success thoughts gave them new, creative ideas from their subconscious minds. They were able to use these ideas to make their restaurant more attractive and to dream up new and delectable items for their menu.

I now want to give you the following twenty-two tips so you can make sure you do succeed in your own business.

1. Know what you can do best and use this talent to build your business. It is one of your greatest strengths, and no one can ever take that ability away from you.

2. Always promote the strengths of your business. Remember that your competitors are selling their strengths, too.

3. Compete by saying how good your products or your services are. Don't try to compete by badmouthing your competitors. Tactics like that will always backfire and hurt you in the long run. Politicians who don't have a good record to run on try to win by mudslinging, and they always lose as a result.

4. Remember that your customer's welfare, not yours, is always his first concern. He wants to know exactly what you can do for him, not what he can do for you.

5. Treat your small accounts with respect, understanding, and the expectation that some day soon they'll be big ones.

6. Don't think that your prospects are ignorant if they don't understand your sales pitch the first time around, or even the second or third time that you give it. Could be it's your sales pitch that's off base rather than their understanding.

7. Always think in terms of your customer's needs and then determine how you can fill those needs for them.

8. Don't become too dependent on your "good" accounts. Who knows, tomorrow they could be persuaded to take their business somewhere else. Keep on your toes to prevent that.

9. Don't let temporary successes cause you to lower your standards, forget your ultimate goals, or cause you to let up—even a little.

10. Don't make the assumption that everyone is as honest as you are, but don't think that everyone else is dishonest either.

11. Selling good-quality merchandise is your best bet if you want to succeed in business. Cheap-quality merchandise will not win you lasting customers.

12. Two strong statements you can use to sell your products or your services are these: (1) I can save you money and (2) I can help you make more money.

13. Don't try shoddy scheming to sell the customer. "Once burned, twice shy" will be the end result of that.

14. Keep up with what your customers want and need. Business is never static. Change is constant, so stay up to date. If some item isn't moving, get rid of it. Don't keep it in your inventory. Free that money for other uses.

15. Remember that someone else will always have a lower price. This means you must have better quality to justify your higher price.

16. You can never stop learning. You can never have too much information about your business. Organize your know-how and use it when and where it is needed to become successful.

17. Build a reputation for honesty and integrity. It will win you customers who will stick with you.

18. There are no shortcuts to your business success. Those all lead down blind alleys. It takes plain old-fashioned hard work to succeed in business, but if you want it enough, you can do it.

19. Always give your customer more for his money than your competitor does. If you're selling bagels or doughnuts, for example, always give them a "baker's dozen."

20. Give them more than they pay for and make sure they know that when you do. If you sell him a suit, give him a matching handkerchief or a pair of socks to go with it as a special gift. If you sell her an expensive dress, a tiny vial of cologne as a small gift will help bring her back again.

21. Treat everyone you contact in your business with the same dignity and respect that you expect for yourself. This includes your customers, your coworkers, your employees—yes, and even your competitors, too.

22. Finally, realize that you can't sell everyone on everything, so don't be disheartened when you don't.

And now, let's move on to the next chapter, which also deals with business, but this time I want to show you how to succeed in a big corporation using the psychology of self-achievement.

6

How to Use the Power Within to Climb the Corporate Ladder

Not everyone has the desire to start his or her own business or to become an entrepreneur, usually because they do not want to assume the risk for the sake of profit. Many people are quite happy and content to work in a big company or corporation, and they often become extremely successful financially by doing so. A great many benefits are to be gained from being employed in a big company.

BENEFITS YOU WILL GAIN

- Job security, including retirement benefits.
- Health-insurance plans, including hospitalization.
- No risks: You don't run the danger of failure or bankruptcy that you might in your own business.
- The possibility of a huge salary in the upper-management and executive levels, especially if you become the chief executive officer, president, or chairman of the board.
- Stock options and other large bonuses. For instance, just the other day I read that the CEO of a large corporation held more than $200 million in stock options.

ELEVEN ESSENTIAL QUALITIES OF THE SUCCESSFUL CORPORATE EXECUTIVE

In developing these eleven qualities, I was helped by department and division heads, top-level managers, and executives from twenty extremely successful companies and corporations representing a variety of products and services. The information included in this section represents the very latest thinking of top leaders and executives in business and industry. According to them, a successful executive must:

1. **Know Your Business Inside out and Stick to It.** You must be well rounded in your profession, no matter how your knowledge was gathered, whether by formal education or practical experience, or both. To be well rounded means you must have not only a broad and general knowledge about your profession but you must also possess specific knowledge of its most intricate and intimate details.

You must continue to seek out more information about your field. To remain static is to slide backward. You have to know your own job, your subordinate's job, and your superior's duties if you don't want to be left in the dust of your contemporaries.

If you know your business and stick to it, you can gain the respect, confidence, willing obedience, loyal cooperation, and full support of all of your subordinates. You'll be able to motivate them to do their best for you. Anything less than that is not enough. To accept the minimum instead of going for the maximum is like stopping at third base. It adds no more to the score of the ball game than striking out!

2. **Constantly Seek to Improve Yourself.** Knowing yourself and making an honest evaluation of your executive strengths and weaknesses is half the battle, that's for sure, but it's only the first half. For your inventory of yourself to be worthwhile, you must then take definite and active steps to improve—to rid yourself of your weaknesses and build up your strong points.

You'll need to develop such personal leadership attributes as courage, bearing, knowledge, loyalty, enthusiasm, integrity, and a sense of justice. And you'll always need to set an example for your subordinates to follow.

If you take these positive steps to improve yourself and develop your leadership abilities, you'll grow a mile taller in the eyes of those who work for you. And, just as important, you'll really impress your boss, too.

3. Know Your Staff and Look out for Their Welfare. You must make an honest effort to observe your people, to become personally acquainted with them, and to recognize their individual differences if you want to better understand why they do and say the things they do. By anticipating and providing for their needs on the job, you will gain their full support.

If your subordinates feel that you are deeply concerned about their personal welfare and that you're honestly placing their interests above your own, they'll have a much better attitude toward you and the entire company. They'll be most eager to help you succeed and get ahead.

4. Keep Your Staff Informed and Up to Date. We all want to know exactly what is expected of us. We also want to know how well we have done. If you keep your subordinates well informed, you'll find this will encourage their initiative, it will improve their teamwork, and it will enhance their morale.

The person who knows the situation and exactly what you expect will always do a far better job than the one who does not. It is always the unknown that people most fear. Eliminate the fear, and you'll have gone a long way toward improving the overall efficiency of your organization, whether it's a department or the entire company.

Each person and the entire group will appreciate your recognition of their efforts when a job has been especially well done. By the proper use of the awards-and-incentive program along with the use of a well-planned public information program, you'll be able to favorably influence individual morale and organizational esprit. Improved efficiency and increased profits will be the end result of your efforts.

5. **Make Sure Tasks Are Understood, Supervised, and Accomplished.** The first step is to make sure that your orders are understood. Next, you must supervise to ensure that your orders are properly carried out. Finally, you must see that the work assigned is successfully completed.

A wise executive will decentralize the work to be done so that his orders and directives can be carried out more readily. Failure to decentralize the work will prevent the proper utilization of each person's skills.

Your staff will respond more quickly to orders that are easily understood and that, at the same time, allow them to use their initiative and ingenuity. Always use mission-type statements when you can. They tell a person what you want done and when you want it, but they leave the "how-to" up to the individual. If you don't use mission-type orders, you don't need people to do the work—all you need are machines.

6. **Develop a Sense of Teamwork Among Your Staff.** Teamwork is the key to successful operation of any organization. It is one of the most effective tools you can use if you want to be a master motivator of others. To be truly effective, teamwork must start at the top and work its way down to the last person. Each person must know where he fits into the team if you want him to give his utmost to the group effort.

Effective teamwork requires a high state of morale, esprit, discipline, and individual proficiency. At the same time, good teamwork promotes all these, and, in addition, it contributes to the overall organizational efficiency.

You should never neglect an individual's accomplishments in your emphasis on the efforts of the group as a whole. You must always weigh and balance these two very carefully. Both the recognition of the individual and the final accomplishment of the entire group are important in motivating others.

When you give an individual the proper recognition she deserves, you'll help satisfy her needs for attention and importance. By the same token, she will also get a feeling of pride in her accomplishments as a member of the team. She'll also gain a feeling of job security when your organization excels as a result of its teamwork.

7. **Be Able to Make Sound and Timely Decisions.** If you learn how to make sound and timely decisions as a modern business executive should, you'll motivate your people to trust you and have confidence in you. They'll be inspired to do their best for you when you show good judgment and common sense in your business decisions.

The business executive who cannot make a sound and timely decision will never be able to motivate people to do what's needed. Furthermore, such indecision will cause hesitancy, loss of confidence, and general confusion in the whole company.

When circumstances arise that cause a change in your plans, your prompt action will enhance your people's confidence in you. Constant study, training, and proper planning on your part will lay the foundation necessary for professional and technical business competence that is so necessary to make sound and timely decisions.

8. **Develop a Sense of Responsibility in Your Subordinates.** (If you delegate authority which is commensurate with the responsibility you give a person, you will develop a mutual confidence and respect.) By delegating authority, you'll motivate your staff to do its best to get the job done. Such delegation of authority and responsibility will encourage your people to exercise their initiative and ingenuity, and to give you their wholehearted cooperation and support.

Whenever you delegate authority, you show that you trust a person, that you have faith in his or her judgment. You've given that person a vote of confidence. He'll respond by asking you for more responsibility, which is what you want him to do.

9. **Take Total Responsibility for Your Own Actions.** Actively seek responsibility and responsibility will find you. When you do that, you'll develop yourself professionally. Taking the initiative in the absence of orders from your superiors is one of the primary signs that you've learned to accept responsibility.

When you take the responsibility for your own actions *and* for the actions of your staff, you'll gain their respect and confidence. They'll gladly give you their willing obedience, loyal cooperation, and full support.

Don't be afraid to make mistakes. There's a big difference between mistakes and failures. Remember, too, you must still accept responsibility even after you've reached the summit. You'll never to able to abdicate it and stay up there on top.

10. **Always Set an Example for Your Staff to Follow.** Only by setting the example can the image of the leader be created. Your personality will have a far-reaching effect and influence upon your subordinates. In fact, the personality and attitude of the company is simply an extension of your own individual personality.

If you appear in an unfavorable light before your people, you'll destroy the mutual confidence and respect that must exist between you.

In short, to set the example does not mean to do as I say, it means to *do as I do!*

11. **Build Each Staff Member's Self-Esteem.** To do that, you must make each person feel important. Give dignity and respect to her job and you will motivate her to do what you want her to do.

If you make a person and her work important to you, if you are hearty in your approbation and lavish in your praise, you can be sure she will always *want to do* what you want her to do. But if you try to push her to do something against her will, you will never get the job done. Remember the phrase, *the head never hears 'til the heart has listened?* You motivate people by winning people's hearts—not their heads!

WHY YOU MUST LOOK THE PART TO GET THE PART

If you want to reach the top, then you must look like a top-level executive even before you get there. This requires two things: (1) proper dress and (2) proper bearing.

Now I am not going to go into a lot of detail here about how you should dress. That will depend entirely on where you live and what the dress code and customs are for your company. (I live in Florida and I know that the business executives dress code here is much more relaxed than it is in other places.) The important point is to show those above you that you will fit in perfectly well at their level.

In general, however, leave loud clothes like prints, checks, and plaids at home, or wear them when you're off-duty on weekends. The simpler the design of your clothing, the more effective you'll appear.

The most successful executives usually wear subdued colors with only one striking point of interest near the face. For a man, that's usually a tie—not a busy one, please—and for a woman, it can be a necklace or scarf. Regarding colors: Navy and white have been proven to inspire the most confidence in you from your subordinates; black and white run a close second.

When it comes to bearing and poise, you can develop certain physical characteristics that will help you project the power of an executive personality: a steady, unflinching gaze; a tone of voice that implies complete self-confidence and commands immediate obedience; and, above all, a solid presence that lets your superiors know that you are exactly where you ought to be and that you will fit in well at the top.

Lastly, let me say that erect posture with your head up and a ramrod-straight spine projects a self-assured manner and bearing, indicating that you have supreme confidence in yourself and your abilities. As a result, both your superiors and your subordinates will have full confidence in you.

HOW TO TALK YOUR WAY TO THE TOP

A famous psychologist made an extremely detailed study of successful executives—both men and women—to determine the reason for their success. She found that these people all had one thing in common: *their skill in using words.*

She also discovered that their financial success was closely linked to this skill. You can expect not only your earnings to increase greatly when your language skills improve but more rapid promotion to the upper executive levels as well.

I can say without a doubt that when you can command words to serve your thoughts and feelings, you are well on your way to the top.

To conclude, let me say that if you want to sound like an executive who's on the way up, watch what you say and how you say it. Be on guard constantly to keep grammatical errors from creeping in to your writing or speaking. If you aren't sure of something, ask someone who can give you the correct answer. I'm the author of more than a dozen books, but to this day when I encounter a grammatical problem, I pick up the phone and call my granddaughter's high school English teacher. She's never told me yet to stop bothering her. You see, when I ask for her advice, I'm making her feel important; I'm feeding her ego, and that makes her happy.

HOW TO MAKE YOURSELF INVALUABLE

I realize that no one is indispensable, but you can make yourself so valuable that your boss will think that he cannot possibly get along without you. Knowing your job inside out is one of the best ways to make yourself needed.

So become an expert in your field. Be willing to share your knowledge with others, and your reputation for being needed will grow and grow. People will get used to going to you for answers. And that's good, for it builds your reputation and enhances the positive image your boss has of you.

Remember that if you really are tops in your field, there is absolutely no limit to how far you can go. First of all, not every clerk wants to become an executive. Not every draftsman wants to become an engineer. Some salespeople don't want to become the sales manager. Many a sergeant has turned down an officer's commission in the army because he doesn't want to accept greater responsibility.

Many people are content with the jobs they have and where they are right now. And that's perfectly fine if that is what they want. But I assume you want something more for yourself than that, otherwise you wouldn't be reading this book. And no matter what you are doing right now in your work, I know you can be happier by doing your job better, earning more recognition, and by preparing yourself for promotion and advancement to the executive ranks in your company.

How can you best make yourself needed by your boss and by your company? Let's ask Tom McClellan, the sales and marketing vice president of a large nationwide pharmaceutical company.

The best way you can prepare yourself for promotion to the top executive levels is to increase your knowledge of your own product and the products of your company's competitors. You should acquaint yourself thoroughly with company policy, the history of the industry, the whole manufacturing process of your products from beginning to end, your company's research and development program; its marketing operations; and your customers' peculiar and individual problems.

If you will do these things, you'll be able to answer any possible question your customers might have about your company. And in so doing you will make yourself more valuable to your company. You will make yourself wanted and needed by both your superior and your customers by following through and learning everything you possibly can about your job. You'll also be preparing yourself for advancement and promotion far ahead of most of your contemporaries, who are only too willing just to coast along and take it easy.

HOW TO LET YOUR BOSS KNOW YOU CAN BE DEPENDED ON TO GET THE JOB DONE

You should always let your boss know that you can be depended on to do the job and to do it well. About the finest reputation you can build with your superior is to have it said of you that "you can get things done without any excuses for failure."

If you are going to earn this kind of reputation with your boss, he has to be able to rely on you to carry out his orders actively, aggressively, intelligently, and willingly. Don't misunderstand me here: Your boss should not expect blind obedience. A reasonable boss will always be willing to listen to suggestions for improvement from his staff. If he is not willing to do that, then I'll bet that you will soon be his superior.

Sam Utterback, senior vice-president of a large Atlanta-based firm with national markets across the country told me that his company recommends that their employees follow these six specific techniques to develop the quality of dependability:

1. Never make excuses for failure.
2. Don't evade your responsibility by passing the buck.
3. Do every job to the best of your ability, no matter what your personal feelings are about it.
4. Be exact and meticulous about doing the details of your job.
5. Form the habit of always being on time.
6. Carry out the intent and the spirit as well as the literal meaning of the order.

SIX WAYS TO ESTABLISH GOOD RELATIONSHIPS WITH THE TOP EXECUTIVES

It is very important for you to establish friendly and pleasant relationships between yourself and the top executives in your company. You'll never make it to the top in your company unless you do. You cannot afford to have a single enemy above you anywhere. I don't care how good you are technically and professionally, if you're not on good terms with those above you, you're destined to stay in either a lower- or middle-management position. Cordial relationships are a must if you expect to get ahead, so let me give you six techniques for developing good rapport with others.

1. **Never Make a Fuss About Minor Matters.** Always go along with small, insignificant points when you can do so without causing irreparable harm either to yourself or your position. When it is necessary for you to make an issue out of something, make certain that it is a major point. When you do that, your objection will stand out clearly, and you'll be remembered and well thought of by your superiors for your professional knowledge, attitude, and conduct.

If you constantly bicker and fuss over small points, your bosses may react just as Sam Baldwin, president of a large office-supply company in Orlando, Florida, does. Sam told me how irritated he becomes when one of his staff members bogs down a meeting with nitpicking on insignificant matters:

> One of my people makes a federal case out of every little point he doesn't agree with. He holds up the whole meeting and wastes everyone's time. If he wasn't as good a junior executive as he is in other areas, I'd have fired him a long time ago. But one of these days he's going to push me over the edge, and I'll have to give him the boot. I do feel he's reached the top of his capabilities right where he is and that he's not qualified for further promotion.

2. State Your Objection Clearly, Calmly, and Courteously. If you must disagree with a major point, then back up your disagreement with logic, reason, and facts. Objections based on how you "feel" about a certain thing will not carry any weight.

After your objection has been presented and your boss has considered it, if her final decision goes against your recommendation, then don't carry a chip on your shoulder. Always support your supervisor's selected course of action. You'll be respected as a team player if you do that.

Just remember that you are not responsible for that final decision; your boss is. If it turns out that she was wrong and you were right, she'll remember that fact and be sure to listen to you more carefully the next time.

3. Always Develop the "Golden Touch" in Human Relationships. The ability to get along with others is required if you expect to get ahead in the big company or corporation. As I have already told you, you cannot expect to move up the executive ladder if you make enemies out of everyone. In fact, knowing how to handle people successfully is one of the hallmarks of executive leadership. If you cannot get along with your associates, if you are constantly involved in verbal warfare with someone, you'll be let go, no matter what your qualifications and abilities are, for you'll become known as a troublemaker.

Believe it or not, the company will survive without you. As Walter Parkhill, a retired army colonel, once told me, "I didn't think the army would ever be able to make it without me, but to my amazement, they did. In fact, I don't think they even knew that I was retired and gone for at least a couple of months or so! Just think what that does to your ego."

4. Be Enthusiastic About Your Work. Don't expect to move up the executive ladder to the top rung if you don't really have your heart in your work. Your boss can easily tell whether you do or not, for your attitude will always be reflected on your face and in your actions.

If you can't go to work smiling because you love your work and enjoy the people you work with, then I suggest that you quickly get enthusiastic about your job or that you change your job before it's too late to do so.

5. **Never Be Afraid to Take a Reasonable Risk.** Top-level executives do expect their subordinates to have the courage to take reasonable risks. If you always play it safe, you'll never get anywhere. "Nothing ventured, nothing gained," is an old saying that fits quite well here. However, good planning will prevent most major problems and greatly reduce the risks.

6. **Always Look for Greater Responsibility.** If you duck your responsibilities you'll never reach the top. Upper-level executives are always looking for those people who can and will accept more and more responsibility. The person who can do that is always labeled a "comer."

Remember that whenever you delegate a job to one of your subordinates to do, you are not passing the buck. Instead, you're freeing yourself to accept additional responsibility. Top management is always extremely happy to find a competent person who is available to take care of tough projects. If you want to climb the executive ladder to success, then let that person be you.

HOW TO AVOID THE EIGHT MOST-NOTICED EXECUTIVE PITFALLS

A detailed survey of more than five hundred executives in a number of large companies and corporations found the following eight executive and managerial weaknesses to be the most noticeable:

1. Lack of organization and planning
2. Lack of initiative
3. Improper delegation of authority
4. Inability to make sound and timely decisions

5. Inability to communicate with people
6. Failure to develop subordinates' potential
7. Inability to promote effective human relationships
8. Failure to set reasonable standards of achievement

These eight factors were found to be the most critical in the development of managerial and executive potential. To help you develop your own executive abilities so that you can succeed in the big company or corporation, I have made up a list of questions.

I was aided in this task by information provided by the same department and division heads, top-level managers, and executives of those twenty successful companies and corporations that I mentioned earlier. These questions, then, represent the best and most-current thinking of the best managerial and executive minds in America.

Fourteen Ways to Plan and Organize Your Work

1. Do you understand your job responsibilities and the authority you have to carry them out?
2. Can you draw up sensible plans with realistic schedules for getting the job done?
3. Do you subdivide the work into easier (and progressive) phases, setting intermediate goals to be attained?
4. Do you use your resources of money, people, time, materials, and facilities properly to get the job done with as little waste as possible?
5. Do you use overtime only as a last resort to get the job done on time? When overtime is absolutely necessary, do you inform your people as soon as possible to prevent inconvenience and worker dissatisfaction?
6. Do you reevaluate the work load of each person periodically to cut down on overtime and to ensure that every individual is doing a full day's productive work?

7. Do you effectively establish priorities for the work to be done, both by yourself and by your people?

8. Do you conduct *effective* meetings and conduct them only when required, avoiding unnecessary or routine ones that waste productive time?

9. Are your meetings held to help people or harass them?

10. Do you make sure that each person knows the duties and responsibilities of the job? Is each one doing the assigned work in a satisfactory manner?

11. Do you make full use of all the skills and abilities of your people?

12. Do you have a program for cross-training?

13. Do you make sure that your people have the equipment and materials they need when they need them?

14. Do you have a method of accounting for everyone and their activities during the workday?

Seven Ways to Put Initiative and Ingenuity into Your Work

1. Do you recognize problems and solve them or correct situations that need improvement even in the absence of your superior?

2. Do you come up with fresh ideas for solving problems?

3. Do you make the most of a new plan or promising idea?

4. Do you encourage your people to submit new methods and ideas to you?

5. Do you use worthwhile suggestions made by your subordinates? Do you give them the proper credit when you do that?

6. Do you think and plan ahead?

7. Do you look for additional responsibility?

Nine Ways to Delegate Authority

1. Do you effectively delegate authority to do the job?
2. Do you avoid interfering after you have passed on to a subordinate the authority to do the job?
3. Do you realize that you still retain the full responsibility for the success or failure of the mission?
4. Do you use mission-type orders effectively?
5. Do you push the decision-making process down to the lowest level possible?
6. Do you keep from getting bogged down in details of work that belongs to someone else?
7. Do you do the difficult jobs yourself for fear they will not get done if you do not?
8. Do you make sure the work is being done properly?
9. Do you ask your people to participate in setting work objectives, priorities, and schedules?

Nine Ways to Make Tough Decisions

1. Do you make tough decisions or do you try to pass the buck upstairs to your superior?
2. Are your decisions consistent with established company policies and procedures?
3. Do you stay within the bounds of your own authority in making your decisions?
4. Do you use a realistic problem-solving process in reaching your decisions?
5. Do you ask for the advice and help of others in reaching your decisions?
6. Do you give your employees a chance to actively participate in the decisions that will affect them?

7. Do you accept the full responsibility for your decisions?

8. Can you make up your mind without unnecessary delay?

9. Do you have the courage to act after your decision has been made?

Twelve Steps to Better Communication

1. Do you know the actual status of your people's morale?

2. Do you encourage your subordinates to express their opinions?

3. Do you get the ideas of the group on important matters that affect them before making your decision?

4. Do you listen with patience and understanding to new ideas?

5. Do you answer your subordinates' questions satisfactorily, with patience and understanding?

6. Do you have an "open door, open mind" policy for listening to gripes and complaints as well as to suggestions?

7. Do you keep people informed on changes in company policies and procedures that affect their work?

8. Do your subordinates know what qualities you value most in them?

9. Do you recognize good work and express appreciation for your people's efforts?

10. Do you show your people how each individual job is important and essential to the entire group effort?

11. Do you explain the "why's" of your decisions?

12. Do you inform your superiors of the accomplishments and development of your subordinates?

Twelve Ways to Develop Your Staff's Potential

1. Do you select properly qualified people for jobs in your department?

2. Do you help new employees adjust to the job and to the group?

3. Do you motivate your people to do a better job? How?

4. Do you systematically evaluate the job performance of each one of your people and keep them informed on how they're doing?

5. Do you have a standard and consistent procedure in recommending your people for promotion?

6. Do you inform your employees of weaknesses and mistakes in their work orally rather than waiting for a written performance report?

7. Are you willing to help your people solve their work problems?

8. When someone fails to meet his established commitment, do you determine the cause and take corrective action?

9. Do you use constructive criticism that reflects a helpful attitude?

10. Do you discuss career opportunities with your people?

11. Does your assistant or the senior individual in the group know of upcoming projects in your department? Would your assistant be able to carry them out in your absence?

12. Are you training someone to take your place in case of your temporary absence or promotion?

Nine Ways to Get Along Well with People

1. Are you able to give a brief background on each person under your supervision?

2. Are you firm and fair in dealing with all your people?

3. Do you give recognition for a job well done and compensate for overtime to prevent low morale?

4. Do you enjoy working with people?

5. Do people enjoy being a member of your group? Do people try to get into your department when there is a vacancy?

6. Do you make it easy for people to talk with you?

7. Do you visit your people and your associates in their workplaces and their offices?

8. Do you participate suitably in the social events of your employees?

9. Can you tactfully adjust to diverse personalities?

Five Ways to Set and Maintain High Standards

1. Have you established credibility with your subordinates?

2. Do you use systematic methods to measure the performance and progress of your subordinates?

3. Do you give your people goals, a sense of direction, something to strive for, an objective to achieve?

4. Do you establish the proper managerial climate for your people to work in?

5. Do you evaluate continually to raise the work standards of your group?

WHAT TOMORROW'S EXECUTIVE NEEDS TO KNOW AND DO

Again, I contacted the presidents and chief executive officers of those same twenty companies. Their consensus is summarized in this section. By the way, I am sure you will be pleased, perhaps even surprised, to learn that seven of these twenty top company executives were women.

Here's what tomorrow's executives will need to know and do to succeed:

- Executives in the future will need a much greater understanding of human nature than in the past if they expect to provide the kind of leadership needed to accomplish the goals and objectives of both the business enterprise and the people who constitute it.

- People work most productively when the pattern of organized human relations reasonably satisfies the basic needs and desires of employees. Besides understanding the needs and desires of each individual, the executive of tomorrow will also be required to understand organization as a process of relations between persons and as a means for attaining corporate objectives. She will be expected to know how to maintain conditions in which people can work most efficiently to gain their basic needs and desires and achieve the corporate goals all at the same time.

- Since knowledge is becoming so vast and complex, multiplying year after year, no person will be able to know everything he needs to know about any one particular field. This situation will demand more teamwork and cooperation from employees than ever before. To lead this kind of complex enterprise, an executive will need to understand fully all the facts of human behavior. He will be required to be an expert in the field of human relations and applied psychology.

- The executive of tomorrow must be acutely aware of the importance of human relationships. She must tap both individual and group resources to get the maximum results. This means that management must develop and use the skills of people more than ever before. Despite advances in computer technology, profits in the future will depend increasingly upon human performance in business and industry. The executive who can lead and direct people will be in demand as never before.

How to Keep from Catching CEO Disease When You Become the Boss

What is CEO disease? Simply said, the chief executive officer of the corporation begins to think that he or she is God Almighty. He or she becomes an egomaniac. You think that can't happen to you? Be careful—it most certainly can if you don't watch out.

Douglas D. Danforth, former CEO of Westinghouse Electric Corporation, says, "Many CEOs take on a level of self-importance that goes far beyond reality. They view the company as their own. Some people's personalities change completely after they become the CEO. If you're not careful, you, too, can be seduced."

What are the symptoms of CEO disease? Let me give you these eight so you can keep your eyes open and stay on guard:

1. The CEO feels he or she can do no wrong and refuses to concede or admit to any mistake.
2. The CEO spends excessive time on the boards of other companies or civic groups, playing the role of elder statesman.
3. The CEO surrounds himself with sycophants and parasites who "yes" his every whim.
4. The CEO wants to make every decision but doesn't bother finding out all the details.
5. The CEO always trys to be one up on counterparts in salary, headquarters, aircraft, limousines.
6. The CEO is overly concerned about where she sits in meetings or whether people rise when she enters the room.
7. The CEO relishes media attention—not especially for the company but for personal gain and ego gratification.
8. The CEO hangs on to the job far too long—often undermining candidates who might someday be successors.

What can you do to get rid of the disease if you discover that you are infected? Here are some suggestions:

- *Impose Limits on the Job's Perks.* The trappings of the CEO's office often put distance between the CEO and the workers. That is one of the reasons the CEO of one of

America's largest airlines shuns perks that other chief executives take for granted. "I don't want to suggest to anybody that aside from my ability to do the job I'm any different from anyone else," he says.

- *Stay Focused on the Job Itself.* Many of the most-admired chief executives limit their outside board commitments. Wise CEOs will not serve on more than two boards of directors of other corporations. "You have to know when to say 'no,'" says Douglas D. Danforth, former CEO of Westinghouse Corporation.

- *Don't Assume That Toughness Defines Leadership.* In his book *Servant Leadership,* Robert K. Greenleaf says that a leader is the servant of his followers in that he removes obstacles that prevent them from doing their jobs. In other words, "He who would be the greatest of all must be the servant of all." Does that ring any bells?

- *Keep the Communication Lines Open.* The CEO of one of America's largest airlines hosts annual "presidential conferences" in which he and other senior executives meet employees across the country to discuss business and to answer questions.

   The CEO of one of the largest pharmaceutical companies in the United States eats his lunch in the company cafeteria right along side his production-line employees. "That's where I get a lot of my information," he says. "The research and development people can't wait to tell me what they've accomplished. And I stay very current on other matters as well." This practice serves two functions for the CEO. It tells everyone that he is accessible and it helps keep him informed and up to date.

- *Turn the Organizational Chart Upside Down.* One CEO turns the company organizational chart on its head in staff meetings so that the customer is at the top and the chairman at the bottom. Then he tells his top executives, "Your job is to find ways to be helpful to those above you on the chart."

- *Get Rid of the "Silent Pause."* The silent pause often follows the CEO when he walks around the organization. To combat the silent pause, this same chief executive officer got in the habit of walking around the company with his coat off and his hand outstretched, ready to shake, to put people at ease. Is that technique effective? "It most certainly is," he says, "for it makes everyone feel comfortable with me."

- *Get Rid of "Yes" People.* The most effective CEOs insist on being told what they have to hear, not what they want to hear. Since they insist on getting all the facts from their people, they are willing to surround themselves with strong managers rather than spineless and weak mediocrities.

Executive officers who follow the above suggestions for curing the CEO disease aren't likely to catch it. And they'll have a much better chance of leading a profitable company, with executives, managers, and production employees who are dedicated to its success.

7

How to Use the Power of Imagination to Achieve Success

I have already touched upon how important imagination is in your becoming successful with the power of self-achievement psychology when, back in Chapter One, I told you that you become what you think about. Then, in Chapter Two, I discussed with you how to use the psychology of self-achievement to deactivate and defuse your mind's failure mechanism. This technique also requires the active use of your imaginative powers.

In Chapter Three, I showed you how to use your imagination to make your goals exciting and worthwhile as well as how to visualize what you wanted in your subconscious mind—a technique that requires you to use your imagination. In Chapter Four, I talked about how you could use your creative thinking to succeed, and in Chapters Five and Six, you discovered how to become successful either in your own business or in a large corporation, both of which require use of your imagination and your creative talents.

In this chapter, I show you how the power of your imagination affects everything you do.

SUCCESSFUL IDEAS DEPEND UPON
IMAGINATION AND INSPIRATION

Today we have microchips and transistors in our radios, our television sets, and our stereo systems instead of the old-fashioned vacuum tube that served us so well for so many years. Why? Well, microchips and transistors do not produce heat as vacuum tubes do, so they do not burn out. They are virtually trouble-free and will last indefinitely. But that doesn't really say why at all, now does it? Then why? *Because someone used his or her imagination to come up with a better idea for how to do something.*

Every invention you can think of—from the first crude wheel to the intricate and highly sophisticated control system of the space shuttle—had its beginning in the deep, dark recesses of the subconscious mind.

And how did that happen? Well, a tiny seed of inspiration was planted deep in a brain furrow. It was plowed under by the conscious mind and allowed to germinate for a while. Then it was watered and fertilized by the subconscious mind, and suddenly one day it bore good fruit. And all of us benefited because someone came up with a better idea for doing something.

Imagination is the golden key that will unlock the door to the abundant life for all mankind. As Albert Einstein once said, "Imagination is more important than knowledge."

Little things that you and I take for granted and use every day came about as the result of someone's imagination: the paper clip, which made its inventor a millionaire many times over, by the way; the safety pin, which made the fortune for one of the great aristocratic families of the United States; Scotch tape, the stapler, carbon paper. Then there's the eraser on the end of the pencils you and I use. That person also became a millionaire from his idea. The ballpoint pen we use did the same thing for its inventor.

In the field of electronics there are cordless microphones for entertainers and cordless telephones that almost all of us use every day. Even the loudspeakers for my stereo system are cordless. Now I can put my speakers anywhere I choose and not have to worry about hooking them up to the amplifier and stringing wires all over the place as I used to do.

I could go on and on with other examples, but these should be enough for you to see how important imagination is, so now I want to tell you about . . .

BENEFITS YOU WILL GAIN

- You'll discover new and better ways of doing things.
- You'll save time, labor, and money when you find new and better ways of doing things and put them into effect in your own company or your own business.
- If you're in business for yourself, you can increase your profit margin and be able to make more money.
- If you work for a big corporation, you can gain promotion and advancement to a better position if you use your imagination to come up with a new and better way of doing things.
- And who knows, when you use your imagination to think up something new or a better way of doing things, you might become a millionaire, too. Eighty percent of America's millionaires made their millions by themselves; they didn't inherit their fortunes.
- You can even discover solutions to your personal problems when you use your creative imagination.

HOW TO ESTABLISH A CREATIVE CLIMATE SO YOUR IMAGINATION CAN THRIVE

One of the basic principles that all successful businesspeople and super salespeople follow is this: Find out what a person wants and needs and help him get it. I've already told you this, but I am repeating it here, because you may not realize that this same basic principle of business and sales success also applies to the way your subconscious mind functions.

You see, unless you give your subconscious mind a reason to work for you, it never will. You must give it a goal to reach or an objective to attain before it will go into action for you. If you do not do that, your subconscious mind will just sit there waiting for you to tell it what you want it to do for you.

For instance, if you could coax a fish to jump out of the water into your frying pan, you would never have to figure out a better way to catch a fish. There'd be no reason for you to do so. So the most important motive or incentive in getting your subconscious mind to work for you and come up with a new idea or a new way of doing things is to exert pressure on it. You must give your subconscious mind a goal or an objective to reach before it will go into action. Within reason, the pressure of deadlines and time limits helps bring out a person's best creative and imaginative powers.

Unless a sense of urgency exists, your subconscious mind will not come up with a new idea for you. It will not try to figure out a better way of doing things unless you've given it a valid reason to do so. That's why it's so important for you to impress your subconscious mind with your need for its help.

Here, then, are five important steps you can use to establish that necessary creative and imaginative climate for your subconscious mind to use so new ideas will come your way:

1. Tell Your Subconscious Mind What You Want. Be specific about the goal you want to reach, the objective you want to attain. You must give your subconscious mind a target. Exactly what is the problem you want your subconscious mind to solve for you? Precisely what is it that you want to have improved? Unless you can answer that concretely for your subconscious mind, you have no goal at all to give to it.

Thinking with your conscious mind only in general terms is not enough. The creative instincts of your subconscious mind will remain sound asleep. It would be like thinking, I'd like to be rich. That's not enough for your subconscious mind to work on. You must tell it how rich you want to be and when. Then you must ask it to give you the ideas you need to use so you can reach your goal.

2. **Believe That Your Subconscious Mind Has the Answers.**
You must have complete confidence in the power of your subconscious mind to do the job for you. Not only should you tell your subconscious mind precisely what you want, but also, you must tell it exactly *what you expect* from it. However, do not tell it *how* to solve your problem for you. You must leave that up to your subconscious mind. If you simply relax and not interfere or worry, it will do the work that you have asked it to do.

3. **Collect All the Facts.** Feed those facts into your subconscious mind along with your request for an answer.

4. **Relax.** Wait patiently and watch diligently for the answer to your question or the solution to your problem. The answer or the solution that you are looking for will usually come to you as a hunch or a flash of inspiration or intuition.

Will this method work for you? It most certainly will. Let me give you some concrete examples:

The chief of research of a large pharmaceutical company told me that nearly all the discoveries in their laboratories come as hunches or flashes of inspiration after a session of intensive thinking, brainstorming, and fact gathering.

A friend, Bob Walters, who writes mystery and suspense novels told me this:

> One of the most helpful discoveries I made long ago was that some power within me continues to work while I am sleeping, relaxing, or engaged in some other kind of work not even related to writing.
>
> When I'm having a problem with my story, I turn it over to this power to solve for me when I go to bed. I usually wake in the morning to find a problem of technique, plot, or character that had been troubling me completely solved while I've been sleeping!

I accept the answer I get without question, for I have
found that the judgment of this power—whatever it
might be—is infallible. Evidently it represents inherited
instincts and the accumulation of all my experiences,
none of which has been forgotten. I always trust the
judgment of this power over any conclusions arrived at
through a long process of thinking by my conscious
mind.

The unnamed power Bob is using is his subconscious
mind, even though he doesn't realize it. He just knows that
something within him is helping him solve his writing problems and find the answers that he needs.

This procedure of sleeping on the problem to get the solution from the subconscious mind works extremely well for
many people. It could be the best procedure for you, too. It's up
to you to experiment so you can find out for yourself. If you
feel more comfortable using the spiritual approach to contact
your subconscious mind, then do as another friend of mine
does. As he says, he always sleeps with his mind open to God.
He expects answers and he gets them.

And, in my own case, when I first started writing, I was
having trouble using examples to illustrate the points in my
first book. My editor had pointed out to me that I needed lots
of examples and case histories to add authenticity to my writing. She said that this came easy for some writers but much
harder for others. I guess I was a slow learner, for I just
couldn't seem to get a handle on it.

I thought about it for a long time, and then I finally gave
up and turned it over to my subconscious mind to solve for
me. It took only a few days to get the answer. I remember dis-
tinctly how it came to me. I was driving west on Sunshine Avenue and was just across from the Holiday Bowling Lanes
when a thought came to me as clearly as if a voice had spoken
out loud. "You do it this way," the thought came to me, and
then just as if I were reading a printed page right out of a book,
I saw the format for using examples and case histories as clear

as crystal. That was sixteen books ago and I have used the same style successfully ever since.

5. **Take Immediate Action.** When you get the answer that you need to solve your problem from your subconscious mind—and you most certainly will when you learn to relax and let it do the work for you without trying to force it—then put the solution you have received into effect immediately. Don't hesitate. Go ahead and solve your problem now that you know its correct solution.

How will that answer come to you? Well, most people receive their instructions or their guidance in terms of *feeling* what ought to be done. Remember as I told you before: your conscious mind *thinks;* it uses logic and deductive reasoning. But your subconscious mind *feels* to get its answers for you.

So you will usually receive your instructions as hunches or flashes of inspiration. Many people have told me that when they receive guidance from their subconscious minds, they know that guidance is right, for they feel a mighty reassurance come over them from a source outside themselves.

Now whether or not this mighty reassurance comes over you as it does some people, you will feel compelled to do things a certain way. In fact, sometimes the instructions from your subconscious mind may seem completely ridiculous to you. I'll give you an example of that in the next section, but let me say here that even if the instructions seem to defy all logic and reason, unless they are obviously harmful to you or to someone else, you should follow your hunches or your intuition exactly. That is the way your subconscious mind will give you the solution to your problem.

I cannot tell you how long your subconscious mind will simmer away. But sooner or later, the idea—the answer you have been waiting for—will bubble up to the top. And when it does, it usually surfaces with the speed of a hooked game fish. So you must be ready for it, no matter what you are doing—shaving, eating, driving the car, working, reading, whatever.

You must be ready to write down the answer the moment the message comes to you, for it will never appear as clearly as it does that first time. In fact, in most cases it will never come to you again. Your subconscious mind can be very stubborn indeed. It figures once is enough; take it or leave it!

So when the idea does come, write down enough of it so that it will be clear and understandable a month or a year later. I didn't always do that. Today, I have some cards in my files that have only one or two words written on them. I was so sure that I would never forget the message when I wrote it down, but I've had some of those cards for years now, and I still don't know what they mean.

Where All New Ideas Originate

Inventions, great musical compositions, poetry, fiction, and all great ideas for original accomplishment come from a person's imagination and his subconscious mind.

Now you, too, can be just as creative. You may not be an inventor as such, a composer of great music, a poet, or a writer of best-selling novels, but you can still use your imagination and the mighty magic of your subconscious mind to come up with a better way of doing things in your profession or in your business, no matter what it is.

You see, inventors, composers, poets, and writers do not have a monopoly on creativity or the use of their imagination. All you need do to be creative yourself is give your subconscious mind the thought or the raw material it needs to go to work for you, then keep it going with a deep-rooted desire for accomplishment, and you will get the results that you want. Now let me give you that example I promised you a moment ago.

"I don't care how fantastic or how ridiculous a person's idea might sound to you at first, hear him out," Paul Nolan, a top engineer for a Canadian construction firm once told me.

> Several years ago we took a contract to run electricity to a trading outpost in northern Saskatchewan. We were able to get the powerhouse built; we had the generators and

the engines installed, and we had all seventy houses and the three stores wired up.

We had less than a mile of high wire to string when we got caught with an early winter. Temperatures dropped to fifty below, and we had no way to set the poles for that final stretch of line. Unless we got that line in by the first of December, we'd lose a big chunk of money, but no one could figure out how to dig holes in ground that was frozen more than four feet deep. And you can't set a pole in the ground without a hole; nor can you string a power line without a pole.

Then an office clerk came up with what at first sounded like a ridiculous idea. "Blow out holes in the ground with dynamite," Sally said. "Fill the holes with water and set the poles in the water. The water will freeze to ice, and it will hold the poles solid as a rock until the spring thaw comes. Then you can set them up properly with dirt."

Well, we tried her idea and it worked! We had a lot of other bugs to work out, like getting the dynamite into the ground to blow the holes, but we solved each problem as we went along. For instance, the dynamite hole was made by pounding a steel rod into the ground with a sledgehammer. But first we had to heat that rod red hot to get it into the frozen ground. And we had to heat it forty to fifty times for each dynamite hole, but we did it. We used a portable forge that we dragged along from one hole to the next.

We blew out nearly eighty holes in the ground that looked like giant coffee cups. We carried the water from the river with bobsleds, using two 100-gallon drums with faucets welded onto them. We had to thaw out the faucets each time with a blow torch to get the water out of the barrels and into the holes for the uprights.

But we got the job done on time. And we did it by using Sally's imaginative suggestion that sounded completely idiotic when we first heard it. In fact, she told us afterward, she came close to not telling us about her idea for fear we'd laugh and make fun of her since she was a woman and an office clerk.

As you can see from this example, you don't have to be an inventor to come up with a new way of doing things. All you need is a problem to solve. I think there is something else you can learn from this example of using your imagination, and that is that you should listen to the ideas of your people when they give you suggestions and recommendations for doing something a new and different way. If you go to all the effort of establishing the right creative climate to coax some new ideas for improvement from your people, then it doesn't make any sense to turn a deaf ear to a person's suggestions.

Many ideas may sound ridiculous at first, as in the example I just gave you, but it is important that you not act scornful or impatient. There is no surer way to discourage people's original thinking than to make fun of them or to ridicule one of their ideas. They'll make no more suggestions to you for improvement, and for all you know, the very next idea could well be the one you really need, so you'd better make sure that it's easy to come by, no matter what that person's job is.

Why Imagination and Initiative Must Go Hand in Hand

In business and industry, good, usable labor-saving and money-making ideas are hard to come by. Not that people don't come up with good ideas. They do, but sometimes they don't let you know because they're afraid of being laughed at and made fun of. Then at other times, they simply don't follow up and develop those ideas for a variety of reasons. For example, "I just had the most brilliant idea," Tom Brown exclaims. His face glows with enthusiasm; his eyes sparkle with imagination, but only momentarily, for then he says to himself, "But it would take . . . and then there would be . . . and the boss wouldn't and I couldn't . . . forget it. It wasn't such a good idea after all, I guess."

And so a fresh new idea dies before it was even decently born. Tom's subconscious mind gave him that idea, but he didn't have the drive and the initiative to follow through on it.

Imagination without initiative would more properly be called idle daydreaming. Daydreams have no goals. They have no root or purpose, no objective or goal to attain. They are only wishful thinking that not only accomplishes nothing but also gets in the way of useful imagination. It's the "I want to be rich" daydream, but "I don't want to have to think or work to get it."

The best way to actively use your imagination and not just coast along daydreaming and frittering away your time is to know exactly what you want to get done. Go back and review those five steps I gave you on how to establish the necessary creative and imaginative climate for your subconscious mind to work so that new ideas will come your way. Then you won't waste your time daydreaming.

Let me sum up this section by saying that imagination and initiative—*the power of commencing*—makes the difference between the thinker who does something and the daydreamer who accomplishes nothing.

HOW TO WORK SMARTER—NOT HARDER

When you learn how to use your imagination properly, you'll discover that you can work smarter—not harder. I was born and raised on an Iowa farm, and I watched my father work his fingers to the bone fourteen to sixteen hours a day only to lose the farm to a private moneylender in the depression of the 1930s. So although I didn't know what I wanted to do for a living, I knew that I did not want to be a farmer.

There is one tremendous advantage you can gain when you learn how to work smarter—not harder. And that big advantage is money. Of course, money brings a great many other advantages, too, as well as the responsibility to use it wisely.

Certain names have become historically synonymous with money in these United States. There are hundreds and thousands more than I will mention here, and a lot of recent ones, too. (You can still make a million dollars in spite of taxes; it just takes a little longer, that's all.) But most people recognize immediately such names as Ford, Firestone, Schwab, Carnegie, Morgan, Chrysler, Rockefeller, and the latest one: Perot.

Since most people associate these names with huge financial undertakings, massive corporations, and huge conference tables in thick, carpeted board rooms, few could imagine that the famous John D. Rockefeller was the central figure in this short episode.

As big and important as he was, Mr. Rockefeller knew that the continued growth of his huge personal fortune depended mainly on the imagination and new ideas of his employees. One day Mr. Rockefeller stopped by the desk of a young junior executive who had recently joined the firm. That young man was burning with energy. He read papers at a furious pace; he shifted a piece of business correspondence from his in-basket to his out-basket every fifteen or twenty seconds.

Mr. Rockefeller watched him in silence for a few minutes. Then he put a hand on the young man's shoulder and said gently, "You mustn't work so hard!"

The young junior executive was astounded by Mr. Rockefeller's words. He had thought the best way to impress Mr. Rockefeller was to show him how busy he was. But he was completely wrong. This was not Mr. Rockefeller's idea of how a young, up-and-coming junior executive should work at all.

"You should teach your secretary how to handle all that paperwork," Mr. Rockefeller said. "That's what she's getting paid for. Then you can put your feet up on your desk and think up new ways to help Standard Oil make more money! That is what I'm paying you for."

And when I see the price of gas and oil today, I think that young man took Mr. Rockefeller's advice.

How to Test Your New Ideas

To judge the value of a new idea, either one of your own or one given to you by one of your staff members, you should run it through at least four questions before you decide whether to accept or reject it.

1. **Does the Idea Yield the Desired Results?** Does it give you what you're really looking for? Is it a better way of doing things? Will it actually increase your profits? Will it save you time in a particular phase of your operation? This is an important one to check, for any ideas that will save you time will usually make more money for you. If the idea won't do any of these things for you, chances are it is not the answer you are looking for. But don't give up; have your people keep on working to submit more new ideas to you.

2. **Is the Idea a Real Improvement?** Some ideas that people come up with are impractical to put into operation, not because they won't work, but because nothing really important is gained. Suppose one of your people figured out a button that would replace a lever on a certain piece of machinery. The question is not so much whether it will work or not, but whether it's a better way of doing things. That's the real test of an idea.

By the way, if the button that replaces the lever would not make more money for you, but it would improve safety in the workplace, then it is well worth your consideration.

3. **Does It Cost Too Much?** It doesn't make good economic sense to spend a thousand dollars to install some apparatus that will save you 93 cents a week, for example, especially if the life expectancy of the equipment you're improving is only five more years.

Your amortization, or recovery rate in dollars and cents, has to be realistic. Even if you see where the cost can be recovered in a reasonable length of time, keep in mind that another new idea six months later could make this one old-fashioned. We are advancing so fast in technical and scientific knowledge today that the long-range value of a product is often less predictable than the length of a woman's dress or the size of a man's tie next year.

4. Is the Idea Well-Timed? This ties in closely with the previous point. Some youngsters today have never seen an old-fashioned butter churn like Grandma used to have in the kitchen, and which I hated with a purple passion for it took so long and required so much energy to get butter out of cream.

With the continual inflationary climb of food costs, an electric butter churn might seem like a good idea. However, the inconvenience of churning butter at home makes it about as timely as an improved buggy whip. My point is that if a new idea is to be worthwhile, it must be usable in the time frame in which it is to be implemented.

Never Let Others Dampen Your Creative Spirit

I believe I've already told you that out of every one hundred people only five are leaders; ninety-five are followers. And those ninety-five out of every one hundred usually think like this: "We've been doing it this way for as long as I can remember. So it must be the best way. Why should we change it?"

Now I would be the first to admit that I am a strong believer in the principle of "If it ain't broke, don't fix it." But by the same token, I'm always willing to accept change, if I can be shown that it isn't change just for the sake of change. If that change will result in a better and less-expensive way of doing things, then I'm all for it.

But as I've indicated, 95 percent of people don't like change at all. They resent progress of any sort. Remember the phrase, "that old-time religion"? People also protested the automobile, for they felt that horses were plenty good enough for their transportation.

And many more protested against the airplane than against the automobile. The saying of that day was, "If man were meant to fly, God would have given him wings." An old gentleman I once knew refused to believe that man had landed on the moon. He insisted that it was all a government hoax. He died still believing that the moon landing was impossible. And so it goes, on and on. But as Dr. von Braun, the gifted German scientist, once said, "Man belongs wherever man wants to go."

The best way to keep that 95 percent of people, or anyone else for that matter, from turning off your creativity is to keep all transactions with your subconscious mind a deep secret all to yourself. If you tell others, especially the 95 percent, what you are doing, many of them will misunderstand and think you're completely off your rocker. They'll criticize you, even ridicule you. Criticism and ridicule from others can quickly and completely destroy your confidence in yourself and in your subconscious mind's ability to help you.

So the best way to keep others from planting negative ideas in your conscious mind, which would then be transferred into your subconscious mind if you are not on guard, is to tell no one anything at all about your techniques, your methods, or your procedures.

I have found, for instance, that when I talk to someone about a proposed writing project or if I ask a person an opinion about it, I scatter my forces. I lose my close connection with my own subconscious mind, and more often than not I find I have to start all over again.

The only exception I make to this rule is to have a close personal friend of mine proofread my material before it is submitted to the publisher. Marion catches typographical errors and awkward wording as well as certain other mistakes. I trust her judgment fully, for after all, she is one of the 5 percent, so she is the only person who has both the privilege and responsibility of reading my unpublished manuscripts.

Don't Let Negative Ideas Work Against You

Let's say you are in bed at night sound asleep and you wake suddenly, sure that you've heard a strange noise out in the kitchen. Or worse yet, let's say that your security system alarm goes off. Immediately your heart starts to pound wildly and you are almost afraid to breathe for fear the burglar might hear you.

Do you have any idea of what has actually happened within your body? Your fight-or-flight mechanism has gone into action automatically for you. Your blood pressure is increased and your heart rate speeds up. There is a marked increase in the blood flow to your arms and legs; more adrenaline is pumped into your bloodstream. All this because of a noise you heard at night out in the kitchen.

But when you finally get up the courage to look, after you've heard nothing more for a long time, you find there was no burglar after all. Only a bag of trash that had been placed too close to the edge of a kitchen counter had finally fallen off, breaking a bottle that made the clatter you heard which set off the alarm. That is how easily negative ideas can be fed into your subconscious mind by your conscious mind, keeping it from working properly for you.

This reminds me of the French writer Montaigne, who said in his latter years, "My life has been filled with terrible misfortunes, most of which never happened!" That is exactly what negative thinking can do to you, too.

To end this chapter on a positive note, I want to tell you . . .

How Les Giblin Used His Creative Imagination to Become a Highly Successful Speaker and Author

Les Giblin had been a successful salesman and sales manager for many years. He had done some public-relations work and had gained a reputation in the field of human relations. He liked this kind of work, and he wanted to continue in it, for his big interest was people. After years of both study and experience he felt he had some answers to the problems people often have with other people, and he wanted to lecture on the subject of human relations. But he felt that his one big obstacle was his lack of experience in public speaking.

One night while lying in bed thinking of his one big desire, he remembered the success he'd had in talking to his salespeople and in talking to groups of soldiers as an instructor in the army. But in spite of these successful experiences, he was still afraid he could not get up in front of a big audience and speak.

Then in his imagination he pictured himself standing up before a large audience and making a talk on human relations. He also imagined himself having the same confidence and self-assurance he'd had when he talked to smaller groups of people.

He pictured in detail just how he would stand and what he would say. He imagined the expressions on people's faces, and in his mind he could hear their thundering applause. He saw himself making a successful talk and going over with a bang.

His feeling of success was so real to him that he knew he could do it, for he had combined his feeling of confidence and success from his past with the picture he held in his imagination of his success in the future as an expert in human relations.

Although there seemed to be no opportunity for him at that time, he booked himself, and in only three years he saw his dream come true, almost in the same exact detail as he had imagined it, for he soon had more opportunities to speak than he could possibly fill.

Today Les Giblin is known as an authority on human relations. Hundreds of the largest companies in America have paid him to hold human-relations seminars for their employees. His book *How to Have Confidence and Power in*

*Dealing with People** is now a classic. And it all started in his imagination.

You can have the same sort of success, no matter what profession or occupation you are in, if you will use your imagination to get everything you want out of life, too. Your only limitation is you, yourself, and you alone. So go to it—you can do it.

---

*Les Giblin, *How to Have Confidence and Power in Dealing with People* (Englewood Cliffs, NJ: Prentice Hall, 1956).

8

How You Can Become a Winner in Everything You Do

As far as I am concerned, *a winner is always a leader and a leader is always a winner.* For all practical purposes, the two terms are interchangeable. You cannot be a winner without being a leader, nor can you be a leader and not be a winner.

To become a winner, you must constantly program your subconscious mind with positive, success-oriented ideas. When you do that, your mind's mighty magic powers will go to work to transform you into a winner.

What is it about successful people that gives them the winning edge? Why is it they never seem to lose? What is it that sets them apart from the rest of the crowd? Well, first of all, if you study winners and their actions carefully, you will discover that there are twenty-four specific hallmarks that mark them as leaders and set them apart from losers.

Second, you will find that winners always take winning for granted. *They always expect to win.* In fact, they never even consider the possibility of defeat. They do not allow themselves to think about losing. To them, winning is the natural way of life. They believe wholeheartedly in the philosophy expressed so succinctly by Vince Lombardi, the famous coach of the Green Bay Packers, who said, "Winning is everything; losing is nothing!"

With this kind of attitude, a winner is comfortable in any business situation or social environment. He can walk into the midst of any group and immediately become the focus of attention. The manner, the bearing, and the aura the winner projects instantly attracts others to him. When you, too, learn how to carry yourself like a winner, and when you act like one,

YOU WILL GAIN THESE BENEFITS

- You'll never risk having your position or your authority challenged. People will respect you and have full confidence in you. You will easily gain their willing obedience, loyal cooperation, and full support.

- You'll gain the reputation of being a "born leader." People will automatically turn to you for answers. They'll trust you and ask you for your help and your advice. When you act like a winner and carry yourself like one, you'll gain much power over others, for people will follow your lead without question.

- You'll gain your own fair share of fame. You might not become president of the United States when you act like a winner, but you will become famous and well known throughout your community, your city, or your state. Just how far you want people's recognition of you to spread is entirely up to you. The only limits to your success are the ones you place upon yourself.

- You'll be transformed into a positive, magnetic, outgoing, and powerful personality when you learn how to act like a winner. You'll have an important new look, a masterful bearing, a new charm; in fact, you will have a whole new status.

- You'll be able to attain a successful new life as a winner. You will build a truly effective system for coping with stress—both physical and mental—establishing rapport with others and leading them, and moving your life forward to greater expectations and bigger rewards.

Do these fantastic benefits sound too good to be true? Like a miracle? I'm sure they do, but I can assure you that they will all come true when you know how to program your subconscious mind with the positive concepts and attitudes that tell it you are a winner and not a loser.

THE TWENTY-FOUR HALLMARKS OF A WINNER

1. Optimism and Cheerful Enthusiasm

Winners have learned to look on the bright side of things. They know that the smile is the universal language of love. It melts away resistance and opposition, quiets fears, and instills hope and courage in other people. Winners know that a sour-faced, pessimistic attitude is for losers, not winners.

Winners also know that the physical body expresses what concerns or occupies the mind. They know that a person usually gets what he or she actively expects. Fears and worries turn into anxiety that is distressful in many ways: resistance levels are lowered, and the person becomes much more susceptible to disease and accident.

So if your mental attitude is negative, you can be plagued with a variety of problems ranging from headaches, low back pain, ulcers, and asthma to certain allergies that are often associated with mental and emotional problems rather than true physical ones.

But if you mentally expect good health and exhibit optimism and enthusiasm, your body will be blessed with better health, energy, and a feeling of total well-being.

In short, when you expect the best out of life, you are preparing yourself physically as well as mentally to be a winner. Leadership—the ability to attract the obedience, support, and cooperation of others—is a natural byproduct of optimism and cheerful enthusiasm.

One other aspect of the optimistic and cheerful winner is that she does not take herself too seriously. Winners have developed a sense of humor that allows them to find the cheerful side of any situation.

A close friend of mine puts it this way: "I tried for many years to be successful, but I was never quite able to make the grade. I finally decided I must have the whole thing turned around somehow. So I decided to change my goals. I decided to become a failure, and I was a success overnight!"

Of course, Barbara is just joking. She is an overwhelming success as a stockbroker. But, she has learned not to take herself too seriously. She knows how to smell the roses without getting pricked by thorns.

2. An Overpowering Urge for Action

In every group, you will always find certain key individuals who naturally seem to take over. I call them "pivot people," for the action of the entire group pivots around what these people of action say or do.

You can usually spot these winners, for they will always be in the center of the action. They do not stand on the sidelines, just looking on. They are not spectators. They insist on getting into the act. Unlike so many people, they do want to get involved.

A winner is a leader. He is the kind who automatically takes charge when some tragedy, say, for instance, an automobile accident occurs. He'll send someone to call for an ambulance and the police. He'll appoint someone else to direct traffic. He'll see that the injured people receive first aid.

The winner always seems to be pushed by an inner urge for action. She has an internal drive to keep things moving along at a fast clip, "chomping at the bit" to get things done. This kind of person is able to harness the physical drive to solve mental problems, too. For instance, that person will have that natural ability to take a good idea—either hers or someone else's—and ramrod it, promote it, and sell it to the group.

And it doesn't matter what kind of group it is—PTA, city council, school board, church group, employees in a department or section—those certain individuals always seem to be able to influence and control the entire group through their leadership abilities. If you can identify these key people, you, as a winner and a leader, will be able to control the entire group through them.

3. Skill in Solving Problems

A winner is almost always able to come up with a workable solution to a problem. One of the hardest parts of solving any problem is simply getting started on it. As a winner and a leader, you no doubt will have several suggestions for solving the problem. Your ideas may not always work, but you at least are able to get things moving when a situation has bogged-down, and that's really important in solving a problem.

I've already told you about the time I was attending the Infantry Officers Course in Strategy and Tactics in Fort Benning, Georgia, but it bears repeating here. Our instructors at Fort Benning, all battle-hardened veterans, used to needle us when we were hesitant about making a decision.

"Do something," they would say. "Don't just stand there. Do something, even if it's wrong. If it's wrong, you can correct it. A poor plan carried out enthusiastically is better than the best plan in the world that is not carried out at all."

In contrast, I can well remember the time when the battalion I was in was engaged in mock warfare in military maneuvers in Louisiana. The lieutenant colonel commanding that battalion must never have gone to Fort Benning, nor had he ever heard those words from the instructors there, for he hesitated and refused to commit his reserve company to the battle for fear that he might be making a mistake.

Finally, to keep the problem from stagnating completely, the umpires in charge of the maneuvers forced him to commit his reserve company. They actually made his decision for him. As a result of his timidity, he was relieved of his command when the mock battles were over. Although he was a lieutenant colonel, he was not a leader or a winner.

4. An Authoritative Manner

As a winner and a leader, you will stand out in any group, for you will always act with authority. Your manner, your bearing, your way of speaking will all attract attention. As a winner, you will tend to take command of the situation, no matter what it is. Without appearing to force yourself on others, as a winner you will just naturally assume authority and take over the leadership of the group.

"You can always spot the leader in a group by watching the way the others turn to her for guidance," says Janet Power, an executive in a large Atlanta industrial firm. "For example, a supervisor issues an order, turns her back, and walks away. Immediately all the employees gather around one individual to get her opinion. She speaks; they listen. Then they go back to work and carry out the supervisor's order. But not until they get the go-ahead from the informal leader of their group."

5. Drive, Stamina, and Endurance

A winner has to have these three qualities to see things through to the end, no matter what. As a winner and a leader, you must be able to stick to the job and finish it when others want to give up and quit. Or if you happen to be looking for someone to carry out a long-term project or one that has a large number of details, this is just the kind of person you want and need to find to complete the job for you.

6. Wide-Ranging Interests and Knowledge

One of the best people to have around in a tough situation is the one who has a vast range of interests and broad general knowledge. This is especially important if you are looking for new ideas and new ways to solve a problem. You see, new ideas usually spring from the old ones, so the person with a broad range of information has the background and the potential for coming up with them. When the boss is looking around for someone like that, that person will be you. It's one of the best ways to be both remembered and promoted.

7. A Good Memory

If you want to become a winner and a leader of others, a good memory is essential, not only to the acquisition and retention of knowledge, but it can be of great value when you need a quick solution to a pressing problem.

The kind of person who can remember how a similar problem was solved last year can be invaluable in a crisis. A person with a good memory may be the first one to come up with information or help when it is needed in a hurry. If you are to be a winner and a leader of others, you will be that person with the fine memory. Having a good memory is such an important subject that I have devoted all of Chapter Ten in this book to it.

8. Creative Thinking

A winner with leadership abilities will always be an action person. A winner can often be recognized by the way he hates the routine way of doing things.

Winners refuse to accept the status quo and are constantly looking for new and more efficient ways to get the job done. These are the kind of people you want around to help you because they can often solve your problems before the problems happen.

This kind of person will be a creative thinker—many times a true nonconformist. A really creative person will usually be a wellspring of ideas and will strongly resist any efforts to restrict and channel his or her thinking.

If the creative urge is strong enough, it will show up in the person's efforts to find more challenging jobs, or, at the least, to acquire additional knowledge about other departments and other people's work. This may well be your first clue to the presence of a winner or a leader who can help you solve your problems or achieve your goals.

And if you, yourself, are that kind of person, so much the better, although it always helps, of course, to have allies who can help you.

9. Accepting of Responsibility

One of the most noticeable qualities of a winner is his or her charisma, often called *presence*. Winners literally radiate authority to those around them. They have the knack of assuming command of a situation, no matter what it is. People automatically defer to winners and let them take over. Why is this so?

Because a winner and a leader always takes charge even when she lacks the authority to do so, and since most people do not care to accept responsibility, especially in a bad situation, they are only too glad to defer to someone who will.

Let me give you an example of what I mean by that. An automobile accident had occurred out in the country north of Des Moines. Over a dozen people had stopped to look, but no one had tried to help. Then a car stopped, and the woman who got out took charge of this bad situation at once.

First, she checked the occupants of both cars and found that only one person had been badly hurt. His face had been badly cut and was bleeding, one arm was broken (it turned out to be a compound fracture) and a cut artery was spewing blood. The man was also in deep shock. Since this was the dead of winter and the temperature was below freezing, shock was doubly dangerous.

The woman immediately applied a tourniquet to the broken arm to stop the loss of blood from the artery. Then she checked to be sure the injured person had no spinal injuries that would keep him from being moved. Next, she turned and issued a series of rapid-fire orders to the men who were just standing around.

> You there. Go in that house and call an ambulance. Then call the highway patrol. You over there, go with him. Bring back two blankets to cover this man and a

sheet or towel or anything we can use to immobilize his broken arm.

The two of you there, go find something we can use to carry him into the house so we can get him out of this freezing weather. Get a folding cot, some boards, a door, anything at all that will support his weight.

You two there, go down the road to the south and keep more cars from stopping. You two go up the road to the north and do the same thing. We don't want another accident here. The rest of you get in your cars and leave right now!

Where before there had been only confusion, in only a few moments there was now order and organization. All because one person had taken control of a bad situation. This woman's manner and conduct were so positive and authoritative that no one questioned her orders or her right to give them. People jumped to obey her commands. They were really eager to help but needed someone to lead the way and assume the responsibility for making the decisions.

Taking charge in a bad situation and assuming the responsibility for making the decisions is one of the most important characteristics of a leader, and it makes the person a winner every time. So if you have the inner courage to make decisions and then to accept the responsibility for your actions, you will find that people will acquiesce and let you take over the position of leadership every time.

You will be surrounded by an aura of authority that, even though invisible, is still so easily recognizable that a person can almost reach out and touch it. People will automatically regard you as a winner, and they will look to you for leadership whenever a difficult problem arises.

10. An Air of Control

From the previous example, you can see that when two people meet for the first time, one will automatically become the leader and assume control of the situation. The other person will then become the follower. I'm sure you realize by now that winners are not followers; they are always leaders.

You, too, can seize control of any situation if you simply remember that *most people are waiting for someone else to tell them what to do.* If you want to be a winner, then let that someone be you. That strategy alone will single you out of any crowd as the leader and the winner every time.

All you need do is take the initiative, and you will instantly have the momentum on your side. If you adopt a positive attitude and assume the other person is going to do what you want him or her to do, you'll find that 95 percent of the time your orders or your commands will be carried out without hesitation or question. In 5 percent of the cases, all the other person needs is a little extra push for motivation.

I do not mean by this that you should force your opinions on others. There must be a legitimate reason for you to assume control of a situation. Don't, for example, do what the person in this story did. If you do, you'll be unpopular wherever you go.

I attended a small social gathering one afternoon at a friend's house. One of the guests was a talkative man who constantly forced his opinions on everyone. Whatever subject was brought up, he'd either done it before or knew all about it. He was an expert on everything, at least according to his account of it.

"Great Scott, Jim, is there anything that man doesn't know?" Bill Jones asked me.

"Evidently not, Bill," I replied. "But I doubt if he will ever be invited back here again."

When I say you should take charge of the situation, I do not mean that you should be a know-it-all and take control of the conversation just to show off and let people know how smart you are. A know-it-all rubs people the wrong way. This kind of person embarrasses others, makes everyone uncomfortable, and is highly unpopular. Nobody likes the perfect person who has all the answers to everything. No one feels at home with perfection.

So let me say again: You must have a specific reason for taking charge of the situation and assuming responsibility for it and for your decisions.

11. A Positive Self-Image

Winners make more honest self-appraisals than most people do. They also have an excellent understanding of how others see them.

Winners also have a deep-down feeling of their own worth. They realize that liking themselves and feeling super about themselves in their own special way is not being overly egotistical. Winners take a deep pride in what they are doing and accomplishing right now, and they enjoy being the unique persons they are.

Most successful people believe in their own value and their own worth. A positive self-image and high self-esteem are the means to high achievement and total happiness.

Behaving out of character results from not having a positive and realistic self-image. Children often pretend they are someone they are not: cowboys, firefighters, police officers, astronauts. That's fine for children. I did it, and I'm sure so did you.

But if when you're an adult you still pretend you're someone you're not, something's wrong with your thinking. Losers always think they'd rather be someone else. Winners are perfectly happy with who they are. To tell you the straight truth, although there have been times when I was not the happiest person in the world, perhaps, I have never wanted to be anyone but who I am.

12. A Good Example for Others

When you do that, you'll be able to motivate people to want to do what you want them to do. The attitudes and actions of your subordinates will be deeply influenced by the personal qualities you have and exhibit.

Remember that leaders and winners are examples to be followed, not models to be admired. Setting the example isn't an easy task. It means you're going to have to develop or strengthen some of those old-fashioned personal qualities we heard about as children.

Setting the example means developing such personal traits as courage, integrity, tact, unselfishness, dependability, and a host of others. Setting the example means sticking to what you know to be morally right even when it would be so much easier not to do so.

As Albert Schweitzer, the medical missionary to the country of Gabon in west central Africa and winner of the Nobel Peace Prize, once said, "Example is not the main thing in life; it is the only thing." So set the proper example and you'll not have to preach a sermon to your people. They'll need only to follow in your footsteps to do the right thing.

Your subordinates will always look to you to set an example for them to follow, for everyone tends to do as her superior does. If you set a bad example for your staff, don't expect good work from them. That is not possible, and it will never happen. Just remember this thought if you will: *Once you have lost the respect of your people, it is almost impossible to regain it.*

In addition, if you do not set the proper example for subordinates to follow, they will always use you as the excuse for their own mistakes and shortcomings. If your people can't climb up to your level, they will always try to drag you down to theirs.

Let me give you eight specific techniques that winners and leaders use to set an example for others to follow:

1. Set high standards for your people to live by.
2. Set the example by working hard yourself.
3. Keep yourself physically and mentally fit.
4. Master your emotions completely with self-discipline and self-control.

5. Maintain a cheerful and optimistic outlook and attitude.

6. Conduct yourself at all times so your personal habits are not open to censure or criticism.

7. Always use tact and courtesy with everyone.

8. Your word must be your bond. That means:

   • Never make a promise you cannot keep.

   • Never make a decision you cannot support.

   • Never issue an order you cannot enforce.

Personal integrity is a must if you are going to make your word your bond. Without integrity, you'll never be able to set an example for anyone to follow. Integrity is that quality or state of being of sound moral principle. It means uprightness of character, absolute truthfulness, and deep sincerity. Above all, *you must be honest with yourself.*

Let me give you five guidelines that will help you develop the highest standards of personal integrity and moral character:

1. Practice absolute honesty and truthfulness in everything at all times. Don't allow yourself the luxury of even one little white lie.

2. Be accurate and correct in everything you say and do.

3. Remember that your signature on any document is a certification of the truthfulness of that document. When you write a personal check, your signature is a certificate to the effect that you have sufficient money in the bank to cover your check. Your signature in your work and business must carry exactly the same weight.

4. Stand up for what you believe to be right. Have the courage of your convictions, regardless of the consequences. Never

compromise your standards; never prostitute your principles. If you are ever tempted to compromise your principles, then remind yourself to place honesty and your sense of duty and personal honor above all else.

5. Duty and honor come first. If you can grasp, understand, and practice the ideas of duty and honor, you cannot help but develop personal integrity.

13. Self-Motivated

A winner and a leader must be goal seeking and purpose oriented. In other words, what you get depends on the goals you set for yourself. If you're going to be a winner, you must be your own self-motivator. You can't depend on someone else to motivate you to do your best.

Unless you have a powerful urge to be a leader of others, to assume more responsibility, and to reach the top level as an executive or manager, you will not. Many capable people set their goals too low, for they are not motivated to shoot for the moon.

Let me give you an example here of two different people with two different goals to achieve so you can better see what I mean.

Tony Atwood and Curtis Scranton were both under consideration for promotion to the position of production superintendent in one of the plants of a large industrial corporation in Atlanta, Georgia. Arthur Harper, the plant manager, would make the decision.

Both men were qualified, not only by education, but also by experience on the job. Each one was a department foreman. Tony was a good administrator; his office records were meticulous. His production figures were high. He competed vigorously with other departments and hated to lose. On paper, he had a slight edge over his competitor in his specialty, both in production and administration. He was somewhat weak, though, in his understanding of the problems of other departments in the plant and his appreciation of company problems as a whole.

When asked what his career goal with the company was, he said, "To be the best department foreman in the plant." And as Arthur Harper says, "He is!"

Curtis Scranton was perhaps not quite as good an administrator as Tony. He admitted he hates to be confined to his office doing paperwork. His production met plant standards in both quantity and quality. He knew how to work with other departments for everyone's benefit; he cooperated with people. He made every effort to identify company goals and objectives and coordinate them with his own. Curtis also tried to expand his knowledge of the entire plant by spending some of his off-duty hours visiting other departments so he could better understand their problems and how they function.

When asked what his career goal was, he said, "To be the company president."

With these facts in mind, which man would you select for promotion? I myself would pick Curtis Scranton. In fact, so did Arthur Harper. Here are his reasons for that selection:

> Tony Atwood is the best department foreman in the plant because that is exactly what he wants to be. That's fortunate for us, perhaps, for we do need good department foremen, but unfortunate for Tony. By setting too low a goal for himself, he has limited his opportunity for advancement and promotion.
>
> On the other hand, Curtis Scranton has shown us that his career objective is much higher. He wants to be the company president, and he knows he can't begin to achieve that goal unless he knows everything there is to know about every department in the plant. Personally, I think he'll make it clear to the top and become the company president and CEO. And I hope he does.

My point is that if Tony cannot visualize a higher goal for himself, he will never go any higher than that. And the same holds true for you. Unless you visualize a goal that's way up there for you to reach, you will never get there. If you want to succeed, then shoot for the moon. Give it your all. Go for broke!

14. Self-Confident

If you are going to be a winner and a leader of others, you must have confidence in yourself and in your decisions and your actions. If you are certain you have made the correct decision, you should never back down. And, if you are confident, you won't lose your head or panic in a crisis.

If you lack confidence in yourself, other people will also lack confidence in you. So the first step in winning people's confidence is to have confidence in yourself. How can you gain that self-confidence so you can win the confidence of others? One of the best ways is to *know your business inside out and keep on knowing it.* In other words you need to be the expert and the authority in your own chosen field.

The person who knows his or her business, who is the authority and the expert in his or her own field, has complete confidence in his or her own abilities. That kind of confidence comes from extensive study, research, long experience, and plain, old-fashioned hard work.

My chiropractor spends four to six weeks every year attending lectures and clinics to keep herself up to date on the latest developments in her profession. Is it any wonder that she is regarded as one of this country's top doctors in the field of chiropractic? Or why her office is always jammed full, often with patients from a hundred and more miles away?

If you want to be the authority and expert in your own field, no matter what it is, then you will have to do the same. Don't stop studying just because you have graduated from school or have a degree. You'll never live long enough to know everything there is to know about your chosen profession.

Not only must you retain what you have already learned, but you must also keep up to date on new techniques and procedures so you can be ready for the future. No matter what you do, you will always need to keep on learning, for each new day brings change, and, if you want to retain your position as a winner and a leader, you must continue your professional education and development. There simply is no other way to do it.

15. Decisive

Since indecision is nearly always one of the worst mistakes a person can make, you as a winner must learn to be decisive. Every day as a business executive you will need to make dozens of decisions. Some will demand the greatest skills that you can muster, for certain decisions will have long-lasting and far-reaching effects.

If you put things off, or if you call a meeting to get a joint decision from your subordinates so that you can blame them if things go wrong, or if you farm out the problem to a committee for more study or to wait for further developments, you are never going to become a winner and a leader of others.

This kind of indecisiveness is contagious. It infects everyone in your organization, causing hesitancy, confusion, and loss of confidence in you. If you do that, you will never become a top executive. Instead, you will find yourself pushed off on a siding in a dead-end position or looking for another job with a different company.

If there is one thing I want you to learn from this it is that *you cannot command by committee. You must make that final decision all by yourself* if you want to get to the top of the totem pole. As President Harry Truman once said, "Somebody has to make decisions around here." To make sure that you are that somebody, here are ten guidelines you can use to make the right decisions:

1. **Plan Ahead for Any Possible Emergency.** Consider everything that might possibly ruin your plans. Use the phrase

"What will happen if . . ." so you can force yourself to think of every possible thing that might go awry.

2. **Take the Initiative.** Don't wait for your boss to tell you what to do. Seize the initiative. That's the only way you will ever learn how to make sound and timely decisions on your own. You'll never get anywhere by avoiding the tough assignments or the hard decisions that have to be made.

3. **Act Decisively.** Develop your ability to make quick decisions. Don't beat around the bush. It's easy to say, "Facts first, decisions second," but it doesn't always work out that way. Sometimes an immediate decision is more valuable than one reached after weeks of study and debate. Learn to develop your intuitive instincts. Of course, experience helps. As an old business saying goes, "An experienced executive makes decisions by instinct; the inexperienced one has to work at it." I would also add that the timid one has to work at it even more!

4. **Set a Reasonable Deadline for Your Decision.** A specific deadline can force you to come to grips with the problem so you can reach a decision.

5. **Take a Few Chances.** Nothing attempted, nothing gained is an old cliché that is applicable here. There's also an old army saying that only a small, thin line exists between a general court martial and dishonorable discharge from the service and the Congressional Medal of Honor. Remember that people who never stick their necks out once in a while never become winners and leaders, either.

6. **Try to Limit Your Choices.** For example, if you are picking out a new carpet for your office and you are confused by the wide number of choices available, narrow them down by looking at only three at a time and picking the best one. Then look at the next three and pick the best one, and so on. Then take the best ones you've already picked out and repeat this process until you have only one left.

You can use this same system to pick out the best person for the job or for promotion, especially if there are many eligible applicants. On a personal note, you can also use the same procedure to pick out your suits, shoes, dresses, ties, and so on.

7. **Reevaluate Decisions.** Doing so will help you determine if the decisions you made were sound and timely.

8. **Analyze Decisions Made by Others.** If you do not agree with them, determine if your reasons for disagreement are sound and logical.

9. **Broaden Your Viewpoint.** Study the actions of others so that you can profit from their successes or failures.

10. **Don't Make Major Decisions on Minor Matters.** Save your real efforts for important decisions. Don't give yourself a migraine headache trying to decide whether to have peas or corn when you're standing in the company cafeteria line, or you might get run over by the people behind you.

Remember that when you know how to make sound and timely decisions, people will trust you and have confidence in you. They'll be motivated to do their best for you.

16. Sound Judgment

Good judgment is a quality you'll need to develop if you want to be able to make sound and timely decisions. It allows you to logically weigh all the facts and apply all possible solutions to the problem so you can make the proper decision.

To improve your judgment, you should be as technically and professionally qualified as possible. Education, experience, and common sense will all be important to you when the moment comes for you to use proper and good judgment in reaching your decisions.

Judgment must be completely unemotional. Just because you don't happen to like the way a person looks or dresses, for example, you should never allow it to influence your decision one way or the other.

If you want to improve your ability to make proper judgment calls, then follow these three simple guidelines:

1. **Make Estimates of the Situation.** Always look ahead. Anticipate those situations that require decisions from you if they would happen to come up. Then you'll be prepared to handle them if the occasion requires you to do so.

2. **Don't Make Rash Decisions.** Although as a winner and a leader you will be expected to make timely decisions, don't let that force you into making spur-of-the-moment or snap decisions. Many times those aren't really decisions at all, they are only guesstimates.

3. **Use Common Sense.** To develop a sense of good judgment, approach your problems with an attitude of common sense and an understanding of people.

Let me elaborate on the idea of an understanding of people with this example that Paul Newport, director of personnel management for a large industrial company in Dayton, Ohio, told me:

> Every time I'm inclined to give up on a person and say to hell with it all, I remember a fellow named Scott Brady. You see, I was in the army then, a training company commander at Fort Riley, Kansas. Scott Brady was transferred to my unit. He'd been in the army twenty-one weeks and still hadn't finished his first eight weeks of basic training. He'd been AWOL or in the stockade most of that time.
>
> When he came to the company, my first sergeant recommended that we process the paperwork to get him out of the army since it seemed that he never would be a worthwhile soldier. However, I felt that it was wrong not to give him at least one more chance. I called him into my office so I could make our status extremely clear to him.

"I don't care what you've done before," I told him. "All that matters now is what you do for me. If you'll soldier for me, I'll back you all the way. Your past will be forgotten completely. It's all up to you."

Well, Scott ended up as the company's honor graduate. He wasn't really bad at all. He'd just gotten off on the wrong foot, and everybody expected the worst from him. I started him out with a clean slate. I held no prejudice whatever against him for his past mistakes. All that counted as far as I was concerned was what he did for me. I gave him the chance to prove his worth and succeed, and he did.

So every time I'm tempted to give up on someone here, I remember Scott Brady. I made the proper judgment call when I gave him a chance, and he showed me that I'd made the right decision in doing so.

If you can develop an understanding of people the way Paul did, it will help you make proper judgment calls, too. To be a winner and a leader of others you'll need to be able to do that.

17. Respected

A winner and a leader not only has to be well liked but he must also be respected by them. Being well liked by others and getting along with them is such an important subject that I cover it in detail in Chapter Fifteen. For now, I want to limit myself only to how to gain the respect of others.

If you want to be a winner and a leader of others, if you want people to look up to you and respect you, then you must accept full responsibility for everything you do, especially your mistakes. You cannot pass the buck to others for your mistakes. No one ever said it better than President Truman when he said, "The buck stops here!"

When your subordinates know that you are not going to pass the buck or blame them for your own mistakes, you'll

most certainly gain their wholehearted respect, their willing
obedience, their loyal cooperation, and their full support.

Here are five simple techniques you can use to program
yourself to accept responsibility, earn the respect of others,
and be a real winner and leader in the eyes of those around
you.

1. You must seize every opportunity that offers you increased responsibility. Don't wait to be told what to do;
   take the initiative yourself and act on your own good
   judgment and inner guidance from your subconscious
   mind.

2. Always do every job you've been given, large or small, to
   the best of your ability. I know that it's a cliché for me
   to say that any job worth doing is worth doing well, but
   it's true, so I'm going to say it. I will say that if there are
   details in your work that you feel are unnecessary, then
   recommend to your boss that they be eliminated. But unless and until she gives you her OK to do so, you have no
   choice in the matter. Like it or not, you must do it.

3. Accept honest and deserved criticism and admit your mistakes. Only a coward refuses to do that. Don't indulge in
   self-pity, or as another old saying goes, "Don't sit on the
   pity-pot." Correct your mistakes, put them behind you,
   and move forward with complete confidence and courage.

4. Always take full responsibility for the failures and mistakes of your subordinates. Always act as a buffer between
   your subordinates and your superiors. When you do that,
   you'll find that your people will go all out to keep mistakes from happening. *When you keep them out of trouble, you'll discover that they are eager to keep you out of
   trouble, too.* Taking full responsibility for the mistakes
   of your subordinates really determines whether you are a
   true winner and leader of others.

5. Always assume full responsibility for your actions—
   for your failures as well as your successes. Most people

are perfectly willing to accept the credit when things go right, including the successes of their subordinates. But they are not willing to accept the blame when things go wrong, either for their own mistakes or those of their people. But if you want to be a winner and a leader of others, you must take the bitter along with the sweet.

18. Accepts Criticism, Admits Mistakes

This is the third technique for winning the respect of others, but it is such an important point it deserves additional discussion.

Mistakes are hard for the average person to handle. But criticism for those mistakes is even harder to take. I have long been an advocate of using praise rather than criticism to get better results from people. Let me give you an instance.

Let's say one of your subordinates asks you to check her work so you can show her what she's doing wrong, or where she might be making some mistakes. Now do you really think that's what she wants you to tell her? No way. She doesn't want you to criticize her and point out her errors. She wants you to praise her and tell her what a terrific job she's doing. I've yet to meet the person who asks for criticism and who really means what he or she says.

If you are going to be a winner, you must know how to handle another person's mistakes properly. Now let me give you a quick sixteen-step checklist that will help you correct the mistakes of others without using criticism.* Then I'll tell you how to take care of your own.

---

*How to correct a person's mistakes is discussed in complete detail in Chapter Seven of *Conversational Power*. If you have even as few as three people working for you, it is an extremely valuable book for you to read, for it gives you the detailed techniques you can use to correct mistakes without criticism so that you can get the best results from your subordinates. James K. Van Fleet, *Conversational Power* (Englewood Cliffs, NJ: Prentice Hall, 1984).

HOW TO CORRECT A PERSON'S MISTAKES WITHOUT USING CRITICISM

1. Get all the pertinent facts bearing on the problem first.
2. Call attention to a person's mistakes indirectly.
3. Decide whether a formal counseling session is needed.
4. If it is, pick the right time and place. Privacy is an absolute requirement.
5. Never lose your temper when counseling an employee.
6. Always begin your counseling session with *praise* for the person's work.
7. Let him know you've also made mistakes to make the person feel more at ease with you.
8. Let him tell his side of the story first.
9. Weigh all the evidence and facts carefully.
10. Discuss *only one mistake* per interview.
11. Be specific about how to correct the mistake.
12. Always fit the penalty to the offense.
13. Close your counseling session on an up-beat note.
14. Motivate the person to improve by praising the slightest improvement he makes.
15. Give your employee a good example to live up to.
16. Follow up with another counseling session if necessary to correct the mistake.

Now let me tell you how to handle your own mistakes with good grace like a winner should. All you need do is recognize where you went wrong, admit your mistake to yourself, pick yourself up off the floor, and move forward with confidence and assurance. No recrimination or sense of guilt is necessary. It's like getting bucked off a horse or falling off a bicycle. You simply get up, dust yourself off, and get right back in the saddle again. If you don't do that, you'll become paralyzed with fear of making the same mistake again, and even more important, you don't want mistakes programmed into your subconscious mind where they will form a pattern for the future.

Handled the right way, mistakes can help you. They build expertise. You'll know what doesn't work so that then you can concentrate all your energy and efforts on what does. Children learning to walk fall down again and again, but as long as they get up and try again, they will eventually succeed. You are no different. You can handle your mistakes in the same way a baby learning to walk does. The method is exactly the same.

19. Able to Plan and Organize Their Work

Winners and leaders are able to plan and organize. Then they make sure that their plans are carried out through the orders they give their subordinates. Unless they supervise the work, chances are their orders will not be obeyed to the letter. *Never inspected, always neglected* is a good management rule of thumb to follow.

Let me now give you five questions to ask yourself that will help you plan and organize your work as well as your time.

1. **Whose Decision Is This?** Ask yourself if this is really your decision to make or if it belongs to someone else. Here you must know the boundaries and limitations of your own job. You must know which decisions you and you alone must make and which ones your subordinates can make.

   Don't interfere with your people's work. Let them carry out the details of their jobs. If you do decide that no one but you can make a certain decision, then prepare yourself so you can make the right one. But if the decision belongs to someone else, then get rid of it. Unload it as if it were a hot potato. Give the problem to the right person to solve. That in itself is a wise decision.

2. **What Do I Have to Decide?** In other words, is there really a problem that is screaming for your attention? The best

way to find that out is to get something pinned down in writing, preferably in one short, simple sentence that says exactly what you will lose if this problem isn't solved. Doing this will quickly bring things into proper focus.

3. **When Must I Decide?** Is time a critical factor in your decision? Must you act right now or can you wait without complicating or increasing the possible bad effects of this problem? If you can wait, it could be that time alone will solve the problem for you. Don't, however, use that as an excuse to put decisions off. Deciding whether to wait or whether to act now is a tough decision in itself and takes a tremendous amount of good judgment.

4. **What Else Do I Need to Know Before I Act?** Do you have all the facts necessary to make a sound and timely decision? Where can you get more information? Who might be able to advise you in reaching your decision? Have you also considered all the consequences or the results of your decision? Will it affect other people? If it will, you'd better check with them first.

5. **How Shall I Make This Decision?** With all these assembled facts—and their consequences—clearly in mind, set up a balance sheet. Weigh carefully the advantages and the disadvantages of each course of action. A careful comparison of these possible solutions should allow you to pick the right one. Once you've picked it, once you've decided on your course of action, then there is only one thing left to do: *Act!*

20. Delegates Authority

If you do not delegate authority to your subordinates to do the job, you will be wasting your time on details or work that belongs to others. Let me tell you what Raymond Jamison told me about his own experience with the president of a bank:

> This bank president, I'll just call him John, has been president of this bank for more than thirty years now. He

personally approved the first loan I ever made there back in the fifties—a five-hundred-dollar college loan—and he also *personally* approved the last loan I made there when I bought a vacation cottage on Lake of the Ozarks last summer. And that, no doubt, will be the last loan he ever makes to me if he reads your book, Jim!

Now that bank has doubled in size and doubled again during those years, yet he has followed the same routine every morning of *personally* sorting and opening every single piece of mail and distributing it to his officers, tellers, and other bank employees.

What could this bank president have done to stop wasting his time on work that could easily have been done by others? Well, he might at least have given some clerk the authority to open and distribute the bank's mail. He might also have appointed one of his vice-presidents to be in charge of all loans below a certain figure.

Had he done that, he'd have had more time to analyze his bank's new business opportunities, to study his biggest customers' operations, to use his more than thirty years of valuable banking experience to help his own vice-presidents solve their problems, and to make friends with the owners and top executives of new businesses—and, therefore, new customers—who'd moved to his town.

You may think that this is an unusual example of improper delegation of authority. That is not true at all. A great many so-called leaders do not trust their subordinates. They try to do all of their own work and a sizeable part of their subordinates' work as well. This results only in inefficiency on the part of the "leader."

If you insist on keeping your hand in the details all the time, you'll discourage your subordinates by competing with them. Then the capable ones will leave you; the weak ones will sit back and let you do all the work. In the end, you'll have no time left for your real job as a winner and a leader: thinking, planning, organizing, supervising.

One more point before I leave this section. Many managers and executives try to delegate responsibility for work and think they are delegating authority. That is not true. Responsibility for the success or failure of those under you belongs only to you. If you try to delegate your responsibility to those who work for you, you are not a winner.

21. Takes Orders Well

Just because you have to take orders from your supervisor does not mean that you are a follower as such. Even leaders and winners must take orders at times. For instance, if you are the owner of your own business, you still cannot do just as you please. The other day I was in one of those fast-food restaurants for a quick lunch, and I saw a sign on the wall that read:

> Rule Number One: The customer is always right.
>
> Rule Number Two: If the customer is wrong, refer to Rule Number One!

Even five-star generals have a superior, as General Douglas MacArthur found out when he was relieved of his command by President Harry Truman in April 1951. So, no matter how high you go, there will always be somebody who is your boss, and you have to take orders from that person, even if that person is the customer. In almost all cases, top-level executives have achieved their positions of leadership because they were able to carry out their superiors' orders.

You can usually spot a winner and a leader, for that person will be willing to accept advice whenever necessary. One of the characteristics of winners is that they know when to get more information before taking action. They are not reluctant to go out and get it from the CEO, from their immediate superior, from an associate of equal status, or even from the newest person in the company.

22. A Good Communicator

"Why don't they let me know what's going on?" "Why don't they tell me what they want?" "Why can't they make up their minds?" "Why is it always hurry up and wait?"

Have you heard comments like these before? I'm sure you have. So have I; too many times, when I was in business. And when I heard them, I knew that I wasn't keeping my people properly informed.

If you want to be a winner and a leader, you must not run your organization in such a way that people have to ask questions like these. Every single one of your subordinates has the basic right to work and to think in the clear.

She should be told the why and the wherefore of whatever she is expected to do, as well as the what and the how, unless it is a mission-type order. Your employees' efficiency, morale, confidence, and enthusiasm will depend primarily upon how well you keep them informed.

For instance, if you have the bad habit of constantly brushing off your subordinates, not keeping them properly informed just because you think it's not important for them to know, then you're doomed to work in an information vacuum yourself. If you don't keep your people informed, you can be sure that they'll never tell you anything you need to know either.

But if you believe in the importance of giving your subordinates full information in a straightforward manner and then do exactly that, they'll always keep you well informed, too.

TEN TECHNIQUES YOU CAN USE TO COMMUNICATE WITH YOUR PEOPLE

1. Let people know exactly where they stand with you.
2. Use a checklist to rate a person's job performance.
3. Tell a person when the work is not satisfactory.
4. Always praise a person for a job well done.
5. Learn to praise a person without using flattery.
6. Make your employee feel like a VIP.

7. Brief your major subordinates at an early stage on any planned changes in operation.

8. Prevent and eliminate misunderstandings by keeping people well informed and up to date.

9. If a planned company change affects some of your people, let them know.

10. If a planned company change *does not* affect anyone, let them know that, too, to squelch rumors.

One of the most important things your subordinates can ever do for you is to tell you the straight truth and let you know what's actually going on in your own shop. I learned this lesson early in my business life from a wise old foreman who told me, "Don't let your employees tell you what you *want* to hear. Let your wife do that. Make your employees tell you what you *have* to hear. That's the only way you can be sure of hanging onto your job."

His advice has proved most valuable to me over the years. I know it will be valuable to you, too.

Even though you are the leader of your group, no less than 40 percent of your time in communication will be spent in listening to the other person. Yet it is a proven fact that managers and executives retain less than 25 percent of the information their subordinates give them. Here's how you can do a much better job than that.

TEN TECHNIQUES TO HELP IMPROVE YOUR LISTENING ABILITIES

1. Give Your Wholehearted Attention to the Other Person. Listen with all the intensity and awareness that you can command.

2. Really Work at Listening. Listening is hard work. You will know whether you're really working at listening or just faking it.

3. Show an Interest in What the Speaker Is Saying. Look directly at the person. Establish eye contact and hold it.

Show by your alert posture and intense facial expression that you are deeply interested in what he's saying.

4. **Resist Distractions.** Give the speaker your total attention so that she can tell you what you need to know.

5. **Practice Patience.** This is largely a matter of waiting, watching, listening, and sitting silently until the person who's speaking is completely through.

6. **Keep an Open Mind.** Remember that you are listening to your subordinate to gain information. If you happen to hear something with which you don't agree, that doesn't mean that everything else he says is wrong, too.

7. **Listen for Ideas.** A poor listener tends to get lost in trivia and details. A good listener watches for ideas, concepts, and principles. Don't fret if you can't remember all the details right now. That can come later.

8. **Judge the Content, Not the Delivery.** Don't concern yourself with a person's personality, style of delivery, grammar, use of words, and so on. You should be interested only in finding out what she knows and what she wants to tell you.

9. **Hold Your Fire.** Too many times a listener will spend most of the time trying to figure out how to rebut the speaker rather than actually listening to what's being said. Forget your own pet ideas and listen; you might learn something brand new and profitable for you.

10. **Learn to Listen Between the Lines.** Lots of times you can learn more by what the person does not say than by what he does. Watch the facial expression, mannerisms, gestures, body movements. To be a good listener means you must use your eyes as well as your ears.

23. Grows on the Job

A winner who does not get better on his job ceases to be a winner and a leader. You can recognize the person who has come to a standstill by remarks like, "I must be getting old; I just can't seem to keep up with those young guys any more," or "I guess you can't teach an old dog new tricks," or "My memory isn't as good as it used to be." You can also tell when a person has stopped growing on the job if he says, "Nothing new to learn in this job any more," or "This job has no challenge for me any more."

Winners never lack challenges on their jobs, nor do they ever stop growing in their current positions. They know that the more they learn now, the more prepared they will be to step into a bigger and more challenging job in the future when it is offered to them. It is also true that leaders and winners make their own opportunities. They don't just wait for one to come their way.

24. Focuses on the Present

Winners live in the present by keeping themselves busy with daily challenges and current goals to achieve. Dreamers live only in the future, while losers get lost in the past, crying over missed opportunities, thinking to themselves, "If only I had done this," "If only I'd been there," "What if this had or hadn't happened."

When you focus your attention on the present, you can become completely responsive to it, aware of your present goals and what you have to do to reach them. If you find your mind wandering back to the past or straying forward to the future, bring it back to the present immediately. It is only through perseverance and self-discipline of your conscious mind that you can break your negative concepts and replace them by programming your subconscious mind with positive ones.

A positive concept of yourself and your own abilities to succeed is necessary to maintain a winning attitude. If you program your subconscious mind with the winning self-image of a leader, you can change the course of your entire life so that it will become what you desire.

You are limited only by your imagination. As Albert Einstein once said, "Imagination is everything; it is the preview of life's coming attractions." So imagine yourself to be a winner and a leader. Program your subconscious mind with positive concepts and attitudes of love, success, and self-respect. As you think, so shall you become.

▽ ▽ ▽

Let me now summarize for you the twenty-four hallmarks of a winner:

1. Optimism and cheerful enthusiasm
2. An overpowering urge for action
3. Skill in solving problems
4. Authoritative manner
5. Drive, stamina, and endurance
6. Wide-ranging interests and knowledge
7. A good memory
8. Creative thinking
9. Accepting of responsibility
10. An air of control
11. A positive self-image
12. A good example for others
13. Self-motivated
14. Self-confident
15. Decisive
16. Sound judgment
17. Respected
18. Accepts criticism, admits mistakes
19. Able to plan and organize their work
20. Delegates authority
21. Takes orders well

22. A good communicator
23. Grows on the job
24. Focuses on the present

▽ ▽ ▽

One final thought about winners: Winners know they must give before they can get. That's why they plant shade trees under which they know they will never be able to sit.

9

How to Use the Power Within to Improve Your Memory

Why do some people have a poor memory? Because they have programmed their subconscious minds with that negative concept. They have constantly made such remarks as "I can't remember," "I always forget," "I really have a bad memory," "I always got bad grades in school because my memory was so poor," and the like, until they have drummed that idea into their subconscious minds, and, as a result, yes, they do have a poor memory.

If you have that problem, don't worry. You can train yourself to remember all the things you want to remember, all the things that are important for you to recall. The benefits you will gain from having an excellent memory are tremendous, and I'll tell you about them a bit later, but first, I want to tell you . . .

HOW TO RID YOUR MIND OF THE IDEA THAT YOUR MEMORY IS POOR

Most people with a poor memory have programmed their subconscious minds with the idea that they are not able to remember. They have fed that failure idea into their subconscious minds with devastating effects. As a result of that negative programming, they do have a poor memory. Usually teachers and parents are responsible for initially feeding this negative concept into the child's mind.

For instance, if a child is scolded and criticized for having a bad memory or for poor grades in school, or if she is told that she is stupid, dumb, a nitwit, and so on, you can be sure that her response to that will be so negative that she can barely remember her own name, home address, or telephone number.

If you have a problem with memory recall, the first thing you need to do is program your subconscious mind with positive attitudes and concepts; in other words, convince yourself that you have an excellent memory. Then you can remember anything and everything you want to remember.

To motivate yourself to achieve that goal, tell yourself of all the benefits that will be yours when you have a good memory. Tell yourself that having a good memory is not only important in your studies, if you are still in school, but that it is also of great value in your work and in your daily life. In some occupations, especially acting and music, it is extremely important to be able to memorize easily.

All of your retained knowledge is based upon what you have learned in school or on the job, including all of your experiences in life. The more you are able to use the knowledge that you have, the more you will be able to use the extraordinary mental powers that you possess. The purpose of this chapter is to help you draw on those great intellectual abilities that you have, some of which are no doubt lying dormant, buried deep in the memory files of your subconscious mind, or possibly even blocked by the negative input you have programmed into your subconscious mind.

BENEFITS YOU WILL GAIN

- Your self-esteem will increase and your self-confidence will soar when you discover that you do have a good memory and that you can easily recall whatever you need to whenever you want to.

- A good memory can increase your success on the job and in business in many ways. Not only can it help you better remember the tasks to be done, but it can also keep you from forgetting to do certain essential things.

- A good memory can help you remember details you didn't write down. In fact, when you have a good memory, you won't have to write down all the little details; just the main items will be enough. For example, if you're shopping for groceries, instead of writing down chicken, steak, roast, pork chops, hamburger on your list, all you would need do is write down one word: *meat.*

- A good memory will help you at social and business affairs. For instance, when you remember people's names, you increase your chances of getting new jobs and new clients. If someone gives you the name of a possible prospect, you can remember that person's name for later contact. Remembering people's names is so important that I'll cover it in greater detail later, but for now let me say that to remember a person's name is a compliment. To forget it is an insult.

- An excellent memory can help you give a better sales presentation to a prospective customer. Or it can be a tremendous asset when giving your boss an important and detailed briefing on something. It can help you remember the correct words and grammar to use in written and spoken communication. In fact, your memory can make or break your chances for promotion and advancement.

- Whether it's a business or social gathering, a good memory can make you more interesting company. It can help you remember humorous jokes and stories, interesting anecdotes, or the news of the day. In other words, it can help make you a first-rate conversationalist.

YOUR SUBCONSCIOUS MIND: YOUR MEMORY BANK

First, let me tell you that everything that has ever happened to you, all you have read, studied, been told, seen, or experienced, is retained in complete detail in the memory bank of your subconscious mind. Information storage takes place in your subconscious mind. Storage of this magnitude would be absolutely impossible for your conscious mind. If you were to be simultaneously aware in your conscious mind of all the millions and millions of bits of information stored in the memory bank of your subconscious mind, you would be unable to function. You would be bombarded with all this stored information and go completely mad.

Nothing that has happened to you is ever forgotten. What has been programmed into your subconscious mind is never completely removed. However, since much of that information is not required at all times, it is not allowed to surface until it is needed for some reason or another.

Most of us do have temporary lapses of memory, finding to our frustration that we cannot immediately recall something we most definitely know—someone's name, for example. The harder we try to remember, the more elusive the name becomes. But then when we stop trying to remember the name, it usually comes to mind in a very short time; in fact, most of the time, almost immediately.

This temporary lapse of memory can also happen when a student is about to take an examination. Before that student enters the room, it seems as if everything he needs to know can readily be remembered. But the moment he sits down at the desk and looks at the questions on the examination, everything seems to go blank. Then he panics, and the more scared he becomes, the harder it is to recall the answers.

The only way this situation can be resolved is to calm down and realize that the answers are stored in the brain and that as soon as the panic leaves, the answers will come back.

A brilliant neurologist and neurosurgeon proved by her experiments that past events—which the patient thought were completely forgotten—came vividly back to the person's conscious mind when an electric probe was used to stimulate those portions of the brain that contain the memory banks of the subconscious mind.

For instance, one patient remembered being with some children when she was around five years old. She had not thought of them for years and years. She not only remembered what they were doing but exactly what they were wearing. She could actually hear them talking and laughing. The most amazing thing about this memory was that, not only did she recall the past event, but she also seemed to be reliving the experience.

How Hypnotism Stimulates Memory Recall

Hypnotism can also help the conscious mind recall events that have been programmed into the subconscious mind but that seem to have been forgotten. One of the most interesting results of this is what is called *age regression*. As with the electric probe, when a person is hypnotized, he can be caused (this time by suggestion) to return in time and to relive his past experiences. This is much deeper than mere remembering. As with the electric stimulation of the brain, all five senses function. Very early experiences in a person's life, even in infancy, can be relived in this way. The fact that a person really has a perfect memory can be demonstrated in this way.

I tell you this to demonstrate that you do not have a poor memory. Frankly, I personally feel that unless there was brain damage at birth, every person is born with a perfect memory. Memory blocks are a result of improper programming of the subconscious mind, which then affects the person's ability to recall readily.

When this is reinforced and the person is constantly bombarded with the idea that he can't remember, the idea may become fixed and further dull the person's memory.

Repetition: Your Key to Your Memory Bank

Just as repetitive suggestion is most effective in programming an idea into your subconscious mind for easier retention, so, too, is it a must for easier recall by your conscious mind. This is not to say that your subconscious mind cannot remember something that you have seen or heard, but that repetition makes it easier.

For instance, memory experts say that if you want to memorize something simple, like a short poem, for example, it takes approximately forty-two repetitions to make a permanent imprint in the memory banks of your subconscious mind. They also say that if you want to learn something long and difficult, say Lincoln's Gettysburg Address, for example, it will take nearly five hundred repetitions before you can recite it without a mistake or without hesitation.

Repetition is a powerful factor in effectively programming your subconscious mind. It serves two major purposes. First, your subconscious mind cannot act on what it does not understand. Repetition, especially when a proposition is presented in a variety of ways, serves to make the idea clearer. Second, repetition wears down the resistance of any contrary or conflicting ideas that are preventing the ready acceptance of the proposition.

As Job said in effect, "The water wears down the stones." That simple sentence is one of the clearest pictures of the power of repetition.

How Your Subconscious Mind Stores Memories

As I've said, everything that has ever happened to you, all that you have read, studied, been told, seen, or experienced, is retained in complete detail in the memory banks of your subconscious mind. This recorded information can be divided into three main types: *experiential*, *word*, and *attitude* or *conceptual*, which is derived from an interpretation of the first two types.

- *Experiential storage* in your subconscious mind comes from everything that has ever happened to you, everything you've been told, seen, heard, smelled, or tasted. Remember, an imagined experience is just as real to your subconscious mind as an actual event, for it cannot tell the difference between reality and fantasy.

- *Word storage* in your subconscious mind is derived from everything you've read or studied and your understanding of the meaning of individual words.

- *Attitude or conceptual storage* is your subconscious mind's interpretation of the first two storage systems. For example, if someone were to describe a dog to you, but never mentioned the actual word *dog,* you would still know exactly what he was talking about.

Or if a person were to discuss perseverance, enthusiasm, success, failure, love, anger, or resentment, your understanding of words and your actual experience would cause your subconscious mind to play back to your conscious mind a picture that conveys the attitudes or concepts you have of such terms. Your concept of life and your actions toward people are based upon the attitudes you have programmed into your subconscious mind for permanent storage and memory recall.

WHAT'S IN A NAME? EVERYTHING

"I can't seem to remember your name," is one of the worst phrases you can utter. It can cost you a sale if you're a salesperson. It can ruin a potential friendship. If you're the boss, it can cost you the loyalty and respect of a subordinate.

A person's name is the most important word in all the world to him; it is his most valuable possession. Use it and it can often work magic for you. But if you don't use it—if you don't call a person by name, if you don't even know her name, if you forget it or mispronounce it—the negative impact may last forever.

As a good manager or executive, you should be able to call every single one of your employees, not only by their last, but also by their first names. It is one of the most powerful, most convincing ways you can say to a person: *I recognize you as an important individual.* Let me show you what I mean by that with this example.

"Today I know every single person in the plant by his first name," Jim Wilkins, the president of a Chicago company that employs nearly five hundred people, told me:

> Oh, I miss once in a while, especially if the person is new, but not very often. But it wasn't always that way. Used to be, I never paid any attention at all to any of my employees. I knew the main department heads and I figured that was enough.
>
> One day I saw a bunch of men standing around doing nothing. I went up to them, chewed them out for loafing on the job, and told them to get back to work. Told them I hadn't hired them to stand around and if that was all they could find to do, I'd fire them.
>
> Well, they just laughed at me. So did all the people watching. That made it even worse. I became furious and really blew my stack. Made a complete fool out of myself in front of almost all of my employees. And the company grapevine quickly told all those who didn't see the incident, so everybody soon knew all about it.
>
> Come to find out those people didn't even work for me! You see, I lease the building, and the owner had sent over some furnace people to repair the heating system that I'd complained about. They were just waiting for their own foreman to tell them what to do.
>
> Since then, I've kept everything on a first-name basis here. I know every one of my people. It's paid off for me in friendship, loyalty, cooperation, and quality production with increased profits. Not a bad payoff for remembering a person's name.

If you want the same kind of results for yourself, then treat your employees like people—not cattle. There's a lot of difference between a *team* and a *herd*. People want to be known by their names, not their clock numbers, "Hey you!" or "Fellas." It doesn't cost you a cent to call a person by his or her first name, but it makes that person feel like a million bucks.

Yelling at a person with "Hey you!" will get you absolutely nowhere. My letter carrier, Dick Jones, told me about this story:

> I was delivering mail one day and I heard a man behind me yelling, "Hey you!" I knew perfectly well he was calling to me, for no one else was on the street, but I kept right on walking and paid no attention. He yelled several times, "Hey you!" but I didn't stop.
>
> Then he called, "Mr. Mailman." I immediately stopped, turned around, and said, "Did you call me?"
>
> "I sure did," he replied, with an angry tone in his voice. "I called you several times, but you never listened."
>
> "And how did you call me?" I asked. "I only heard you call 'Mr. Mailman' once, and I immediately stopped and answered you."
>
> "Well, several times I called 'Hey you!' but you never paid any attention, and you knew darned well I was calling to you."
>
> "Well, I don't answer to 'Hey you,'" I told him, "and I'm sure you don't either. But I do answer to 'Mr. Mailman,' whenever you call me by that name."

These two examples demonstrate how important it is to call a person by his name, or in Dick's case, to call the person by his title.

One other important point: Never yell at a person unless he or she is really too far away to hear you properly. Even then, it's not a smart idea.

Five Simple Ways to Remember Names

Memory courses always plug the idea of association for better recall. They often suggest using rhyming words like *myth* for *Smith*, *bones* for *Jones*, and that sort of thing. That's okay, I suppose, as long as you don't forget the rhyming word. But I use a completely different system, and, frankly, I think it's much better. Here's how:

1. **Listen closely.** I've often heard it said that when you don't remember a person's name, it's because you're so busy listening to your own and making sure it's properly pronounced that you don't even hear the other person's name at all.

To remember a name, you must listen closely and really concentrate on it. Ask that the name be repeated if you miss it the first time. Even if you didn't miss it, it helps to have it repeated anyway. If it's a difficult name, ask the person to spell it for you. Don't worry; you'll never offend anyone by showing such interest. In fact, the person will be complimented by all the attention you're showing him or her. She'll know that you're making an honest attempt to learn the name and to remember it.

2. **Repeat the person's name.** Repetition is essential to remember people's names. As soon as you learn the person's name, say, "I'm ever so happy to meet you, Mr. Stone." Then repeat his name over and over to yourself silently while memorizing his features. Insert his name into the conversation whenever and wherever you can. Use it again when you part company. Don't worry about using his name too often. Everyone likes to hear his name as much and as often as possible.

3. **Write the person's name down.** Do this at the first opportunity you have. Try to visualize the person's face and appearance for even better association. If the person has some striking feature, a Roman nose, a mustache or a beard, so much the better. It will be that much easier for you to remember the name by associating it with a specific feature.

4. Be interested in the person. This is one of the most important points in remembering people's names: being truly interested in them and really wanting to remember them. I take pride in being able to call a waitress by her name even if she has waited on me only once before, no matter how long ago it was.

A dinner companion of mine is often amazed at my ability to do this. The other morning we had breakfast together at a little restaurant called the Blueberry Muffin. A waitress walked by who had waited on us a few weeks before, and I said, "Good morning, Gretchen." All my companion could say was, "I don't believe it. I couldn't even remember her face or that she'd ever waited on us before, let alone recall her name!" But it can be done if you make an honest attempt to do so.

I also make it a special point to remember the names of the messengers who pick up and deliver packages for me. It is not enough for me just to remember their names only; I try to remember everything I can about them.

For example, Pete is of Italian heritage. He loves pasta, is slightly overweight, and has a problem with high blood pressure and his cholesterol level. But he always has a cheerful smile and a pleasant greeting, even at 7:30 in the morning! He is no longer surprised that I remember his name or that I can inquire specifically about certain aspects of his health.

The other day Dan, another delivery man, whom I'd met only once about six weeks before, was dumbfounded that I could call him by name. That is all I know at the moment about Dan, but as time goes on and if he keeps coming to my house I can assure you that I will soon know much more. This kind of memory work can be a lot of fun if you are really interested in people and are willing to concentrate on remembering not only their names, but also everything else that you can about them.

5. Learn the ethnic derivation of a person's name. This is also an excellent way to remember people's names. You will never insult anyone by asking what the ethnic derivation of her name is. I always say, "It's a hobby of mine to learn the ethnic derivation of a person's name. I'm always interested in knowing. Is yours French, Italian, Belgian, or what?"

Most people are eager to tell you all about their names, where their parents and grandparents came from, and everything else they can think of. Knowing something about the name and the person will help you remember it. And you learn a great deal in the process.

My wife is not as good as I am at remembering names. But she always knows the color of the person's eyes and hair. She also notices the style and color of the dress a woman is wearing as well as the jewelry she has on. She observes these points and remembers them and thinks it strange that I do not. But it's merely a matter of interest and emphasis. I place my emphasis on remembering names. She places hers on appearance.

HOW TO RECALL HARD-TO-RECALL EVENTS

Usually, when your conscious mind cannot recall something from your subconscious mind's memory files, it is for one of three reasons: (1) The event is too distasteful, too embarrassing, or too painful for your conscious mind to recall; (2) your conscious mind did not consider the event or the incident important enough to record; (3) or too much was happening at one time to permit concentrated recording by your subconscious mind. Let me now discuss these individually.

1. **The Event Is Too Distasteful to Recall.** Your conscious mind then simply blocks out the memory and does not allow it to be recalled from your subconscious mind. It simply refuses to live the experience over again.

Victims of violent crimes, such as incest or rape, sometimes do this. So do some people who have committed illegal or immoral acts while under the influence of drugs or alcohol.

2. **The Event Wasn't Important Enough to Record.** At the time it happened, no strong impression was transmitted to your subconscious mind for permanent retention. This is not to say that your subconscious mind did not record and remember the incident. It did, but it regards it only as trivia since

your conscious mind did not consider it important. Therefore, only a very light imprint of the event was made in the subconscious mind. Under hypnosis, however, it could readily be brought back to the conscious mind.

No two people will attach the same importance to an event. My wife and I have been married for more than fifty years, yet she vividly recalls incidents that I just don't seem to remember at all. By the same token, I remember certain events that escape her memory completely. The simple reason for this is the amount of importance each of us attached to the experience.

3. Too Much Was Happening at One Time. Your conscious mind cannot concentrate on all the details at the same time. It tries to absorb everything that is happening, and, as a result, almost nothing is recorded and absorbed. That is why when eyewitnesses to an accident or a robbery are questioned by the police, they provide so many conflicting or different versions of the same incident.

Four Ways to Improve Your Recall

Here are four specific techniques to improve your memory and your ability to recall: (1) concentrating harder on the event, (2) avoiding distractions, (3) visualizing and (4) learning to be more observant of what you see and hear. Let me discuss each one of these in detail with you now.

1. Concentrate Fully. By doing so you can absorb much more with your conscious mind. As a result, a deeper imprint is made on the neurons in that portion of the brain that houses your subconscious mind, and memory recall will be much easier. Being able to concentrate intently and keep your conscious mind from jumping from one distraction to another is one of the keys to a better memory.

A great many times a lack of concentration can merely be a bad habit that is a carryover from younger years. For example, if during your school days you daydreamed and fantasized, and let your mind wander when you should have been either studying or listening to the teacher, this could well have been the beginning of a bad habit.

And if you still have this habit, then your subconscious mind assumes that the material is not important to you. So it makes very little effort, if any, to record the information permanently in its memory banks. Only a shallow imprint is made, which makes recall extremely difficult.

One way to force yourself to be more observant and concentrate on the subject at hand is to follow the advice of E. Joseph Cossman, a mail-order millionaire, who said, "Look at each piece of correspondence or a document, think about it, make a decision, pass it along for action, file it if absolutely necessary, or destroy it—but never, never handle the same piece of paper twice." Your fidelity to this one simple rule will always save you an untold amount of time, and it will also keep your desk clean and clear.

Not only will this save you time and keep your desk clear, but it will also give you an incentive for developing a better memory. If you box yourself into a corner by not allowing yourself the "luxury" of looking at the same piece of paper again, you will have no choice but to concentrate fully on the subject at hand and develop a better memory.

To sum up, then, if you want to improve your memory, you must force your conscious mind to concentrate totally on the point you want to remember and completely disregard distracting and extraneous input. And that's the next technique I want to discuss.

2. Avoid Distractions. In World War II, aircraft-manufacturing executives found that production increased sharply, quality improved, and even safety records got better when the women on the assembly line wore uniforms instead of street clothes.

An office manager of a large insurance company discovered that placing extra-thick pads under typewriters dramatically cut the distracting noise in his office. The result was more efficient typists, clerks, and executives.

Both street clothes and noisy typewriters were distractions. They kept people from paying full attention to their work. And like many distractions, they could easily be eliminated.

Some techniques are even subtler. For example, the employees in a small factory got a big kick at first out of the many "THINK" signs the boss had placed around the plant. But as it eventually turned out, the boss knew what he was doing.

"I found that when my employees saw enough of these signs, they finally got the point that people actually were thinking about their work and what they were doing," he said. "They also realized that loud talk and useless chatter don't go together with job concentration, so now they keep the conversation down."

3. Visualize. This technique has many applications. For example, you can visualize a "lost" object. Think back to the last time you were using that object. Where were you? What were you doing with it? Visualize yourself using it. Then, when you were finished with it, see yourself putting it away so that you can remember where you put it. In other words, *relive the experience* so that you can bring it up from the memory banks of your subconscious mind to your conscious mind.

I use this system myself. Although I have a cabinet in my garage in which to keep my tools, I must admit that I sometimes fail to put a hammer, a screwdriver, or a pair of pliers back where they belong.

Now you know nothing is ever really lost for me—it is just misplaced temporarily. It will always be exactly where I left it. I have found every tool I have ever "lost" in the exact place where I last used it and where my subconscious mind told me to look.

So when I can't find some tool that I want to use, I simply sit down, close my eyes, concentrate on the "lost" object, and ask my subconscious mind to tell me where it is. After a few moments of meditation the answer will come and I will be led immediately to the correct spot.

For instance, a few days ago I couldn't find a small hand-saw I wanted to use. After a few moments of meditation, I saw it clearly in my mind's eye. It was on top of the carport, where I'd been fixing a leaky plastic pipe for my swimming pool's solar-heating unit a few days before.

I have taught this art to others with great success, for they've told me that they've found such "lost" items as small tools, airline tickets, keys, business papers and plans, glasses, wallets, jewelry, and so on.

Just recently, I taught this technique to a friend who has a tough time finding things. She always says, "Oh, it's here somewhere in my apartment." And of course, it always is. Her problem is that she files papers well, but she doesn't recall which file they are in, for she doesn't concentrate on that when she puts them away. And that's really the key to finding those lost items: *constant concentration on what you're doing at all times.*

You can also use visualization to remember a road route without a map. If you've already traveled the road or street before, you shouldn't have to refer to a map to go the same way again. Just see yourself in your car as in your original experience. Don't try to retrace your route backward. Instead, visualize exactly where you started your trip. Now see yourself leaving from this starting point. Remember the surroundings as you pass them, and look for significant or outstanding landmarks or route markers. Pay careful attention to your route when you make a turn. Keep retraveling this route in your mind until you reach your final destination.

I have traveled across these United States from coast to coast many times. Once I travel a highway, I never have to refer to a road map again, unless there have been so many changes that the original route is no longer unrecognizable.

4. Be Observant. One of the best ways to become more observant is to pay exact attention to what you are doing or what a person is saying. When you do that, you will be able to eliminate or avoid any distractions. It's also wise to follow the system of *who, what, when, where, why,* and *how.*

A good way for you to practice this technique is to look at a person for ten seconds, starting at the head and moving down to the feet, observing everything you see as you go: color of hair, color of eyes, complexion, scars or blemishes on the face, estimated height and weight, type of clothing, color and cut of coat, trousers, pants, skirt, blouse, color and kind of shoes, watches, rings, and other jewelry.

Then turn your eyes away and see how well you remember all those details. If you practice this technique carefully, within a week or so, probably even less, you will find that your powers of observation will have increased tremendously, and so will your power of recall.

In conclusion, let me say that there are a great many advantages to be gained from developing a good memory. It sure beats spinning your wheels and wasting precious time trying to remember something.

10

How to Rid Yourself of Worry and Fear

To be afraid at times is perfectly normal. Most people will be afraid if real danger threatens them in some way. Courage is not the lack of fear but a matter of facing danger when you are afraid.

The normal physical reactions to fear are increased heart rate, increased flow of blood to the arms and legs and a decreased flow to the abdominal area, increased respiration, and a greater flow of adrenalin through the body. This is known as the *fight-or-flight syndrome,* a normal physiological phenomenon.

Some fears of physical injury are perfectly valid and are just plain common sense. For instance, if you are at a zoo or a circus and the lions and tigers break out of their cages and start running around loose through the crowd, you would have a perfect right to feel afraid. Frankly, I would be terrified. Your body would respond to this legitimate physical fear.

But imaginary or psychological fears can cause the same sort of physical reactions. An old classic Arabian fable illustrates this well.

Pestilence met a caravan on the road to Baghdad.

"Why are you in such a hurry to get to Baghdad?" asked the leader of the caravan.

"To take five thousand lives," Pestilence replied.

On the way back from the city, Pestilence and the caravan met once more.

"You lied to me," the caravan leader said angrily. "You did not take five thousand lives; you took fifty thousand!"

"No, I did not lie to you," Pestilence said. "I took only five thousand lives and not one more, just as I said I would. *Fear took all the rest!*"

PROGRAM YOUR SUBCONSCIOUS TO ELIMINATE IMAGINARY FEARS

As you can see from this old story, many of our fears are imaginary or psychological rather than physical or real. And most of these psychological fears come from negative programming of a person's subconscious mind. To get rid of them, a person must reprogram the subconscious mind with positive ideas of courage and success.

One way of doing that is to do as General George Patton of World War II fame did. When he was asked by a reporter if he ever experienced fear before a battle, he replied, "Of course I do. Only a fool would say he was not afraid at times, but I never take counsel of my fears."

A psychological fear many people have is the fear of death or injury to oneself or some member of the family—a wife or husband, a son or daughter. But death is inevitable. There is no other way out of life that I know. As George Carlin, the comedian, once said, "I knew that everyone had to die, but I thought God would make an exception in my case!" To sit around in fear of when it is going to happen to you or someone you love is to engage in useless self-torture.

Our nephew, the son and only child of my wife's sister, was killed in a hunting accident a few years ago. His mother and father were grief-stricken, as we all were. But that did not mean that John's parents had lived in fear of that happening all those years. Nor did his wife and his two children. They had all enjoyed a happy life together. And that is the way it should be. Life is meant to be enjoyed, not feared. My own grandson died tragically when he was just twenty years old. Naturally, we all grieved. But life goes on and so must we.

As a result of his death, I could have become overly fearful if I allowed myself to do so, for I have four young granddaughters ranging in age from six to thirteen. If I allow myself to think all the time about what might happen to them, I could easily be consumed by uncontrollable fear.

But rather than let that happen, I program my subconscious mind with positive thoughts that my two sons and their wives will do everything in their power to safeguard and protect their daughters. And that is all that I can do.

BENEFITS YOU WILL GAIN

- Freedom from stress
- Freedom from fear of people
- Better health
- More self-confidence
- And best of all, serenity and peace of mind

THE ELEVEN MOST-COMMON PSYCHOLOGICAL FEARS

What does everyone want out of life? Well, according to psychologists everyone wants to be loved, to win fame, fortune, and power, and to stay healthy.

And the primary cause of fear in most people is that they will not achieve these goals, or that they might lose them if they already possess them.

Almost everyone, at one time or another, will suffer from one or more of these eleven basic psychological fears:

1. Fear of failure
2. Fear of criticism

3. Fear of making the wrong decision
4. Fear of not being important
5. Fear of poverty
6. Fear of loneliness or loss of love
7. Fear of loss of liberty
8. Fear of sickness
9. Fear of old age
10. Fear of death
11. Fear of the unknown

You can learn to conquer these fears if you use the power within—the psychology of self-achievement—to program your subconscious mind with positive ideas of health and success. When you do that, you'll have much more confidence in yourself and in your abilities to achieve your goals.

What People Worry Most About

Statistics gathered by life-insurance companies to help determine the cause of heart disease show that people worry most about the following things:

1. Forty percent worry about things that never happen.
2. Thirty percent worry about things they cannot change.
3. Twelve percent worry needlessly about their health.
4. Ten percent worry about petty, miscellaneous, and unimportant things.
5. Only eight percent actually worry about *real* problems.

As you can see from this, 92 percent of the things people worry about the most are either psychological or things they are unable to control.

To worry about things that never happen, that you cannot change, or that are psychological in nature not only destroys your health, causing stomach ulcers and heart irregularities, but can also lead to a complete nervous breakdown, or, at the very worst, suicide.

It is said so often that I suppose it is a cliché, but worry is the interest people pay on trouble before it actually becomes due. Worry never solves any problem; it only complicates it. Worry is destructive and disintegrating. Still, a lot of people spend many of their nights worrying instead of sleeping. Loss of sleep and fatigue in itself can lead to ill health.

Worry is actually a malfunction of the mind and can easily result in disease. I suppose you could say that it is against the law to worry. Buddhists say that "the two devils of the mind are anger and fear. Anger is the brain passion while fear is the freezing passion." In short, fear causes you to freeze up so that you are not able to do anything.

When excessive worry consumes the mind, it can lead to *abulia*, the loss of the power to make decisions, created when the mind becomes divided and cannot act. Abulia often results in a complete nervous breakdown, for the person quits struggling and becomes completely depressed and passive. He literally becomes a living vegetable.

To conclude, worry is injurious both to the mind and the body. It is injurious to social fellowships, business relationships, and family affairs.

How You Can Conquer Worry

There is another emotion that will conquer worry and get rid of it for you, if you will but use it. That emotion is *enthusiasm*. Enthusiasm is the vital quality that will stir you to take action to solve your problem, whatever it is, rather than sit around and worry about it. Enthusiasm is the emotion that will direct your action and lead you to become positive, powerful, and self-confident so that you can overcome the destructiveness of worry.

Let me give you a couple of examples so you can see for yourself how you can overcome worry with enthusiasm.

Before Frank Bettger became one of the most successful life-insurance salesmen this country has ever known, and the author of the classic best seller, *How I Raised Myself from*

*Failure to Success in Selling,** he was a professional baseball player.

He started out with the Johnstown, Pennsylvania, team in the Tri-State League. But he was fired by the manager of that team. Frank went to him and asked him why he had been fired.

"Because you're lazy," the manager told him. "You drag yourself around the field like a veteran who's been playing ball for twenty years. Why do you act that way if you're not lazy?"

"Well, Bert," Frank said, "I'm so nervous and so scared that I try to hide my fear from the crowd, and especially from the other players on the team. Besides, I thought by taking it easy, I could get rid of my nervousness."

"It will never work, Frank," the manager said. "That's what's holding you back. Whatever you do after you leave here, get rid of your fear and put some life and enthusiasm into your work!"

Shortly after that, Frank received a tryout from the New Haven, Connecticut, team, a member of the New England League. No one knew Frank in that league, so he made up his mind to be the most enthusiastic ballplayer they'd ever seen. From the minute he appeared on the field, he acted like a man electrified. He threw the ball around the diamond so fast and so hard that it almost knocked the infielders' gloves off.

Did Frank's newfound enthusiasm work for him? It most certainly did. As Frank said, three good things happened, and here's what they are:

- His enthusiasm entirely overcame his fear.
- His enthusiasm affected the other players on the team, and they, too, became more enthusiastic.

---

*Frank Bettger, *How I Raised Myself from Failure to Success in Selling* (Englewood Cliffs, NJ: Prentice Hall, 1949).

- He felt better during the game and after it was over than he had ever felt before.

Two years later Frank was playing third base for the St. Louis Cardinals. While playing a game in Chicago against the Cubs, he had a bad accident. On a full run, he picked up a bunt and tried to throw it in the opposite direction. Something snapped in his arm, and the injury forced him to give up baseball. Perhaps that was best in the long run, because had it not been for that injury, Frank would never have become the outstanding success he became in the life-insurance business.

Frank said that enthusiasm in what you are doing will help you overcome fear, get rid of worry, become more successful in business, make more money, and enjoy a healthier, richer, fuller, and happier life.

How can you, too, become so enthusiastic that you eliminate worry and fear? Well, Frank says: *To become enthusiastic—ACT ENTHUSIASTIC!*

And now let me tell you about the famous American showman P. T. Barnum. He managed the highly successful United States tour of the Swedish singer Jenny Lind, better known as the "Swedish Nightingale." Then, in 1871, Mr. Barnum opened his famous circus, known as "The Greatest Show on Earth." In 1881, he merged it with that of his chief competitor, and the circus continued as Barnum and Bailey.

Mr. Barnum was a positive-minded person filled with enthusiasm and self-confidence. Once he was awakened from a sound sleep in the middle of the night to be told that one-fourth of his circus had been completely destroyed by fire.

Mr. Barnum sat up, blinking his eyes. "What are you going to do?" the messenger asked, expecting him to leap from his bed and start issuing orders.

"Do?" Mr. Barnum asked. "I'm going to go back to sleep, for there's nothing I can do about it tonight. I'll do something about it tomorrow."

Mr. Barnum had learned a long time before that worry accomplishes nothing; it only destroys. So he lived his life without fear, but with positive enthusiasm and self-confidence.

HOW TO GET RID OF FEAR IN FIVE EASY STEPS

1. Admit Your Fear

This is the first and usually the most difficult step to take. We all tend to rationalize our fears to some extent, so it's often hard to admit the whole truth, even to ourselves.

In addition, most people do not like to admit their fear. They think it is a confession of weakness, but actually the exact opposite is true; it is an act of courage. An unacknowledged fear is the one that often causes the most trouble. You know it's there even when you refuse to admit it to yourself. But stuffing your ears with cotton won't make the knock in your car motor go away, no matter how hard you try to pretend it's not there. It's the same with your unadmitted fears. They're still there to haunt you.

But once you admit that fear, you've taken the first big step toward solving your problem. Take an alcoholic, for instance. When he admits that he's powerless over alcohol, he's on the road to recovery. The same thing happens when you admit your fear to yourself. You get it out into the open, where you can pin it down and do something about it.

So just remember this simple rule: *When you're afraid, admit it.* Do that and more than half of your problem will be solved. When you've done that, you're ready to move on to the second step.

2. Analyze Your Fear to See If It's Justified

Once you've admitted exactly what it is you're afraid of, then you need to analyze your fear to see if it's truly justified. If it is, you can do something about solving it. If it isn't, you can stop worrying about it.

Let's say, for example, you fear other people because you're afraid they will criticize or ridicule what you say or do. This is one of the most common fears people have. And even though the fear of criticism is only a man-made devil, it is still one of the greatest killers in the world.

Your fear of being ridiculed or criticized can murder your ambition, initiative, ingenuity, daring, achievement, and self-confidence. Fear of people and what they might say about you or about your ideas and suggestions can cause unnecessary worry, indecision, frustration, procrastination—yes, and even eventual failure.

"Your subconscious mind has unlimited power to make all your dreams come true and to fulfill your deepest desires," says Dr. Earl Conway, a clinical psychologist from Tulsa, Oklahoma. "But there is no other fear that will close a person's mind more quickly and more securely than the fear of criticism, ridicule, or being laughed at. This fear of what people will say about you can stop you before you even get started."

This is ever so true. The fear of criticism will even influence the kind of dresses a woman buys, the shoes she wears, the style of her hair. It will decide for a man whether his suit will have two or three buttons, or if it's going to be single- or double-breasted. If the current style is long hair, a man will grow long hair even if he dislikes it. That's how sensitive most of us are to being criticized.

Take the employee who trembles every time his supervisor stops to speak to him; the office secretary who shivers in her shoes whenever the boss calls her; the salesperson who's afraid she might lose a sale and get chewed out for it; the teacher who worries excessively about making a mistake in front of his class; the junior executive who fears she won't be able to handle increased responsibility; even the company president who frets and stews about losing his position to some aggressive, young subordinate beneath him. All these people are committing slow and painful mental suicide because of their unreasonable fear of what other people might think or say about them.

But let's talk specifically about you now. Are you afraid because something bad happened to you in the past? Have you had some unfortunate previous experience? We've all had them. They're over and done with; forget them. Not many people can cross the river of life without getting their feet wet.

Or maybe you're afraid of your boss, as is true of so many people. Why should you be? Are you afraid he's going to raise

Cain with you for something you've done? Why? Have you really done something wrong? Are you afraid he's going to fire you? Why? Do you deserve to be fired? Has your work been sloppy and inefficient? Do you come to work late all the time? Have you been stealing from your boss? If your answer to all these questions is no, then you have nothing at all to worry about. You're giving yourself stomach ulcers and cardiac flutter for no reason whatsoever.

I would tell you one thing right here that I feel you ought to remember, and that is, you are not responsible for what other people think about you. *You are responsible only for what you think of yourself.*

3. Get Your Fear Down in Writing

It's always helpful to write down your fears on paper. Force yourself to put them all down in black and white. This will let you see, once and for all, what it is that's really troubling you. In many cases, you'll find that you have nothing at all to fear or worry about. All you've been doing is making yourself miserable by nursing a vague, uneasy feeling of dread that has no real foundation whatsoever. Although this is the shortest step of all, that does not mean it is unimportant. In spite of its brevity, it's still a must.

4. Don't Concentrate on What You Fear

Fear requires an active imagination. Unfortunately, it's the wrong kind of imagination, for it can turn fishworms into snakes and lizards into dragons.

Here in Florida there are all sorts of harmless chameleons and lizards. But some people are deathly afraid of them and insist that they are deadly poisonous. The other day an old gentleman sitting on a park bench sunning himself warned me not to go too close to the "scorpion" that was a few feet away on the sidewalk.

"That's not a scorpion; it's a harmless lizard," I said. I was quickly informed that I was mistaken, and that the lizard was a deadly scorpion, so I let it stand that way without argument. The old gentlemen's imagination had convinced him that the chameleon was a deadly scorpion, so there was nothing at all to be gained by arguing with him.

Remember that Job once said, "For the thing which I greatly feared is come upon me, and that which I was afraid of has come unto me" (Job 3:25). So take a lesson from Job's experience. Keep in mind that whenever you fear anything, that thing is much more likely to find you and harm you.

If you fear failure and concentrate on that, you will fail. Absolutely nothing can keep it from happening. Worry about criticism and ridicule from others and you will be criticized and ridiculed, for your excessive worry and fear will cause you to make stupid and ridiculous mistakes.

To keep this from happening to you, program your subconscious mind with positive thoughts instead of negative ones. *Don't think about what you fear.* Instead, concentrate on the solution to the problem rather than on the problem itself.

5. Do the Thing You Fear and Gain Power Over It

I've discussed this technique at some length in Chapter Two, so I'll just touch on it lightly here. But I do want to say that in one hundred out of every one hundred cases, this is the best—and usually the only—solution for getting rid of your fear.

Take yourself, for example. As I said, most people fear other people, so let me ask you, is this one of your major fears? If it is, then go out of your way to meet people and become friends with them. You will soon find that your fears were completely unfounded and unreasonable.

Or are you afraid to speak to a group of people? If so, stand up and talk every chance you get. (I'll discuss that point more fully later on in this chapter.) Whatever it is that you dread or fear doing, force yourself to do it until you've reached the point where you no longer fear doing it. Then you'll know you have complete control over your fear.

Take it from me, life will improve if you just remember this one simple idea: Do the thing you fear to do and you will gain the power to do it. If you do not, you will never have the power to do it. Honestly, it's that simple.

As the famous poet and philosopher Ralph Waldo Emerson, one of America's most influential authors and thinkers, said, "Do the thing you are afraid to do, and the death of fear is certain."

HOW TO OVERCOME YOUR FEAR OF SPEAKING IN PUBLIC

In previous chapters, I have discussed at great length the fear of poverty, the fear of failure, which is the greatest fear of a businessperson; and the fear of making the wrong decision. These are the major fears most of us have. However, there is one more fear that causes a state of near panic in most people, and that is the fear of speaking in public.

I'd like to discuss how you can develop your abilities and your confidence to speak to a large group of people. You say that you never talk to large audiences, that you don't address large numbers of persons, and that you're not a professional speaker?

Well, that could all be true, but when's the last time you *wanted* to stand up and speak your piece yet didn't because you were too afraid? How many people are in your class? Twenty? thirty? fifty? That's a lot of people to stand up in front of, right?

Or what about the times you've wanted to express your opinion at a PTA meeting, present your viewpoint to the town council, address a convention or a union meeting—yet you didn't because you were completely overwhelmed with fear. So whether you are a professional speaker or not doesn't really matter. It will pay you dividends to lose your fear of speaking in public, no matter how many people are in the group or who they are.

Let me tell you this. You are not alone. The person who isn't afraid of speaking up in public is as rare as a blacksmith or a good cribbage player. A large midwestern university surveyed its speech classes and found that over 95 percent of those students suffered from stage fright both at the beginning and at the end of the course.

I know that I nearly panicked the first time I stood up in front of a large audience. My throat was dry; my voice was raspy. My palms were sweaty, and my heart pounded. But as soon as I got the first sentence out, I felt better. As I continued to speak, my fears quickly faded away. Confidence came to me, for as soon as I did the thing I feared to do, I gained the power to do it.

Why Some Nervousness Is Beneficial

A certain amount of nervousness is actually useful to you. This is how your body prepares itself for this strange, new, and unknown situation. More adrenalin is pumped into your bloodstream. Your pulse rate speeds up, your breathing becomes faster, and your muscles become tense. Don't be alarmed at this. It's just nature's way of doing things to prepare you.

By understanding the basic physiological functions of your own body, you can keep this normal preparatory nervous tension from developing into uncontrollable panic. That extra shot of adrenaline will help you think faster, talk more easily, and speak with greater emphasis and intensity than under normal circumstances.

"A certain amount of nervous tension is always present before I speak," John Erskine told me. "It lasts through the first few sentences of my talk. That is part of the price I pay for earning my living as a professional platform speaker; it's an occupational hazard, you might say. But if I weren't built that way, I doubt if I could be a professional lecturer."

Now John is an old-timer in the business of speaking to a large audience. He's traveled over a million miles and spoken to more than a million people during his highly successful career, and he's still going strong. John is also a member of the speech faculty at a large university and holds a master's degree in communication, yet he still gets nervous before he walks out on stage.

So don't worry about this kind of nervous tension. It's quite normal and to be expected.

How to Pinpoint Your Major Ideas

If you don't know why you're getting up to say something, then you should stay seated. Every speech or talk must have a worthwhile purpose or it should remain unspoken. If you don't know what you want to achieve by speaking to the group, then you definitely are not ready to go before your audience.

If you find it hard to isolate and define your exact objective, then your talk cannot possibly be effective. If it is not clear to you what you want to gain by speaking, then it cannot be clear to anyone else either. But if your specific objective is clear and distinct to you, then your talk can be effective.

"Successful speakers know that deciding what to leave out is sometimes more important than what to put in," says Stanley Graham. Stanley teaches public speaking in the adult education division of a university here in Florida. I would add that this is just as important in writing—my biggest problem is usually not what to say, but what *not* to say. Ideas might be interesting as such, but unless they contribute to your listener's understanding of what you are trying to achieve, they should be left out.

Preparing your talk, then, is primarily a process of sifting and discarding until you have only one clear purpose or single objective to reach and the main ideas required to gain that goal.

How to Organize Your Presentation

Once you know your specific objective and you've pinpointed your main ideas to support it, then you're ready to outline and organize your talk so that you'll know exactly what you're going to say. If you don't, you could sound like a speaker I once heard at a convention in Miami.

This highly educated man, a doctor in fact, rambled and wandered around for five minutes or so without coming to any point whatever. His audience grew nervous and restless. Realizing this, he stopped talking for a moment and then said, "Please be patient with me. When I get through talking here, I'm going to say something!" Only his sense of humor saved the day—you might not be so lucky.

There are many ways to outline and organize a presentation. I have found that the format most successful salespeople use is the most useful to me, and that is:

- The opening
- The benefits to be gained
- Techniques to be used to gain those benefits
- Examples of people who've succeeded by using those techniques
- The conclusion

1. **The Opening Sets the Theme.** It is always wise to use a "grabber" to get your listeners' immediate attention. You can use any one of these five methods to do just that:

- A startling statement
- An unusual anecdote
- A strong example
- An authoritative quotation
- An arresting question

As Barbara Parkhill, a highly successful professional speaker, once told me, "Your opening sentences must shock your audience, startle them, or get their attention in some way. If you don't grab them with your first few sentences, you'll end up talking to the wall." Barbara also advises against opening with a joke. "Leave that to a comedian like Bob Hope," she says.

2. **Stress the Benefits to Be Gained.** This will enable you to keep your listeners interested and show them how your

talk will help them. If I'm trying to persuade my audience to do something, I often combine steps 1 and 2, beginning immediately with the benefits to be gained.

3. **Present the Techniques to Be Used.** In this step, you tell your listeners how they can achieve the results they desire.

4. **Provide Examples.** By telling your audience about people who've succeeded, you demonstrate that what you say is true. Choose concrete examples that show that the techniques you've offered really do work. Your examples must be specific and give names, dates, places, and so on.

5. **Your Conclusion.** If your talk is meant to persuade, then your conclusion should be an appeal for some sort of action. If your talk is primarily to inform, then your conclusion should be a summary of your main points.

The Bonus You'll Get From Speaking in Public

Before I conclude this section, I want to say that speaking in public offers a special bonus. It will expand your life and its meaning. It will give you a sense of personal power and fulfillment unlike anything you've ever experienced before. And the more you express your ideas and feelings to an audience, the more you'll want to do it. You'll have a tremendous feeling of accomplishment that nothing else can ever give you.

DON'T WORRY, BE PREPARED

Preparing for the worst is not fear, it is plain common sense. As Dionysius, the ancient Greek, once said, "Forethought is better than repentance." For example, when my wife and I go to a theater to see a movie or a play, the first thing I do is check the location of the nearest fire exit. And if possible, we seat ourselves close to that exit.

Many years ago I made several trips across Arizona, New Mexico, and Utah, as well as Wyoming and Montana. In those days, filling stations and rest stops were not as plentiful as they are today, so we always carried two water bags in case of emergency. Fear never entered my mind when we did this; it was only proper preparation. Only a fool would try to cross arid land without enough water.

When I lived in Iowa, snow tires were a must in winter. They prevented many an accident. Again, the purchase of snow tires was done, not from fear, but from common sense and proper preparation for ice- and snow-covered roads.

Today I live in Florida, hurricane country, so we prepare for the worst here, too. All our windows have hurricane shutters that can be closed tight to prevent glass breakage. When a warning comes, people stock up on canned goods, candles, and fresh water. In fact, I always have a good supply of these items on hand. That way, I'm always prepared and can avoid the last-minute rush.

Insurance, whether it's life, car, or house, is also preparation for the worst. Again, it is not a sense of fear but plain common sense to prepare for possible disaster.

Rather than stew and fret and worry about what might happen, prepare yourself for the worst and then forget about it. Sit back and relax knowing that you've done all that can be done. This whole idea might be summed up this way: *Expect the best; prepare for the worst.*

How to Get Rid of Abnormal Fear

1. A person is born with two normal fears, the fear of falling and the fear of loud noises. These two fears are protective in nature. All other fears were acquired, and you can get rid of them. (If you choose to, you can even get rid of the fear of falling.)

2. Normal fear is both good and wise. Abnormal fear is destructive. To fear something without reason causes a sense of panic and terror.

3. Do the thing you fear to do and the death of fear is certain. Say to yourself and mean it, "I am going to defeat this abnormal fear," and you will.

4. Fear is a negative thought. Replace it with a positive concept. Fear has killed millions of good ideas and suggestions as well as people. Confidence is always stronger than fear. Nothing is more powerful than confidence in yourself and your abilities.

5. Fear is a person's greatest enemy. It is behind failure, sickness, and bad human relations. Live in the joyous expectancy of the best, and invariably the best will come to you.

6. You can overcome fear when you know that the power of your subconscious mind can change negative conditions to positive ones and bring about your heart's cherished desires. Focus your attention on your desire, which is the opposite of your fear.

7. If you are afraid of failure, concentrate on success. If you fear sickness, focus your attention on health. If you are afraid of an accident, think of the guidance and protection of a higher power.

8. The law of replacement is the answer to fear. Whatever you fear has its solution in the form of your desire. Mentally concentrate on the good that will replace your fear and know that your subconscious mind will answer you. It never fails.

9. Finally, look at your fears in the light of reason. Learn to laugh at your fears. That is the best possible medicine you can use for them.

11

How to Use the Power Within to Break Bad Habits

Now if I were to ask you which was more important in breaking a bad habit, *imagination* or *willpower*, I'm sure you would say willpower. Most people do. But surprisingly, that is not true. Using your imagination is absolutely the only way you can ever break a bad habit. Here's why.

Just suppose, for example, you make a valiant (but futile) New Year's resolution to stop smoking cigarettes. You are positively determined to quit smoking by using your willpower and proving to yourself that you are stronger than that little white sliver of paper with tobacco in it.

That should be easy enough to do with willpower, should it not? After all, you are a strong-minded person, you say, and, by golly, you can do it. So you say to yourself over and over, "I am not going to smoke a cigarette. I am not going to smoke a cigarette. I am not going to smoke a cigarette. I am not going to smoke a cigarette no matter what." You repeat this phrase to yourself over and over again, but all the time your imagination is reminding you how really good a cigarette would taste. Suddenly you find yourself saying, "I am not going to smoke a cigarette no matter *how good it would taste!*"

Suddenly *how good it would taste* looms up as more important than *I am not going to smoke a cigarette.* Finally you break down and say to yourself, "Well, I'll have just one cigarette. After all, just one won't hurt that much." But after the first cigarette, it's easier to have the next one and the next one and then to put off quitting the cigarette habit until tomorrow . . . and tomorrow . . . and tomorrow . . . ad infinitum.

What happened here anyway? You were so sure when you decided to quit smoking that you could succeed using willpower. But willpower never works; not only won't it help you stop smoking, it won't help you correct or get rid of any other undesirable habit you might have. Let me tell you now why.

You see, just as long as you allow your imagination to keep reminding you how good a cigarette would taste, then sooner or later, usually sooner, you will light up a cigarette and smoke again. Why? Well, the answer is really quite simple. *Whenever imagination and willpower are in conflict—whenever they are pulling in opposite directions—imagination will always win.*

But when your imagination and your willpower are in agreement, when they are harmoniously pulling in the same direction, an irresistible force is created, and success will be the inevitable result.

In this chapter, I show you how you can get your will-power and your imagination working together and pulling in the same direction. By properly programming your subconscious mind, you can stop smoking, stop obsessive drinking, quit overeating, stop putting things off until tomorrow, cure a bad temper, get rid of resentment you feel toward others, and eliminate laziness and any other bad habit you might have.

THE ONE *HUGE* BENEFIT YOU WILL GAIN FROM THIS CHAPTER

I could give you a variety of individual benefits depending on what undesirable habit you're trying to get rid of. However, the one huge benefit you will gain when you break an undesirable habit is . . .

FREEDOM!

You'll no longer be a prisoner or a captive to your habit; you'll no longer be its slave, for you will be free! I'm reminded here of the spiritual quoted by Martin Luther King, "Thank God Almighty . . . free at last!"

HOW TO PROGRAM YOUR SUBCONSCIOUS MIND TO BREAK A HABIT

Now I'd like you to write down on a little card that you can carry with you what undesirable habit it is that you want to break. Whatever it is, write down on your card exactly what you want to eliminate. Make sure you have a specific and concrete goal that is clearly defined.

Do *not* show your card to anyone, and don't tell a single person what you're doing. Above all, don't say, "I'm *trying* to stop smoking or drinking or whatever." That programs your subconscious mind with the idea of "trying to stop," which implies the possibility of defeat or failure.

Look at your card at least three times a day, morning, noon, and night—more often if possible. In a cheerful and relaxed manner, think about your goal and what it is you want to accomplish. Do not become anxious or worried about not reaching your goal. Instead, tell yourself all the benefits you are going to gain when you break your bad habit.

As you look at your card and as you think about the goal that is written on it, remember that *you must become what you think about,* and since you are thinking about what you want, you know that it will soon be yours. To tell you the truth, it already is yours the moment you write it down and begin to think about it.

Here is an extremely important point that you should remember: *Fear is always the opposite side of the coin of desire.*

That is, many people want to gain something, a specific goal, but they are so afraid they won't get it that they concentrate on this fear instead of on the desire or the belief that they will.

And, if you program your subconscious mind that way, I guarantee that you will fail. To keep that from happening to you, do what I told you to do in the last chapter: Stop thinking about what it is that you fear and concentrate entirely on what you want to achieve, in this case, the bad habit that you want to break.

Try the following test for thirty days. Control your conscious mind's thoughts as you never have before. If for one single moment you think about the fear of failure or the fear that you will not attain the goal you have written on your card, force that fear out of your mind and concentrate entirely on your goal. Another way of saying this is *concentrate on the solution, not on the problem.*

If you concentrate on your goal and keep the problem or the fear of failure out of your mind, your subconscious mind will take care of the rest. Its miraculous powers will give you the answers you need to achieve your objective. These five ingredients must be present if you are going to break any habit, no matter what it is.

1. **Reach the Point Where You Can no Longer Stand Yourself.** Let me give you a concrete example of what I mean by this statement. Carl T., a close friend, a member of Alcoholics Anonymous and a recovering alcoholic, told me this story about himself and his own past drinking experiences.

> My wife, my children, friends, business associates, and my boss had all reached the point where they could not stand me any more the way I was. But I hadn't reached that point yet so I kept right on drinking.
>
> Despite all their pleas and threats, I myself had to reach the point where I could no longer tolerate myself the way I was before I would stop. In AA we call that point the alcoholic's bottom. We always laugh and say

that some people's bottoms are lower than others. Some come to this low point in prison, some with their heads literally resting in the gutter, while others have had bottoms much higher. I remember one banker who came to the program because he wore the same shirt two days in a row, but he was a rarity, of course.

In my case, I'd been drunk every night for as long as I could remember. The last night I drank I got home very late, completely bombed out of my mind as usual. But the next morning I was so disgusted that I simply couldn't stand myself any longer the way I was. I stared at my worn-out and tired face for a long time in the bathroom mirror. When I finally came out, I said to my wife, "I'm through drinking. I can't take it any more. I can't stand myself any longer the way I am. I'm just sick and tired of being sick and tired."

Then I placed a bottle of beer on the mantelpiece.

"Why are you doing that?" my wife asked.

"So I know where to find a drink if I want one," I told her. "Then I can kill myself instead."

"I haven't touched a drink for more than twelve years now, but I leave that bottle of beer right there on the mantelpiece as a constant reminder of my previous intolerable situation."

Although Carl's wife had pleaded with him for many years to stop drinking, he had never paid attention to her. It was not until he could stand himself no longer that he did something about his bad habit.

Carl gave me another bit of insight into breaking an undesirable habit, and that is that you can't break a bad habit *for* someone else; you must always do it for yourself. He told me that people who come to Alcoholics Anonymous to please a wife, a husband, or a boss almost always fail. "Unless a person wants to get sober for himself, he won't make the program and stop drinking," Carl said.

That means that if you want to break a bad habit, then you must reach the point where you can no longer tolerate yourself the way you are or the situation the way it is. If you don't reach that point, you will not succeed.

2. Desire to Be Rid of Your Bad Habit More Than to Keep It. Every person with a bad habit that she wants to break always has mixed emotions about it. She may want to break her bad habit—say smoking, excessive drinking, or overeating—but by the same token she does not want to give it up. Such a person will never quit until she wants to be free of the habit *more than she wants to keep it.*

Sometimes the motivating force is better health, sometimes money, sometimes just plain, old-fashioned disgust with one's self. Let me give you a quick example of that.

Sam, noticing that the price of cigarettes had gone up again, complained loudly, but he still put the extra dime in the vending machine. A coworker laughed at him. "You'll pay whatever price you have to," she said. "You have no choice at all, Sam. They've got you hooked."

"She's right," Sam thought. "The tobacco company has me right where it wants me. I'm no longer free. I'm a slave to this disgusting habit. To hell with it." Right then and there he threw away the pack of cigarettes he'd just bought and gave up his three-pack-a-day habit forever.

Did Sam still want to smoke? "Of course I did," Sam told me. "But I wanted to quit more than I wanted to keep smoking. If I hadn't, I could never have stopped."

No matter what the bad habit is, you, too, must want to get rid of it more than you want to keep it. When you reach that state of mind, and when you program your subconscious with that idea, you'll be able to get rid of your unwanted habit, no matter what it is.

3. Establish Tangible Goals. The best way I know of to do this is to tell yourself all the benefits that you will gain when you rid yourself of this bad habit. You can motivate yourself even more by listing all the disadvantages that will still be yours if you insist on hanging on to your undesirable habit.

4. Reprogram Your Subconscious Mind. Remember that your conscious mind furnishes the willpower necessary to take only the first step in breaking your bad habit. It makes the decision to do so when you have reached the point where you can stand yourself no longer the way you are, but that is as far as your conscious mind can go.

Before you can make that decision stick, you must use your imagination to reprogram your subconscious mind with positive thoughts of the benefits that will overcome and override the negative input that caused your bad habit to develop in the first place.

Program all these positive benefits into your subconscious mind until you become as obsessed with the idea of freedom from your undesirable habit as you were with the habit itself. As another friend of mine in the AA program told me once, "I used to have an obsession to drink. Now I have an obsession to stay sober." That's the kind of motivation and desire you need to break that bad habit of yours, no matter what it is.

5. Do It One Day at a Time. This is another helpful concept I learned from my friends in the AA program. As one of them told me:

> When I joined AA, I didn't have to stop drinking forever. I doubt if I could have done that, for that was too long a period of time for me to comprehend. In fact, to stop drinking forever is too much for the alcoholic mind to even imagine.
>
> So we quit drinking just for one day at a time. And since tomorrow never comes, it's always today. I know that's just a gimmick, but it works to keep an alcoholic from drinking, and that's the whole purpose of the AA program, to help the alcoholic who wants to stop drinking.

This last technique also works for stopping other bad habits, such as smoking, weight problems, bad temper, whatever. If an alcoholic can go one day without a drink, then a smoker can go one day without a cigarette, an overweight person can go one day without overeating, and so on. Those days can turn into weeks, weeks into months, and before long, your bad habit will be completely gone.

Before we move on, let me summarize these five essentials:

1. You must reach the point where you can no longer stand yourself the way you are or the situation the way it is.
2. You must want to get rid of your bad habit more than you want to hang onto it.
3. You must establish tangible, specific, and concrete goals.
4. You must reprogram your subconscious mind with these new concepts, goals, attitudes, and ideas.
5. You must do it one day at a time, but do it every day.

How to Stop Excessive Drinking

As a writer in applied psychology, I have done a great deal of research in certain areas of both normal and abnormal behavior. I have gained a tremendous amount of useful and informative material from members of Alcoholics Anonymous.

It might come as a surprise to you, as it did to me, to learn that no less than one out of every thirteen people who drink is troubled with the problem of excessive drinking, in many cases, the actual disease of alcoholism.

I asked Carl how the AA program motivates a newcomer to get sober. Here's what Carl told me:

> We tell the new person all about the benefits he'll gain when he stops drinking. There are a whole slew of them, and that's for sure. For instance, he will never have to suffer from another hangover. There won't be any rubber

checks to worry about. He'll always remember where he left his car. And he won't have to throw up every morning. The newcomer to the program will never fall down and rip the knees out of a new pair of pants, at least when he's drunk, as I always used to do.

Some other big benefits he'll gain are never running the risk of driving his car while he's drunk and killing someone else in an automobile accident. A young man in his late twenties that I know is now facing a fifteen-year prison sentence for killing a policeman in an automobile accident he caused when he was driving drunk.

Nor will he need to panic each time he hears a siren or sees the flashing red and blue lights on the police cruiser. He'll never run the risk of hallucinations or delirium tremens. Nor will he be in danger of cirrhosis of the liver or becoming a living vegetable, as so many alcoholics do. And he won't have to worry about killing himself, either accidentally when he's drunk or purposely when he's sober.

There are a lot more benefits, like regaining the love and respect of your wife and children, your friends, and your boss, as well as dignity and respect for yourself, but I think I've given you enough for starters.

Oh, I would like to add that we always tell a newcomer that there's nothing so bad that a drink won't make it worse.

If drinking too much is your problem, then look over that long list of benefits Carl mentioned so you can convince yourself of the advantages of sobriety.

Then program your subconscious mind with those positive benefits so that you can convince yourself that you are better off not drinking. Get the support you need by giving Alcoholics Anonymous a ring. They're listed in the white section of your telephone directory. You have nothing to lose but your drinking problem.

Don't put off calling AA for fear that all its members are skid-row bums. That simply is not true. You'll be surprised to find out that doctors, lawyers, preachers, and businesspeople—in short, people in all sorts of occupations—are represented in Alcoholics Anonymous.

In discussing this drinking problem, I have used male examples almost exclusively, but Carl tells me that alcoholism is not limited to men only. He says that more than one-third of the members of their AA group are women. As he says, alcoholism is no respecter of age, sex, economic status, social position, or profession.

How to Stop Overeating

One of my friends in our church, I'll just call him Jim, played the role of Santa Claus every year because he had the appropriate build for it. But this year he refused it. "I'm tired of being the jolly old fat man," he said. "I'm tired of being the patsy and the butt of all those jokes about fat people."

"Jim, I'm surprised you've refused to play the part this year," I told him. "No one in our church has ever made fun of you for being a little bit overweight."

"Maybe not here," Jim said, "but the other day in my business I happened on to a group of my employees and overheard them making fun of me. One of them was walking around pretending to be me. He had his cheeks all puffed out and his belt pulled way down and belly pushed out and hanging over the top of his belt. He was walking around with a duck waddle as if he were so fat he couldn't walk normally. Well, enough is enough. I've decided to lose thirty pounds and to slim down like I should. I just don't want to be Santa Claus any more. The church will have to find someone else. Sorry."

Why the sudden change? He had been ridiculed and made fun of by others, something none of us can handle well. As a result, Jim had reached bottom. He had reached the point where he could no longer stand himself the way he was. That's when he decided to do something about it.

For some overweight people, the motivating factor for weight loss is better health. For others, like Jim, it is vanity. But no matter what your motive, willpower is *not* the key to success. You must use your imagination to dream up all the possible benefits you can gain and program them into your subconscious mind so that you can lose those unwanted pounds.

To help you start, let me list some of those benefits for you:

1. You'll have more energy, more vitality, more pep and go-power. You'll no longer be short of breath.
2. Your complexion will be clear; your hair will shine.
3. You'll become regular without laxatives. Your digestion will improve for you'll be free from heartburn and acid stomach.
4. You won't be nervous and high-strung; you'll even sleep better.
5. You'll look and feel five to ten years younger.
6. You'll be the envy of all your "plump" friends.
7. Your sex life will improve dramatically.
8. You'll run far less risk of a heart attack.
9. Your blood pressure will be much lower.
10. Your circulation will improve markedly.
11. According to insurance statistics, you'll live much longer.
12. Your low, nagging backache will disappear.
13. Your arthritis and rheumatism will be much less painful.
14. Life will definitely become worthwhile again.

Now that's a carload of benefits you can gain when you get rid of your excess pounds. And you don't have to use will-power to do it. In fact, you cannot. You must use your imagination and program your subconscious mind to focus on all the benefits that can be yours when you slim down. If you do that, losing weight will become easy for you.

You might try programming your subconscious mind with pictures, just as one of my wife's friends did. Lucille taped two pictures of herself to her refrigerator door. One showed what she looked like when she graduated from high school and was a slim and trim 115 pounds. The other was a current one with her weight at 190 pounds. It took her six months to lose those 75 pounds, but she succeeded because she was motivated by what she saw staring at her from her refrigerator door.

Why Willpower Won't Work

Let me tell you now why you can't rely on willpower to help you lose weight any more than you can use it to stop drinking or smoking, or to break any other bad habit. I can best illustrate this by telling you about another of my wife's friends who had a weight problem.

Irene wanted to prove to herself that she had the willpower to resist her desire for sweets, so she put a box of chocolates on the dining-room table and then sat down to stare at them glumly, vowing not to touch a single one.

What was the outcome? You guessed it. She ate the entire box of candy, of course. What else could she do? Under such circumstances as these, she really had no choice.

But today she's thin. She lost the weight after she learned from me not to use willpower but to use her imagination to concentrate on the benefits she would gain from losing her extra pounds.

You see, when you fight your problem with willpower, as Irene tried to do, allowing yourself to be tempted, you are programming your subconscious mind with the wrong goals. When you do that, you simply give your problem more power over you and deplete your own energy to gain victory over it by the same amount.

At first glance, resistance sometimes seems to be the only way out of solving your problem. In fact, bombarding your problem with willpower can easily cause you to be stuck with it. The opposite course—nonresistance—is the only way out. An alcoholic, for example, uses nonresistance to stop drinking when she finally admits that she's powerless over alcohol and gives up the battle of trying to control her drinking. When you do not fight your problem with willpower but instead use your imagination to visualize all the benefits that you will receive when you attain your objective, your problem will crumble away and disappear from view.

You might ask, then, what use is willpower? It is useful in only one way: making the initial decision to change, whether that change is to lose weight, stop smoking, quit drinking, stop putting things off, get rid of a bad temper, whatever. Once that decision is made, you must use your imagination to program your subconscious mind with all the benefits you'll receive. Then the decision you made with the willpower of your conscious mind will stick.

Remember, when imagination and willpower are in agreement, when they are harmoniously pulling in the same direction, an irresistible force is created, and success is the inevitable result.

How to Stop Smoking

Back in Chapter Three I told you about eight benefits you could gain when you stopped smoking (see page 51). You can refer back to that chapter to read those again. I don't want to repeat that information, but I do want to tell you a bit more about how to stop smoking.

Fear can be one of the biggest motivators in giving up cigarettes. Remember that fear is always the opposite side of the coin of desire. You want to smoke, but the fear of cancer, heart attack, asthma, and emphysema must be stronger than your desire for a cigarette. This is one time when fear can be beneficial.

I had a friend, Tim K., who smoked three to four packs of cigarettes a day. His father had died from lung cancer as a result of smoking, but Tim paid no heed.

But one morning he woke up with a tremendous pain in his chest. "I felt as if someone had thrown a huge spear through my chest and it had gone all the way through and was coming out my back," Tim told me.

This horrible pain lasted for five days, yet Tim continued to smoke. On the sixth day, he made the decision to stop smoking; he had finally reached the point at which he could no longer tolerate the situation as it was. He was scared to death of possible lung cancer. That was ten years ago, and Tim has not touched a cigarette since.

The pain in his chest disappeared within ten days, and it has never come back. His lungs are clean and clear. X-rays show them to be as healthy as the lungs of a person who has never smoked.

"All in all, I have more energy and my food tastes better, too," Tim says. "Not only that, the benefits of not smoking far outweigh the benefits—if indeed there are any—of smoking."

My own daughter, Teresa, had smoked for a number of years. One day she read a magazine article that said that women who smoke have more wrinkles at age fifty than non-smokers do at seventy. Immediately after reading this article she went to the supermarket and there saw an elderly woman sitting on a bench waiting for the bus and smoking. As Teresa told me later, "That woman had more wrinkles than I've ever seen. I swear, she actually had wrinkles on wrinkles!"

As she told me, "If smoking makes you look like that, it just isn't worth it."

I had sent her articles on the dangers and hazards of smoking and potential lung cancer without effect. But one glimpse of what she might look like if she kept on smoking was enough to make her stop. In her case, vanity was greater than fear.

Whatever your motivation, list all the benefits you can think of to convince yourself that it is more worthwhile to quit than it is to keep smoking.

How to Rid Yourself of Anger and Resentment

This is certain: Anger and resentment toward others will give you ulcers and cardiac flutter if you allow such negative feelings to rule your life. I had a problem with that myself one time. I'd had a run-in, you might call it, with a lawyer, and I felt he'd cheated me badly. I resented him and hated him for what he had done.

One Sunday in our morning church service, we were singing a hymn entitled "God Forgave My Sin in Jesus' Name." The words of the first verse go like this:

> God forgave my sin in Jesus' name;
> I've been born again in Jesus' name;
> And in Jesus' name I come to you
> To share His love as He told me to.
> He said, "Freely, freely,
> You have received:
> Freely, freely, give.
> Go in My name, and
> Because you believe,
> Others will know that I live.

As we were singing the hymn, the following words came to my mind just as clearly as if someone had spoken them out loud: "Let the one who is without sin cast the first stone."

And as I wondered about these words, a silent but definite distinct voice again came to me that said, "I have forgiven him for his past sins, but you have not forgiven him for them. You are not without sin yourself, and as long as you do not forgive him I will not forgive you."

I tried to erase the words from my mind, but again they came to me as clearly as they had the first time. Then I not only knew where the words came from, but I also knew that the message was about the lawyer.

As soon as the service was over, I went home and wrote a letter of apology to the lawyer, and I mailed it on Monday morning. But then I felt that was not enough, so I called on him and apologized in person. We have since become good friends.

I will tell you this much about that experience. You probably think my imagination was working overtime that morning and you might laugh at me. I really don't care if you do.

What I learned from this experience was invaluable—not to lose my temper or vent my anger at anyone because doing so hurts me much worse than it does the other person.

I had wanted to cover procrastination in this chapter, for wasting time and putting things off is another bad habit so many of us have. But the subject is far too big to discuss here, so I'm going to take it up in the next chapter.

12

How to Use the Power Within to Make the Most of Your Time

LOST: Two golden hours between sunrise and sunset. Each hour was set with sixty sparkling diamonds.

REWARD: None, for those two golden hours are gone forever.

What benefits are to be gained by getting rid of your habit of procrastinating? Well, I think they'll be self-evident when you reread the two statements I opened this chapter with.

If procrastination is one of your problems, you certainly are not alone. It has been estimated by efficiency experts and time management people that this bad habit affects 90 to 95 percent of the work force.

Why do people procrastinate? Well, primarily because we would rather do what we enjoy doing and put off until tomorrow, or preferably next week or even next month—and if we're lucky, maybe forever—those things we don't like.

If you think you are not a victim of this bad habit, let me ask you these six questions. All I ask is that you answer them truthfully.

1. Do you do something you like to do instead of doing what you know you should be doing?

2. Do you conveniently put the required work out of sight so you can't be reminded of it?

3. Do you tell yourself that you need to rest and relax?

4. Do you get sick or half sick, and therefore decide you just aren't well enough to do the job until tomorrow or maybe even the next day?

5. Do you manage to be late for work and then convince yourself that there's not enough time to do the job today?

6. Do you conveniently forget to bring the materials necessary to complete the job with you; for instance, data sheets, time charts, sales figures, and so on?

If you answered yes to any of these questions, you are guilty of putting things off. How deeply rooted this habit is can be determined by the number of yes answers you gave. If you answered all six affirmatively, then you really need to reprogram your subconscious mind in a big way to get out of your rut.

Let me give you a typical example of procrastination at work. I'm sure you'll recognize some of the symptoms.

Phyllis is a real-estate saleswoman. A lot of her time is spent on the telephone locating potential prospects, although she dislikes this part of her work. In fact, it would be much more accurate to say that she hates it. But one rainy afternoon she decides to do some telephone prospecting since it's too wet to go out. She sits down with a reverse telephone directory, a directory that lists streets and house numbers and the names of the owners.

She sits for a while staring at a page opened to one of the streets in her territory and then decides to have a cup of coffee since it has just been freshly made. That leads her to scan the newspaper with her coffee, and a pleasant thirty minutes pass away before she forces herself to go back to the directory. After another ten minutes of just looking at names, she finally dials a number, and to her joy the line is busy.

What's going on here, anyway? Well, Phyllis decided by force of her willpower to do some telemarketing. But her imagination is working against her. She keeps imagining that the person who answers the phone is going to be rude and ill tempered, so she puts off making the call.

To rid herself of this fear of rejection, all she need do is let her imagination and her willpower work together, believing that the person who answers the phone is going to be pleasant and good-natured. And 95 percent of the time, this will be the case. Phyllis can dismiss the other 5 percent who are grouchy or ill tempered by feeling sorry for them and being thankful that her disposition isn't like that.

Do you recognize yourself in the example of Phyllis? A lot of good plans can go down the drain if you've put things off and are not ready when the right time comes. Pearl Harbor will live forever in our country's memory as the classic historical example of a nation's failure to be ready. All sorts of defense plans had to be scrapped after the Japanese attack was over. Too many of our battleships lay ruined at the bottom of the bay.

But you don't have to be in the military to benefit from using the principles of readiness and preparedness. They can be used in business and industry and most other fields as well.

If you're a teacher, you'll be able to give better instruction with a good lesson plan than if you've procrastinated, put things off, and are not completely prepared to teach your class. Or if you're a preacher and you put off preparing your sermon so that you can play golf on Saturday, you might be lucky and get some inspiration from the Higher Power when you're in the pulpit on Sunday morning. You might also get struck by lightning. Some advance work on your sermon will make you feel a lot more at ease behind your lectern.

If you're a student, you know how uncomfortable and embarrassed you can feel when you're called on and you're not prepared because you put off studying. No examination is ever hard if you're ready for it and know all the answers. Or maybe it would work out better if you first knew all the questions!

BENEFITS YOU WILL GAIN

- You'll never be caught off-guard by your business competitors or your enemies when you don't procrastinate and put things off until tomorrow.
- You'll build a reputation for getting things done and being reliable.
- You'll not miss the opportunity for promotion and advancement.
- You'll actually gain more free time for yourself.

THIRTY-THREE SELF-STARTERS SO YOU'LL ALWAYS BE READY

Now in previous chapters I've given you specific techniques you can use to gain the benefits. In this chapter I'm going to do it just a bit differently. Since not being prepared is usually the end result of plain old procrastination, I'm going to help you shake that bad habit of always and forever putting things off by giving you these self-starters:

1. Pinpoint Your Goal

Don't waste time and energy just because you're not sure of what you want to do or where you want to go. Ask yourself these simple questions: What do I really want to get done? Where do I really want to go? Then give yourself a straight and honest answer. Level with yourself.

2. Make a List of Everything You Need to Do

Make up a list of things that you need to do just as you would a grocery list. Then cross off each item as you do it. That way, you gain the satisfaction of having done part of the job. Your attention will automatically go to the next item down

the line. You can use your own time schedule for doing this;
it depends on what you need to do. The important thing is
do it!

3. Put What Needs to Be Done Right in Front of You

When there's some distasteful task you don't really want to
do, it's always easy to hide it. Your goal should be to do *first
things first.*

An old saying that my mother-in-law always used to
quote is "Happiness lies, not in doing what you like to do,
but in liking what you have to do." I used to hate this idea
and spoof it when I was younger. But the older I get, the more
truth I find in it, although truthfully, I still don't like it!

4. Concentrate on the Essentials

I once knew a plant manager who created nothing but panic
simply because he didn't know how to establish priorities. To
him, every project was a crash. He was always sending memos
marked "Urgent" or "Priority Number One" to his department
foremen and administrative staff.

But nothing ever got done on time, for *when everything is*
marked "URGENT," then "URGENT" becomes "ROUTINE."
He finally gave up and called on me for help. He still uses the
advice I gave him more than ten years ago. He paid me a fabu-
lous fee for showing him how to get things done, but it's yours
for free. Here's what I told him:

> Your problems can be solved only by establishing the
> proper priorities, Ray. Make up a list of the most urgent
> tasks facing you right now. Give each job a different pri-
> ority. No two jobs can have the same number.
>
> Then dig right in on Priority Number One and stick
> with it until it's done. Then go for Priority Number Two
> and do it the same way. Don't worry if you finish only one
> or two jobs a day. The point is, you'll be making progress

where before you were stalemated. You're getting things done by taking care of your most urgent problems first.

In short, use the approach of first things first; one thing at a time. If you can't solve your problems this way, chances are you couldn't handle them in any other way. Once you get this system rolling, stick with it; you'll clear away the debris and solve all the problems that have piled up on you.

5. Keep Reselling Yourself on the Benefits

No salesperson worthy of the name would try to close a sale just once, get a rejection, and then quit. Most people say no the first time around. Remind yourself of this when you're trying to motivate yourself to do a job that's not especially interesting.

For instance, it'd be a lot easier to settle back in your old easy chair in the office, read the morning paper, and have a cup of coffee than gather up some more information to put in your prospect's file. But reading the morning newspaper, drinking coffee, and loafing will not give you the information you need to close the sale the next time you call on your prospect.

So if you want to stimulate yourself to do something that's tedious, but necessary, push yourself to get on with it. Remind yourself of the rewards and benefits for doing it. If there aren't any, then you're collecting the wrong information or you're shooting at the wrong target.

6. Give Yourself a Small Part of the Job to Do

When a person has a big job to do, he hates to start. He puts it off until the last possible moment. Watch a little girl practicing the piano. She'll play the song she knows best over and over rather than start on the new one she doesn't know.

So if you have a big job to do, break it down into parts. If you must call a hundred people, break your list down into five smaller lists of twenty names each. Then do a fifth at a time, and the job becomes easy. To write a 65,000 word book is a tough job. But to write a book with thirteen chapters of 5,000 words in each chapter makes it a lot easier.

As I told you before, people in the Alcoholics Anonymous program don't try to stay sober for the rest of their lives. "Couldn't make it that way," they say. "Too big a job. We do it the easy way: one day at a time."

7. Develop a Written Step-by-Step Plan

Putting your plan down in writing seems to work like magic. A vague and nebulous idea will change to a concrete and specific fact when it's on paper, where you can see it.

The point is that the process of writing it down forces you to be specific. If you check your ideas later on, you can get even more precise. Writing it down will help you clearly see other plans you just couldn't visualize when you were carrying it around up there in your head.

8. Make Up Some Alternative Plans

An amateur is satisfied with herself when she comes up with the one "best way" to do something. But the professional knows you need a pocketful of techniques if the *best* method fails and doesn't work. She knows how to travel the back roads when the freeway is blocked.

9. Make a Decision

Don't be so afraid of making a mistake that you procrastinate and do nothing. Fear of failure and possible embarrassment causes most indecision. But the successful person has to be right only 51 percent of the time.

When you have enough facts to make a reasonable decision, do so. Don't worry about the decision after you've made it. The time to "worry" about a situation is before you act, not afterward.

Worry is like walking on a treadmill. You wear yourself out and you get nowhere doing it.

10. Emphasize Doing—Not Doing Perfectly

When you feel you must do everything just so, you often find that you can't bring yourself to start the new job. As long as you don't do anything, you don't run the risk of failure. When you keep your ideas to yourself, your boss can't tell you that they're wrong. The writer with his stuff in the desk drawer need never fear a critic.

To make an honest mistake is not the end of the world. It's only when you continually repeat that same mistake— *knowing that it's wrong*—that you ought to get concerned.

The person who has never made a mistake has never done anything. Nothing can be predicted right down to the letter, especially when people are part of the act, so you must experiment and watch the results as you go.

11. Figure Out Why You Put Things Off

If you find you simply can't get started on a certain project, then ask yourself these two questions:

- Do I really think the results are worth the effort?
- Do I honestly think I can do the job?

If you cannot motivate yourself to do a certain job, it's either not worth the effort or you're afraid you can't do it. Find out what's wrong. Then correct it.

12. Get Your Problem Down on Paper

If you can figure out problems in your head, you're better than I am. The average person can't even add a single column of a few figures in his head. He has to see it in black and white in front of him before he can get the right answer. Merely thinking about a problem is usually the worst way to solve it. Put your problem down on paper so that you can limit it. Fence it in with verbal barbed wire to clarify your thinking. Define it in specific terms.

When you're tackling any problem, you can solve it more quickly if you ask the time-honored questions: *what, when, who, where, why, and how.*

13. Use Your Energy for Action—Not for Worrying

Worrying uses up large amounts of energy. Ask any experienced worrier; she'll tell you that for sure. If you want to worry, become a professional worrier: be an efficiency expert. That way you'll not only get paid for worrying about troubles, but they'll also be someone else's.

Or if you don't like that solution and you still insist on worrying about your troubles, then hire someone to worry for you so you can forget your problems and get a good night's sleep for a change.

Any action you take to solve a problem will relieve your mind, for you'll be actively doing something to change the situation. Even if the action is wrong, you'll feel better because you're doing something.

And once you get going, you'll find your mind will start to click. Your imagination will loosen up; you'll be stimulated to find new ways to solve your problems. Dig right into the situation; you'll get a better understanding of it. That's why so many of your best ideas come when you're actively working on your problem.

14. Learn from Others

Why do most of us insist on learning everything the hard way? Trial and error is costly and inefficient. Profit from the successes and failures of other people.

The library is full of books on self-improvement. A library card costs you nothing. When you find a book you want to make a permanent part of your reference library like this one, then it's time for you to buy it.

You can tell if you're really trying to learn from others simply by looking at some of the books you've read to improve yourself. In many cases, you'll find that the first four or five chapters will be underlined and have notes along the margins, but the rest of the book will be clean. Did the author run dry, or did you run out of steam and quit?

In either case, it's about like trying to build a house without a hammer and a saw. Learning shouldn't end when you leave school. That's when it usually starts.

15. Don't Wait for Inspiration to Strike

Most people think they must be in the right mood before they can accomplish anything worthwhile. That's not true. Two plus two always equals four for the happy mathematician as well as for the sad one. Moods have nothing to do with it. If something is disagreeable or boring, and you wait for inspiration, chances are you'll never be inspired to go to work on it.

To tell the truth, *successful ideas are 2 percent inspiration and 98 percent perspiration.* Every invention, from the first crude wheel to the intricate and highly sophisticated control system of the space shuttle, had its beginning in the dark caverns of the subconscious mind. Almost every major innovation you can name came into existence because a persistent person with an idea wouldn't give up. And that's why successful ideas are only 2 percent inspiration and 98 percent perspiration.

16. Work Up a Continued Self-Monitoring System

It isn't enough to check on yourself when the job's about to be finished. If you wait until then to make your first progress check, it's often too late. Use a series of checkpoints. For instance, if you want to see fifty prospects by the end of the week, you'd better check yourself on Tuesday and Wednesday to see where you stand. If you wait until Friday noon, it's too late; your week is completely shot.

"Our sales people all work on a straight commission basis," says J. J. Bollinger, president of a health and accident insurance company in Des Moines, Iowa. "I always tell them the week might not be over until Friday night, but they sure ought to know where they stand by Wednesday. The week's more than half gone by then; if they're just starting to get warmed up, it's getting right late. Time runs out fast for a salesperson on Thursday and Friday."

17. Establish Deadlines for Yourself

Besides using a self-monitoring system, another good way to commit yourself is to set exact limits for getting things done. There's a lot of difference between saying, "I'll answer her letter the first chance I get," and "I'll answer her letter before I leave the office tonight."

When you establish deadlines, watch for these two points:

- Make them realistic.
- Stick to them.

18. Make Note Taking a Habit

It's ridiculous to lose a $250 sale simply because you forgot an appointment. Don't pride yourself on your memory; you can be proud of so many other accomplishments. An army officer without a notebook and pencil is more likely to be court-martialed than the one who forgets to carry his weapon.

If you think taking notes is a waste of your time, let me ask you this: How many good ideas have you had that you *never* tried? Why didn't you? I'll bet it's because you forgot them—that's why!

19. Force Yourself to Get Started

If you're like most of us, you associate confidence with action and a lack of confidence with inaction. You can increase confidence in yourself by forcing yourself to take some action. Once you start doing something, your self-confidence automatically goes up. You'll find that you can change your feelings by first changing your actions.

20. Fight Off Purposeful Forgetting

The tendency to forget what you don't want to remember is so strong that psychologists call it "purposeful forgetting." That's why we bury the bad things that happened in the past and remember vividly only the good times.

A reformed drunk tells funny stories about his drinking days, but he never mentions the car wrecks. When old soldiers get together, they never reminisce about death and sorrow. In fact, they never talk about the fighting. They talk only about the comradeship and the good times.

You can defend yourself against purposeful forgetting by:

- Making definite, concrete, and specific plans.
- Fixing deadlines for getting things done.
- Setting up a system to check your progress.
- Keeping records of what you do.
- Analyzing those records so you can correct your mistakes.

21. Start Each Day with a Success Experience

I'm sure you've heard people say, "Something happened this morning that ruined my whole day." If that were really true, then that person would have been better off turning around and going back home to bed. Somehow I doubt if the person's whole day was completely ruined. I think maybe he just had a bad ten minutes that morning and then he nursed it all day!

If you usually feel tops early in the morning, that is the best time to tackle the hardest thing you need to do. However, if you're like most of us, you probably need a little time to "warm up." If so, then you'd best start off with something that you're sure won't go sour on you. Then you can be sure of starting the day with a "success experience."

22. Clearly Distinguish Between Plans and Goals

Most salespeople are always trying to figure out new ways to sell more of their products or services. An aggressive life-insurance sales agent might say, "I plan to write $100,000 worth of business next month." Is this a plan or a goal? Actually, the person has only stated a goal. He or she might not have any plan at all about how to reach that goal. The obvious answer is to make up a specific plan that will show the sales agent how to reach that goal.

23. Use What You Know to Its Fullest Advantage

There's a difference between knowing and doing. Let's say you're a salesperson who knows five different ways to close a sale, but you're using only one, and that one not too successfully. You're no better off than the salesperson who knows only one.

If you think you need improvement in some specific area, figure out what you're doing wrong and look for new methods that can be useful to you.

24. Cultivate Your Use of Time

Get in the habit of putting a mental price on your time; you'll gain new respect for it. Such an approach will also help you decide whether it's really worthwhile to tackle many of the minor jobs that are now eating a hole in your working day. You can better manage your time if you will:

- Learn to say no.
- Avoid telephone traps.
- Discourage interruptions.
- Listen carefully.

- Do it right now.
- Do it right the first time.
- Do it only once.
- Use all the time you have.
- Anticipate your daily needs.

And now I want to discuss each of these points.

25. Learn to Say No

If you don't learn to say no, you'll find yourself besieged by all kinds of do-gooders. You will be lured into doing things and going places you don't want to. Remember, charity begins at home, so be good to yourself for a change. Learn to say no! and stick to it.

26. Avoid Telephone Traps

I'm not suggesting that you write a letter when a phone call would be quicker and do the job just as well. You can't beat the phone as a time-saving device to get information, order supplies, clear up misunderstandings, issue instructions, and make appointments.

But it's also an easy way to waste time through pointless gossip, social chatter, and the like. When you call, protect yourself and your time by knowing beforehand with whom you want to speak, what you want to say, what you want to get done. Then keep your calls on a businesslike basis.

27. Discourage Interruptions

Well-meaning friends and business associates just shooting the breeze can turn your best-planned day into a complete waste. You can keep their friendship as well as your schedule if you let interrupters know in a kind way that you're really pressed for time. It's a lot easier to chatter and gossip and have a coffee break in a real-estate or an insurance office than it is to buckle down and make some phone calls to prospective buyers, but it's not nearly as profitable.

Some people I know face the wall or work with their backs to others. Some juggle their lunch hours around so they can work while others are eating. Wayne Parker, one of the most successful real-estate men I've ever met, has a sign on his desk that makes this point quite well, I think, for it says: "If you have nothing to do, don't do it here."

I, too, am very blunt. I do most of my work at home in a room that acts as a den, an office, and a library. Most of the time my wife answers the phone and the door. I refuse all phone calls unless they are from my publisher, and I'll see no one between 9 A.M. and 3 P.M.

If I do get stuck once in a while and one of those door-to-door sales people shows up while she's gone, I simply tell them what my time is worth per hour. Then I ask them how much they'd like to buy—fifteen minutes, half an hour, or an hour's worth. I don't get many takers!

28. Listen Carefully

You can avoid all sorts of costly mistakes, backtracking, and doing things over if you get your information and instructions right the first time. Before you act, make sure you have all the facts. If you're in doubt, ask.

29. Do It Right Now

It's human nature to put things off; it's also unproductive. Once you know what's to be done, do it; don't put things off. That's what this chapter is all about—showing you how to become your own self-starter so that you can do what needs to be done without delay.

30. Do It Right the First Time

Plenty of rehearsals will ensure success when it's time for the real thing. People hate lifeboat drills, but without dry runs, a lot of lives can be lost when it turns out to be a wet run. So do it right the first time and you'll save more time for yourself.

31. Do It Only Once

Of course if you do it right the first time, you'll not have to do it more than once. After I read E. Joseph Cossman's book *How I Made $1,000,000 in Mail Order,* I put his rule about never handling the same piece of paper twice to work for myself. I gained nearly two hours to each working day. It's a hard rule to live by, but it can be done. The amount of time you gain is well worth the effort.

32. Use All the Time You Have

You can really add to your productive hours if you use every single waking minute. This means using all your travel time, your waiting time, your eating time, every single minute for thinking out problems, planning, reading, jotting down ideas.

"In my twenty years of service in the army, I think I spent fifteen of them standing in a chow line, a pay line, a theater line, a post-exchange line, or a latrine line," says retired sergeant major Vince Reed, now a teacher in Kansas City, Missouri. "The first five years I just stood. The next ten years I used that spare time to get both my bachelor's and my master's degree from the University of Maryland in their army overseas program."

Doctor Freda Maxwell, an Atlanta pediatrician, tells me that she learned every page of *Gray's Anatomy* while riding the bus to and from the college to her home. If you yourself are a commuter, either train, bus, or carpool, you can use that travel time profitably, or you can just sit and stare blankly out the window. It's all up to you.

---

*E. Joseph Cossman, *How I Made $1,000,000 in Mail Order* (Englewood Cliffs, NJ: Prentice Hall, 1963).

If you do enjoy listening to cassette tapes for self-improvement, I'd suggest you get a copy of my six-cassette-tape album entitled *Conversation Power.**

33. Anticipate Your Daily Needs

This one sounds so simple, you probably laughed when you read it. But please use it; you'll soon stop laughing. I know I did.

You can avoid those minor, time-wasting frustrations that whittle away your valuable time and save your temper by looking ahead and planning for those little daily crises.

You should have on hand such simple everyday items as small change for the parking meter, the coffee machine, and the cigarette machine (if you still have that bad habit); stamps, paper clips, rubber bands, stationery, and so on.

If necessary, have duplicates of your keys, shoelaces, glasses, umbrellas, handkerchiefs, comb, electric razor, hose, toiletries, etc. at the office as well as at your home. Decide the night before what you're going to wear the next day and lay your clothes out then.

All this boils down to is simply planning ahead for the basics. It's a lot like making up the grocery list or paying the monthly bills; not exciting, but required. And it should become so routine, as to be second nature. Then you won't have to waste time thinking about it.

▽ ▽ ▽

In summary, then, avoid being caught off guard by your competitors or your enemies, and to build a reputation for reliability and getting things done on time, to not miss the opportunity for promotion and advancement, and to gain

---

*Nightingale-Conant, 7300 North Lehigh Avenue, Niles, IL 60714, or call them toll-free at 1-800-323-5552 for more information.

more free time for yourself, use the thirty-three self-starters I just gave you like this:

(1) Pinpoint your goal by (2) making a list of everything you need to do and (3) put that list right in front of you. Then you can (4) concentrate on the essentials. Do that and it's much easier to (5) resell yourself on the benefits that you'll gain.

If you (6) give yourself a small part of the job to do, it's easier to (7) develop a written step-by-step plan (8) along with some alternate plans. This way, you can more easily (9) reach a decision that will (10) emphasize doing rather than doing perfectly.

If you want to (11) figure out why you put things off, (12) get your problems down on paper. Then you can (13) use your energy for action, not for worrying.

(14) Don't scurry around and work up a sweat, learn from others instead (15) waiting for inspiration to strike (worrying).

You can (16) work up a self-monitoring system by (17) establishing deadlines, (18) making note taking a habit, and (19) forcing yourself to get started so you can (20) fight off purposeful forgetting.

(21) Start off each day with a success experience; you'll soon be able to (22) see the difference between plans and goals and thus realize that (23) knowing and doing are not the same.

Time is one of your most valuable assets. You can (24) cultivate its use when you (25) learn to say no, (26) avoid telephone traps, (27) discourage interruptions, (28) listen carefully, (29) do it right now, (30) do it right the first time, (31) do it only once, (32) use all the time you have, and (33) anticipate your needs.

In conclusion, I want to give you four final pointers that will help you stop procrastinating, putting things off, and wasting time:

1. Indecision is nearly always the worst mistake you can make—it wastes more time than you can begin to imagine.

2. The pursuit of excellence is healthy; the pursuit of perfection is frustrating and a terrible waste of time.

3. If your office is typical, most of the items in your file cabinets should have been put in file 13, the wastebasket.

4. Of all the time-saving techniques ever developed, the most effective of all is use of the word *no!*

13

How to Use the Power
Within to Achieve
Glowing Good Health

Now that you know how to get rid of worry, anxiety, and fear
(see Chapter Ten), your health will show marked improvement. And when you get rid of such undesirable habits as
smoking, excessive drinking, overeating, and resentment (see
Chapter Eleven), your health will improve even more.

However, there are still a great many more things you
can do to gain even better health for yourself. Of course, not
all diseases are caused by improper programming of the subconscious mind, but, without exception, every single disease,
no matter what the original cause, can benefit from properly
and positively programming your subconscious mind for better health.

Amazingly, even such serious problems as cancer can be
helped, as I personally know, since I, myself, have completely
recovered from prostate cancer. In fact, on my last visit to my
radiologist for my semiannual bone scan to check for possible
metastasis, the doctor told me that I had more chance of being
killed by a truck hitting me than I had of dying from prostate
cancer.

So I want to ask you this: Are you a person with just average, run-of-the-mill health? Is your weight far from what it

should be, either over or under? Do you feel less vital and enthusiastic, more depressed and anxious, than you used to? Do
you have violent or angry outbursts of temper, followed by pe-
riods of self-recrimination that make you feel as if you'd like
to crawl into a deep hole to hide and stay there?

Do you avoid social activities because you just don't feel
up to it, or claim that you're too tired and worn-out to go? Do
you look back at your past successes for comfort and consola-
tion rather than ahead to new challenges and more triumphs?

If you answered yes to any of these questions, then this
chapter will be of great value to you. Here are some of the
many good things that will happen to you when you know
how to properly program your subconscious mind positively
for better health.

BENEFITS YOU WILL GAIN

- You'll gain a fresh new look of vigor and vitality. There
  will be a marked change in your mental awareness. In
  short, you'll visibly "brighten." Your performance, both
  physical and mental, in your everyday duties and activities will be greatly enhanced.

- Your new keenness and interest in life will be evident to
  everyone. Optimism, self-confidence, and a more-positive
  attitude will replace your negative and pessimistic view-
  points. Downcast feelings will disappear. Whereas before,
  you had problems with fatigue and that tired, worn-
  out feeling, there will now be stamina, strength, and
  endurance.

- You'll find that even minor illnesses and complaints—
  colds, occasional digestive upsets, miscellaneous aches
  and pains, from which almost everyone suffers now and
  then—will no longer be as frequent or as troublesome and
  irritating to you as they had been.

- You'll discover that your mental attitude will lead you to
  a greater degree of physical activity, including healthful

exercise. Just for example, a brisk walk will now become pleasurable rather than monotonous drudgery (even if you've previously cringed at the very thought of any physical exercise or exertion).

- And perhaps best of all, your sex life will improve when you learn how to program your subconscious mind positively with thoughts of better health. A vigorous and continuing interest in sexual activity and lovemaking with your partner is a positive sign of good health. This interest should continue throughout your adult life, even into the seventies and beyond, with sufficient physical performance to match this interest.

HOW TO PROGRAM YOUR SUBCONSCIOUS MIND TO GET RID OF EMOTIONALLY INDUCED ILLNESS (EII)

If you become sick tomorrow, or if you are sick right now, the chances are better than fifty-fifty that you are suffering from emotionally induced illness (EII).

What is EII, anyway? It is a real disease caused by improper programming of your subconscious mind by your conscious mind. Your conscious mind tells your subconscious mind that you are sick. The subconscious mind accepts that idea as a solid fact, and it proceeds to make it come true for you.

Where the illness strikes and the kind of symptoms you develop depends upon the kind of emotionally induced illness that you have. Just for example, worry of any sort usually causes gastrointestinal problems, such as gas, cramps, and diarrhea. In fact, as I discuss later, the colon is often called the "mirror of the mind."

Now a medical textbook of diseases, listing the symptoms and the pathology of specific ailments, contains an account of nearly a thousand different diseases that we human beings are subject to. The amazing thing is that EII is as common as the other 999 put together.

Hard to believe as that might be, clinical studies have proven that it is true. For instance, the Ochsner Clinic in New Orleans published a report a few years ago that stated that out of 500 patients treated at the clinic for gastrointestinal problems, 74 percent of the problems were emotionally induced. The Yale University Out-patient Medical Department has reported that 76 percent of the patients coming to the clinic for treatment were suffering from emotionally induced illnesses.

How did these people develop their physical problems? By improper programming of their subconscious minds. Their subconscious minds responded to this improper programming by developing full-blown symptoms that caused actual physical problems.

Emotionally Induced Illness Is a *Physical* Disease

The first thing you should know about EII is that the patient *actually has physical symptoms and physical problems,* not just mental symptoms and mental problems.

The following is only a partial list of the hundreds of physical symptoms that EII can produce. The percentages shown after each symptom show how often the complaint is caused by emotionally induced illness.

COMPLAINT	PERCENTAGE DUE TO EII
Pain in the neck	75
Lump in the throat	90
Ulcerlike pain	50
Gall bladder pain	50
Gas and bloating	99.5
Dizziness	80
Headache	80
Constipation	75
Diarrhea	75
Excessive fatigue	95

How do doctors treat EII? Unfortunately, many physicians act as if the patient is guilty of committing some crime. When doctors cannot find a specific cause for a person's problem, they then tend to tell the patient, "You have nothing physically wrong with you. Your trouble is being caused by your emotions. It's just your nerves. It's all in your head."

This does the patient no good whatsoever. He doesn't understand why the doctor cannot find the cause of his illness. He thinks the doctor is either incompetent or doesn't care, so he becomes angry and sets off to find another doctor.

A smarter doctor will give the patient the kind of diagnosis he is willing to accept. He will then proceed to treat the person with a placebo—a harmless preparation, usually a sugar pill—and get the same good results as if he had used some real drug.

The patient never knows that he is not being given some real medication, so his conscious mind programs his subconscious mind with the idea that he will be cured. The end result is that he becomes well, all because he imagined that the placebo the doctor gave him was the real thing.

How the Subconscious Mind Can Be Programmed by Hypnosis. To show you how susceptible the subconscious mind is to suggestion: A person under hypnosis can be told that an onion is an apple, and she will eat it with relish, and without shedding a single tear. Or she can have a toothpick placed against her skin, be told that it is a burning match, and an actual blister will develop. Whatever the conscious mind believes to be true is passed on to the subconscious mind. Then the subconscious mind accepts whatever has been programmed into it and acts accordingly.

Although I am not a professional hypnotist, I have occasionally been able to hypnotize people. As an experiment, I once hypnotized my nephew, Gary. I then gave him a posthypnotic suggestion that when he was awakened he would be very cold.

Shortly after I woke him up, although the room temperature was set at 75 degrees, Gary said he was surprised at how cold he was. He put on a heavy sweater, and a few minutes later checked the thermostat and then turned up the heat.

"What did you do to me?" he asked. "I was perfectly comfortable before you hypnotized me. Now I feel as if I were freezing to death."

I explained to him about the posthypnotic suggestion I had given him, but it did not help, so I finally had to hypnotize him again. I then gave him a posthypnotic suggestion that when he woke up he would be perfectly comfortable. And so he was.

How Dr. Gibson Treats Ell

A close friend of mine, Dr. Martin Gibson, a chiropractor, told me about some emotionally induced illnesses that he has encountered in his practice. Here's what he said:

> I have had patients who had all their spinal subluxations corrected, who were on an excellent diet plan and an adequate exercise program, but who failed to respond completely and still did not feel entirely well.
>
> Cases like that taught me to expand my case history of a patient to include such questions as, "Is anyone causing a problem in your life? Do you hate, despise, or resent some individual? You don't have to name names. Just tell me if anyone is bothering you, and, if so, in what way."
>
> When I asked questions like these, I began to get answers that gave me an insight into what was really wrong with my patient. Let me tell you about a few cases.
>
> One man was worried about cancer of the rectum, although a proctologist had given him a complete exam and discovered nothing wrong. Yet his pain and discomfort persisted. Careful questioning revealed that his employer

was the source of his trouble. His exact words to me were, and I quote, "My boss gives me a pain in the ass!"

When I explained to him that the way he was thinking about his boss was actually programming his subconscious mind to cause him pain and discomfort, he was able to overcome his problem by a change in attitude and positive reprogramming of his subconscious mind.

Another patient, a woman, was troubled by pain in the back of the neck. Cervical adjustments had properly lined up her neck vertebrae, and x-rays proved that. Yet her pains continued. Careful questioning revealed the true cause of her problem. As she put it, a certain person was a "big pain in the neck." Just as with the previous patient, when I explained to her what she was doing to herself, she was able to solve her problem by reprogramming her subconscious mind with thoughts of health.

Another patient was troubled by stomach cramps, indigestion, diarrhea, and occasional vomiting, all without any apparent physical reason. The cause? Someone was making him "sick to his stomach." Just as with the others, the case was easily resolved when he understood he was improperly programming his subconscious mind and making himself sick.

Anger: It Could Kill You

The main external manifestations of anger are reddening of the face, widening of the eyelids, bloodshot eyes, tightening of the lips, setting of the jaw, clenching of the fists, tremor in the arms, and very often tremor in the voice. You can recognize immediately when a person is angry simply by that person's appearance.

But the internal changes are even more profound and remarkable. When you become angry, your blood clots much more quickly than normal. This is significant, because when a person is angry, he or she is apt to have a fight, to be wounded, and to bleed. Therefore, it is beneficial to have the blood clot quickly.

When you become angry, the number of blood cells in the circulation greatly increases to bring extra oxygen to the body. The muscles at the outlet of the stomach squeeze down so tightly that nothing can leave the stomach. The entire digestive tract becomes so spastic that you can have severe abdominal pains either during or after a fit of anger.

Your heart rate will go up greatly when you are angry, often to 180 or even higher, and it will stay there until your anger has passed. Blood pressure also rises steeply from a normal of 120 over 80 to as much as 230 over 120 or even more. This can often cause disastrous results. If you are already troubled with high blood pressure, a fit of anger can cause a stroke (actually blowing out an artery in the brain).

When you are angry, the coronary arteries in the heart squeeze down, often hard enough to cause angina pectoris, or even a fatal coronary occlusion. This happens quite often, especially if the individual is troubled with high cholesterol levels and plaque formation in the arteries of the heart.

John Hunter, one of the greatest physiologists England has ever known, had the misfortune of having a fiery disposition and a bad set of coronary arteries. He always said that the first person who got him really mad would kill him. His wife came close to finishing him off several times, but the one who finally got him appeared at a medical meeting. Dr. Hunter became so angry at the person that he actually dropped dead from a coronary occlusion at that meeting.

While anger, itself, may not be a disease, the end results, such as a stroke or even death (as in the case of John Hunter), make it important enough to treat it as if it were a disease. At the very least, anger can cause indigestion, sometimes, even ulcers. And, if you do already suffer from high blood pressure, losing your temper really could be disastrous for you.

Perhaps you don't get as angry as John Hunter did. Even so, it's best not to get angry at all. Anger hurts you much more than it does the other person. If you don't lose your temper, you won't suffer from any of the symptoms of anger.

EII Can Tie Your Stomach in Knots

The stomach is one of the internal organs that quite accurately reflects the way you feel. When everything is going well, your stomach will reflect your pleasant emotions. But when things are not going well, you suddenly find you have no appetite and that you also have a stomachache.

When a person's stomach muscles tighten up as a result of a variety of negative emotions, the feeling is usually that of a lump in the upper abdomen. Some people describe it as a "stone."

When the stomach muscles squeeze down really hard, pain is produced, quite often very severe. This pain bears a considerable resemblance to the pain caused by a duodenal ulcer. Fully 50 percent of the people who complain of an ulcer-like pain do not have an ulcer but an emotionally induced pain in the stomach.

If your stomach bothers you only when you get upset, chances are great that you do not have an ulcer or any other organic problem. You undoubtedly are troubled with EII, which can easily be resolved by eliminating from your conscious mind whatever is troubling you and by properly programming your subconscious mind with positive thoughts of good health, serenity, and peace of mind.

The Colon: The Mirror of the Mind

The same kind of painful spasm that upsets your stomach can also occur in that part of the intestines known as the colon. More than any other internal organ, perhaps, the colon manifests a person's emotions and how he is feeling. In fact, a famous university physiologist and medical professor once said, "The colon is the mirror of the mind, and when the mind gets tight, the colon gets tight, too."

When a person is worried or nervous, his colon will usually respond to that nervousness with a muscle spasm. The pain can be as bad as a true gall bladder attack or the absolutely excruciating pain of the passage of a kidney stone down the ureter to the bladder.

A friend, I'll leave him unnamed, had a bad automobile accident as a result of drunk driving. He was a major in the air force, and while waiting for the outcome of the investigation, he suffered constantly with severe abdominal pain. At the end of three weeks, when the major found that he was going to receive only a fine and an oral reprimand rather than a general court-martial and dismissal from the service, his abdominal pains ceased and never came back.

Fully 50 percent of the people who are examined for gall bladder attacks are found to have normal gall bladders. Their pains are caused instead by colon spasm resulting from EII.

Again, the key to recovery is to find out what your mental or emotional problem is, eliminate it, and then program your subconscious mind with thoughts of good health.

Stress, Tension, and EII

Stress and tension can cause all sorts of EII, ranging from diarrhea to arthritis and rheumatism. Stress and tension also cause an undue expenditure of the body's energy, resulting first of all in excessive fatigue.

A good example of that is a trip to the dentist's office. Just the anticipation of the pain to come—*even if it never does*—causes a person to tense up and grip the arms of the dentist's chair until the person's knuckles turn white. All the muscles of the body are tight, contracted, and strained. And when it's finally over, the person almost crawls out of the chair, stiff and sore from the stress, strain, and tension, often more tired than if she had done a full day's physical work.

Unfortunately, this situation is the kind so many people find themselves in all day long at their jobs. They are in a constant state of stress and tension from the time they get up in the morning until they go to bed at night.

Since most of them cannot run away from their environment to escape this stress and tension, they must stay and fight the problem, be that a frustrating, dead-end job; a miserably mean boss; an unhappy marriage; or simply the never-ending daily and monthly bills that have to be paid.

Diarrhea can be one of the results of stress and tension. A friend of mine, who happens to be a writer, too, suffered for a long time from constant diarrhea. He had gone to a gastroenterologist for a complete physical examination. He was found to be free of parasites, and a sigmoidoscopic examination also found no cause.

Fred finally gave up and turned to a psychologist for help. A complete history of his life situation revealed that the problem was an emotionally induced illness. Fred's wife was completely disabled from multiple sclerosis. She had been in a wheelchair for more than ten years. In addition to earning a living for them as a writer of nonfiction articles for magazines, Fred also acted, as he put it, as the "chief cook and bottle washer" in the house.

He took care of cleaning the house, washing the clothes, cooking the meals, doing the shopping, bathing and dressing his wife, and on and on. He refused to put her in a nursing home as long as he could take care of her, although his physician advised him to do so to prevent a complete breakdown of his own health.

After consulting with the psychologist, Fred finally realized that his diarrhea was being caused by stress and tension rather than from some physical cause. He was then able to reprogram his subconscious mind so that he could heal himself.

Although he was unable to change his unpleasant circumstances, he was able to accept them. In only a short time, Fred's changed attitude had given him much better mental and physical health. He still had his problems—his wife was still disabled, in a wheelchair, and needed his constant help, but he was determined to be joyful and happy anyway, in spite of his unpleasant circumstances.

How to Rid Yourself of Constipation

Out of every ten people you meet, at least six or seven are troubled with constipation. It seems to be a national malady, no doubt at least partially brought on by a diet rich in junk food and man-made carbohydrates. However, television advertisers for constipation remedies would like you to believe that it is a way of life, it is not abnormal, and that it is normal for even animals to have it!

For some, the problem is a hangover from childhood days, when their mothers made such a fuss about bowel movements. Some children rebelled against parental authority and, just to spite their mothers, refused to have a BM. I know my own mother had a fetish about it. Her solution was prunes. Her daily question was "Have you gone?" If I said that I hadn't, she reached for the prune jar. Eventually, I hated prunes so much that I would say yes even if I hadn't, just to avoid the prunes. Today I can't look a prune in the face without feeling sick to my stomach. But I will admit I never have problems with constipation.

If you have this problem, you can help yourself, not only by relaxation and meditation, but also by programming your subconscious mind to move your bowels at a specific time of the day every single day.

First of all, you should program your subconscious mind to *expect* a normal bowel movement. Most people with chronic constipation have never trained themselves to expect a normal BM. In this negative frame of mind, when the person does try to go to the bathroom, the law of reversed effect goes into operation, and, naturally, there is no result.

So your first step is to program your subconscious mind to expect a normal BM. You can help this programming simply by sitting on the stool expectantly, at whatever time you have chosen. I, myself, have programmed my subconscious mind to cause me to have a normal BM right after my first cup of coffee in the morning. Does this work? It most certainly does. My subconscious mind is so well programmed, I dare not be too far away from the bathroom when I finish that first cup of coffee if I want to prevent a natural disaster!

You can also help your body's digestive system by eating lots of high-fiber foods, plenty of fresh fruits and vegetables, and by avoiding canned and packaged foods that contain large amounts of refined sugar. Remember, you cannot expect your subconscious mind to do everything for you. You must be its partner and cooperate with it if you want to keep yourself in good health.

How You Can Treat Your Allergy

Some allergies, hay fever, for instance, are physical and caused by pollens. The biggest culprit of all is *ragweed*. However, even physical allergies can be made worse by improper programming of the subconscious mind.

For example, when the hay fever season arrives, the allergy victim will start sneezing, his eyes will water, and he will have all the physical symptoms of his allergy, even if he has not yet been exposed to the pollen. He has programmed his subconscious mind to react when the hay fever season arrives, and it does so automatically. Let me give you a classic example of how your imagination can fool you.

Dr. Gibson, the chiropractor I told you about, had a patient who was allergic to roses. A friend had given the doctor a rose made out of velvet that was so lifelike you could not tell it was artificial unless you felt the flower's petals. When this allergic patient entered Dr. Gibson's office, he saw the artificial rose on the receptionist's desk and immediately began to sneeze. The receptionist handed him the rose and called his attention to the fact that it was artificial. His allergic attack immediately stopped!

Even if you have an actual physical allergy to ragweed, for example, you can program your subconscious mind so that your problem will not be as severe as it was before.

Even Neurodermatitis Can Be Emotionally Induced

A man of seventy-two had a terrible case of neurodermatitis, from which he had suffered for several years. He had never had any sort of skin problem before he was sixty-eight. When he was sixty-seven, his first wife died; he married his second wife when he was sixty-eight years old. It was on their honeymoon that he first developed neurodermatitis. It soon became so bad that he had to be hospitalized. After a week in the hospital he was well enough to return home. But as soon as he got home, the rash returned.

Over the years, he had to go out of town on business several times. Each time, his dermatitis cleared up. But as soon as he returned home, his rash would return.

Then his wife had to leave home to care for a sick relative, and to his amazement he found that his dermatitis cleared up even though he was still at home. Now the connection became clear, not only to him, but also to his doctor.

When the doctor asked him if he had any problems with his wife, his answer was immediate: "She's too damned domineering. I can't stand it!" he said. When his wife came back home, the doctor explained the situation to her. Although she didn't like the diagnosis, she agreed that she would cooperate, and she did. Her husband's dermatitis has not come back. Once in a while, if there is a hint of its return, the doctor simply talks to the wife. So far this procedure has worked.

How to Relieve Emotionally Induced Asthma

A bad asthmatic attack is a terrifying experience. If it is severe enough, it can result in hospitalization. Drugs such as inhalers can help the asthmatic breathe and control the condition, but they cannot cure the asthma itself.

Some asthmatic conditions result from infections; others from the emotions. Emotional factors, such as stress and tension, can not only bring on an asthmatic attack but they can intensify it.

The basic pathology of asthma is that the patient cannot expel the air she has inhaled. Muscular tension in the tissues around the lung sacs blocks exhaling. When this tension is relieved, then breathing becomes normal again.

Cases of infectious asthma are easier for a doctor to treat than are those that are emotionally induced, for the emotional conditions causing the problem must be removed before the asthma can be cured. Even the fear of an attack or fear of any sort will cause an asthmatic spasm to start.

Meditation is helpful in programming the subconscious mind. When the patient relaxes, the asthma is always immediately improved. Daily meditation used consistently over a period of time can alleviate the asthmatic condition altogether if the condition is caused by stress and tension and not by a bronchial infection.

How Visualization Therapy Can Help Cure Cancer

Some years ago my urologist discovered that I had prostate cancer. I underwent eight weeks of radiation. While in the cancer clinic, I met a gentleman who also had prostate cancer. His name was Ben. I say "was," for Ben is no longer with us.

After I found out I had cancer, a close friend gave me the book *Love, Medicine, and Miracles** by Dr. Bernie Siegel, the famous cancer specialist. I used the methods in his book along with the radiation to fight my cancer. Using a technique called "visualization therapy," I formed a mental picture of my cancer.

---

*Bernie S. Siegel, *Love, Medicine, and Miracles* (New York: Harper and Row, 1986).

I made this into a game in my mind. My disease-fighting white blood cells became a deadly fighter squadron. I was the squadron leader. My doctor was ground control, guiding and supporting me through my mental battle for my life. After five years of fighting this mental battle, in which I visualized my white blood cells destroying the enemy cancer cells, I am now cancer-free.

Ben unfortunately would not use this procedure. He pooh-poohed it as black magic and the voodoo medicine of a witch doctor. In spite of the radiation he received, Ben died some time ago from metastatic bone cancer.

Ben would never believe that his cancer could be cured. When I said to him that I no longer had cancer, he disputed me and said, "Oh, Jim, you'll always have cancer. You'll never be able to get rid of it completely."

Of course, with this kind of negative mental attitude, it is really no wonder that Ben died in spite of the radiation treatment that he received.

PROGRAM YOUR MIND FOR HEALTH

As you can see from these cases, improper programming of the subconscious mind can cause emotionally induced disease and result in actual physical problems with real symptoms.

One of the best ways for you to control your emotions so you can prevent or help cure such emotionally induced illnesses is not to let other people upset you. As a friend of mine, Jay Barbree, once told me, "They can't get your goat if they don't know where it's tied." So don't let anyone know where your goat is tied if you want to avoid getting EII.

Not only that, don't let your imagination run riot every time you have a pain somewhere. Remember that your subconscious mind cannot tell the difference between a real experience and one that is imagined. So don't imagine yourself to be sick. If you program your subconscious mind with the idea that you are not well, you can rest assured that you will soon be sick. Remember Job's experience. That is why it is so important for you to use your imagination to program your subconscious mind with thoughts of good health, for quite literally, you will always become what you think about.

Scientific studies linking the mind to physical health and disease are now making for exciting fields of research. Investigators have found that negative emotions and severe stress can cause the development of a variety of diseases, including cancer, while positive thoughts, usually achieved through meditation, can heal a long list of health problems.

Research in this new field, called *psychoneuroimmunology*, a term defining the interrelationship among mind, body, and the body's immune system, is causing doctors to rethink one of medicine's time-honored tenets that the mind and the body are distinct and separate entities.

Among the findings leading to this reappraisal are studies showing that (1) severe stress, such as a spouse's death or the diagnosis of cancer, can impair immune system function; (2) people with emotional short circuits that keep them from experiencing emotions or fantasies are at an increased risk for a variety of diseases, including cancer; and (3) severe depression can prevent white blood cells from fighting off disease in the body.

Scientific researchers have found that mental imagery or visualization causes an increase in a certain body chemical known as thymosin alpha-1. This chemical causes an increase in the number and potency of certain white blood cells that attack and destroy cancer cells as well as foreign bacteria.

In conclusion, let me say that if your doctor has told you that there's nothing wrong with you or that he can find no physical cause for your problem and that it's just your nerves or it's all in your head, you can bet your boots that your sickness has been caused by improper programming of your subconscious mind.

To heal yourself, you must dig out the cause of the improper programming of your subconscious mind so that you can eliminate it. Then you must reprogram your subconscious mind properly with thoughts of health and well-being as well as serenity and peace of mind.

I'm sure you realize I could not possibly cover every ailment here that a person is subject to. Were I to do that, this would not be a chapter, it would be a book. However, you can apply the information presented here to properly program your subconscious mind and get rid of any mental or emotional health problem that might be bothering you.

14

How to Use the Power Within to Win Friends and Improve Relationships

When I was growing up in the little town of Sigourney, Iowa, I knew a very successful businessman named Hap Weller. I never did know what his real first name was, for everyone always called him "Hap" or "Happy."

Hap Weller owned the Sigourney Hotel. Traveling salesmen came from miles around to stay at Hap's hotel. Why? Because Hap Weller made every single one of them feel as if he were the most important person in all the world. He always made sure that each customer's needs and desires were completely fulfilled. In fact, he made every person who stayed there feel like a VIP.

I became close friends with his son, Earl, and often spent my evenings in the hotel lobby studying and doing homework with him. Hap always treated me with the same courtesy and respect that he did all his customers, even though I was a teenager and certainly not a paying guest. But that was Hap's way—to be friends with everyone, large or small, rich or poor, young or old.

I never had any idols that I looked up to when I was young, but Hap Weller came close to being one, for I learned from him to make every person feel important if I wanted to become successful in life.

BENEFITS YOU WILL GAIN

You will always become successful, no matter what you do for a living, if you fulfill a person's desire to be important. The need for ego gratification is a person's most dominant desire. Make it a habit; you'll always benefit.

- You'll gain many, many true friends.
- You'll have no enemies.
- People will admire and respect you.
- They'll do what you ask them to do.
- You'll have power with people that works like magic.

Now just knowing that people want to be important, that they want to be heard and recognized, that they need attention is not enough. You must know how to make a person feel important and how to feed her ego so that you can get what you want from the relationship, too. This chapter will show you exactly how you can do that.

HOW MAKING SOMEONE FEEL IMPORTANT CAN IMPROVE YOUR RELATIONSHIP

What can you do on a day-to-day basis to improve the quality of your relationships? First of all, work on improving your own personality. It's a proven fact that the person with high self-esteem and self-acceptance has a natural ability to get along with the greatest number of people.

Everything you can do to raise the self-esteem and self-acceptance of others will increase the quality of your relationships with them. If you do everything you can do to make others feel important and valuable, then you will also feel important and good about yourself.

What can you do to make another person feel important? One thing is to *accept* the other person exactly as she is, totally and unconditionally, without reservation or judgment.

Acceptance of a person without reservation or judgment can best be expressed by this simple statement: "I like you *because* . . . but I love you *in spite of* . . . .

Another thing you can do is to offer your *approval* by praising everything the person does that is right or good. You can also express your *appreciation* or gratitude for what the person does. This causes her to feel that what she's doing or saying is of value and consequence.

Admiration is also a tremendous way of building the other person's self-esteem. You can admire and compliment a person for such qualities as reliability, honesty, and generosity, and for her children's accomplishments, her possessions, and on and on.

HOW TO BUILD YOUR RELATIONSHIPS

Never Criticize

If your aim is to develop high levels of self-esteem in others, to make them feel more valuable about themselves, and to establish superior relationships with them, then you should never criticize them. Nothing destroys friendships, undermines self-esteem, lowers self-confidence, and causes people to thoroughly dislike you more than criticism. In fact, I'll make it stronger: Criticize others, and you'll soon find that they not only dislike you, they hate and despise you. Let me give you a specific example.

Let's say one of your employees asks you to look at his work and let him know where he's making mistakes. Don't be misled by that. That isn't what he wants at all. He wants you to tell him what a good job he's doing. He wants you to pat him on the back and tell him he's not making any mistakes. He wants to be *praised*, not criticized. Read between the lines. Listen to what he really said. Of all the basic desires every person has, to be criticized is not one of them. The best thing you can remember about criticism is to forget it. Never use it. It will accomplish absolutely nothing.

One last point about criticism: Never argue with people, because when you do, you're criticizing them. You're telling them that what they think, say, or do is incorrect. In effect, you're saying that their thoughts, opinions, and values are wrong because they're not the same as yours, and that is pure criticism.

Praise—Don't Blame

Now as I just said, people want to be praised, not criticized. The person doesn't live who doesn't want to be praised or receive a compliment for what he or she does.

You can use this technique to win friends, no matter who they are—your boss; your employees; associates at work, members of your church, or your social groups; it matters not. All you need do to win a person's friendship is to *praise her for what she has done.*

To be praised is a basic human desire. We all want to be told how great we are and what a good job we've done. So praise a person and you'll win her loyal friendship. She'll love you for it. Tell her what a magnificent job she's doing, how you couldn't get along without her, how happy you are that she's your friend.

Above all, be generous with your praise. Pass it around freely. The supply is limited only by you. So don't be stingy about passing out bouquets; they cost you nothing at all. And don't act as if you expected something in return for your praise. Don't pay a person a compliment as if you expected a receipt for it.

Praise a person and you'll make him feel more important, not only to you, but also, because you fed his ego, to himself. Praise, without a doubt, is one of the best tools you can ever use to win and hold a lasting friendship.

Listen—Really Listen

"No one pays any attention to me," "No one ever listens to my ideas," "Nobody's interested in my opinions," "My boss just wants to do things his own way." Ever hear comments like these before? Ever make the same comments yourself? If you've ever felt this way, then you ought to be able to understand that other people feel the same way.

You can make a person feel important by paying attention to him, by asking for his opinions and ideas. When you listen—*really listen*—with rapt attention to what the other person has to say, you'll prove to him that you feel that what he has to tell you is important, that you respect his opinion, that you feel he has something worthwhile to offer.

"When you ask a person for his ideas and opinions, you let him know he's both needed and wanted in your company," says Dale Walters, president of the Walters Supply Company, a wholesaler for the building trades in Des Moines, Iowa.

> No one wants to be a nonentity or just another clock number on the payroll. Every single person in your organization wants to be an important member of your team. Everyone wants to feel he belongs where he is and that he is contributing to the company's success.
>
> Ask your employees for their advice and their help and you'll give them that individual identity they want and need so much. You make them valuable members of your team. They will work that much harder for you when they feel they're making a major contribution to the success of your organization.

There are few faster ways to make a person feel important than to ask her for her opinion, advice, or help. When you do this, you automatically make the person feel more important. And you'll also establish a superior human relationship with every individual with whom you do that.

What You Can Do to Make Your Employees Feel More Important

If you're the boss, an excellent way to make your people feel more important is to keep your door open to them at all times.

Such a policy will let your employees know that you're really interested in them. They will know they have access to you, that they can reach you, talk with you, give you their opinions, tell you their ideas, bring you their grievances and problems—and that you will listen to them and pay attention to them and to what they say.

But if you close your door, if you isolate yourself from your people, you let them know by your attitude and your actions that you're not interested in them and their ideas and you do not consider them to be important at all. You do not need to say anything; your closed door will say it quite plainly for you. John De Butts, former chairman of the board of American Telephone and Telegraph, said that the open-door policy was a major factor in his successful business career. I am convinced that this is true of all relationships—you must keep the door of your mind open to others if you are going to make them feel important.

Take you own son or daughter, for instance. If you won't listen to them with an open mind, if you won't at least expose yourself to their ideas and their opinions, how can you make them feel important and valuable to you? And the same can be said for your relationships with your husband, your wife, your friends and associates. Keep the door of your mind open to the ideas and opinions of others. You'll establish superior relationships with them when you do.

Another fast and dependable way to make a person feel more important to you and your organization is to give him more responsibility. If at all possible, make him the boss in some way—put him in charge even if he has no one to supervise.

Wally Gilbert, now the president of a large rubber factory manufacturing V-belts and industrial belts, gave me an example of this technique:

> I can still recall, although it's been many years ago now, when an employee of ours named Bill was giving us fits. Bill felt as if he'd been cheated at one time by the

company, so he was doing everything possible to make life miserable for his section supervisor, his department foreman, and management in general.

He would prolong his coffee breaks, turn out shoddy work, cheat on his incentive report sheets, clock in late, and leave early. He was the leader of a team of six employees, and as Bill went, so went his team.

Bill was not in my department, but I watched this battle of wits with great interest. Every possible effort was made by his supervisor and his foreman to find a solution to the problem. Nothing seemed to work. And Bill couldn't be fired. He was too smart for that. Time and again management tried to dismiss him—only to lose when the case went before the arbitration board.

Then one day I happened to watch a safety drill in Bill's department. I noticed how, in the absence of his supervisor, Bill immediately took over and assumed command, even though it was not his job to do so.

"Why not give Bill the responsibility for safety in that section?" I said to his supervisor and his foreman. "Make him responsible and see what happens when you do."

Reluctantly, they did as I suggested. The results were absolutely astounding. Bill now had responsibility, and he acted accordingly. He didn't want to lose his newfound authority; almost overnight he became a model employee simply because management had recognized his hungry ego and made him feel important as an individual.

Well, today Bill is our production superintendent. He is directly responsible to me for everything that happens in here. He also takes charge of the entire plant operation when I am gone. And all this has happened because he was given a feeling of importance when he was given additional responsibility.

Will this technique always work? Well, look at the following two examples and see for yourself. A midwestern telephone company used to assemble its telephone books in twenty-one steps—each step performed by a different employee. Now the company gives each employee the individual responsibility for putting an entire book together. The result of this new procedure? There are far fewer mistakes, and employee turnover has been reduced more than 50 percent.

A California steel company was ready to close a continuous-weld pipe mill because it could not compete with Japanese prices. One hundred and fifty workers would lose their jobs. Labor asked management to let them have full responsibility for making their product competitive with the Japanese. Management agreed, and the workers put their collective heads to work.

They overhauled some tools, rearranged the production flow to make it more efficient, and made some changes in scheduling. The result was that production went up one-third, waste dropped from 20 percent to 7 percent, and they were able to keep the plant open.

You see, when you give a person more responsibility, you also grant her more authority to make the necessary decisions. That makes her feel more important and more valuable as an individual.

How to Never Get "No" for an Answer

Let's say you want a certain job done. You could tell someone to do it, but I'm sure you know full well that most people instinctively rebel when given orders to do something. So how do you get the job done and still give the person a feeling of importance? Instead of telling an individual what to do, ask him to show you how to do it so that he can carry out your order and feel important while he's doing it. Let me give you an example of how this technique works.

"One of the toughest problems the average small businessperson has to solve is cutting his costs and reducing his overhead," Woody Jeffries told me.

And when your net profit is figured in pennies, as it is in the restaurant business, you have to cut corners every chance you get without lowering the quality of the food or the service to your customers.

I've found it doesn't do any good for me to preach to my cooks to cut costs or yell at my waitresses to get them to reduce waste. But I do know from experience I can get my own way every time when I ask them to show me how to do it.

The minute I ask my people to show me how to cut costs and reduce my overhead, they go to work on the problem for me. And they come up with workable solutions most of the time. Then all I have to do is ask them to put their own ideas into effect, for *people will always support what they themselves suggest.* I've never had a person refuse to help me when I ask him to show me how to get the job done. By asking my employees for their help, I've made them feel important and increased their self-esteem.

Three Things That Are Important to Everyone

If you are still at a loss about how to make a person feel important, let me give you a little tip. You'll always be right if you *talk to people about themselves, their children,* and *their personal possessions.* You can make the person feel more important simply by discussing one of these subjects with them. Here's why.

People Like to Talk About Themselves.   "Whether they like to admit it or not, people are basically self-centered," says Dr. Edwin Barnes, a psychologist. "They are chiefly interested in themselves. They don't really care whether the government owns the railroads or whether the aircraft industry gets a subsidy or not—unless it's going to hit them in the pocketbook. Then they become vitally interested, for it's going to affect them personally and financially."

There is nothing more interesting to a person than himself sums up what Dr. Barnes is saying. You can put this idea to work for yourself by making sure that your product, your service, or your conversation conforms to this fundamental characteristic of human nature.

People always feel more important when you tell them how handsome or how beautiful they are, how smart they are, how reliable and honest they are, what wise decisions they make, and so on ad infinitum.

If you want to win friends and establish superior personal relationships with people, all you need do is forget your own needs and desires and talk to a person about how important she is. Do that and you are bound to succeed.

People Like to Talk About Their Children.   Next to themselves, people like to talk about their children. They want to let you know how smart little Jenna is, how clever young Bill is, what a fine football player Tim will be, how Sally has the voice to become a brilliant recording artist.

Look at some bumper stickers and you'll see visible evidence of this. For example, you'll see signs that say "My Son and Daughter are Honor Students at Glendale High School." "Let Me Tell You About My Grandchildren."

How many deadly dull children's school or church programs have you sat through just so you could see and hear your own child perform? Why is it you're far less interested in the football game when your son is sitting on the bench?

We relive our own lives through the lives of our children. We try to make them successful where we failed. Our own egos are fed when they do whatever we wanted to do, or when people compliment us for the achievements of our sons and daughters.

You can be sure that when you ask parents about their children and their accomplishments, you'll make them feel more important.

People Like to Talk About Their Possessions.   Tell a couple what a wise decision they made in buying such a beautiful home out in the country; they'll be your friends. Compliment them on how exquisite their choice was in the selection of furniture, mirrors, and paintings, and how their individual taste has made their house into a beautiful home, and you've made a conquest.

People want to know how wise they were in buying their home, their furniture, the china, the silverware, the pictures, the car, the boat, even the golf clubs, and so on. You make people feel more important when you let them know how smart they are and what wise buying decisions they made.

"When you tell a man or woman how good looking their house, their car, their furniture is, you're really complimenting their good judgment," says Dr. Frank Cameron, a clinical psychologist from Memphis, Tennessee. "You make them feel important when you do that. You're letting them know how wise they were to make such intelligent choices."

HOW TO MAKE *EVERYBODY* FEEL LIKE *SOMEBODY*

Industrial psychologists say that one of the biggest mistakes managers can make is treating their employees like machines or equipment; in other words, not treating them as individuals.

Let's face it. If you are a supervisor, a manager, or an employer, not a single one of the people who works for you wants to be a nobody. Everybody wants to be somebody. No one wants to be just another number—a faceless or nameless anonymity. Everyone wants to retain his own special individual identity.

Unfortunately, in today's highly automated and mechanized business world, a person often feels like just another piece of office equipment or an extension of some part of the machinery.

And then, to make matters even worse, since computers depend on numbers rather than names for credit, identification, and billing purposes, each person tends to be converted into a nonentity even when he or she is not working. More than ever before, people just don't seem to be as important as individuals as they used to be.

What can you do to change this situation? What can you do to establish superior human relationships with the people who work for you? How can you make everybody somebody? Well, you can do what Armond Dunlap, the plant manager for a large electrical-appliance company in Atlanta, Georgia, did. Here's exactly what Armond told me:

> We do our best to make everybody feel like somebody. When you walk around the place, you'll see big signs everywhere that say "EVERYBODY IS SOMEBODY." We do everything we can think of to treat our employees as important individuals. And since a person's name is the most individual and distinctive thing about a person, that's exactly where we start.
>
> I insist that every division head and section chief, every single foreman and supervisor, know the name of all of his or her subordinates. We also provide desk or bench nameplates at company cost so that our employees will know that we recognize them as valued members of our organization—not just faceless names or numbers on a payroll.
>
> We also publish a small weekly plant newspaper that carries news about our employees. Of course, we print news events of plant achievements, special events, promotions, and so on. If we have a new piece of equipment, I have the operator's picture taken along with it to go in our company paper. The personnel section also keeps a record of birthdays. When one of our people has a birthday, a notice goes up on the bulletin board and in the plant paper wishing him or her many happy returns. He or she also gets the day off with full pay.
>
> Whenever awards are given out, we have a photographer take a picture of the person and his or her immediate

supervisor giving the award. That gets two employees into the act. Both of them get a copy of the photograph. Another one goes on all the plant bulletin boards. We print the picture and carry the story in the plant newspaper. We also send a picture along with the story to one of our local newspapers.

But we don't stop with events in the plant. We also carry information about people getting married, children being born, graduation of sons and daughters from high school and college, excelling in sports, drama, music, and the like. Entry into the service, return from the army or navy, that sort of news is covered, too. The important point is to get the employee's name or the name of a member of the family into our paper, no matter how.

Now you might ask if all this is worth it. You bet it is. All I have to do is look at our production records and our employee grievance files before and after we started using this procedure of treating everybody like somebody. The proof of how well it works for us is all right there.

The important point for you to keep in mind is that every person with whom you have a relationship needs individual recognition and attention. You'll find that when you treat everybody like somebody, your benefits will multiply like rabbits.

Be Genuinely Interested

I know of no faster way on earth to drive people away from you than to constantly talk about yourself and your own accomplishments. Not even your best friend can put up with never-ending stories about how important you are. Even she will eventually reach the limits of her endurance.

If you think that you can win friends and establish superior relationships with them by getting them interested in you and your affairs, then I must tell you quite bluntly: You are wrong! The only way you can win lasting friends is to always use the small "i" and the big "YOU." In other words, you must become truly interested in other people and in their problems.

People who have no interest in their fellow human beings and their problems always have the greatest difficulties in life and end up causing the most harm to others, themselves included. Such people will always fail until they change their basic attitude toward people. If you happen to be in that rut, here are two giant steps you can take to get out of it:

1. Forget yourself completely.
2. *Think* that other people are important.

Forget Yourself Completely.   All of us are self-centered most of the time. To me—the world revolves around me. But as far as you are concerned, it revolves around you. Most of us are always busy trying to impress someone else. We are constantly seeking the spotlight. We continually want to be in the center of the stage. Most of our waking moments are spent trying to gain status of some sort.

But if you really want to get along with people and have good relationships with them, you must forget yourself completely. And you can do that in the service of others. If you want to better understand people and win their hearts and their support, then you must be willing to help them solve their problems.

To be able to do this with sincerity means you'll have to place more emphasis on the other person's problems than on your own. And you'll need an attitude of complete unselfishness to do that.

Believe People Are Important and They Will Be.   Christ said in effect, "Believe that you have got it and you shall have it." In other words, all you have to do to think that other people are important is just to *pretend* that they are, and they will be.

Simply tell yourself once and for all that other people and their problems are much more important than you and your problems are. When you adopt this attitude, it'll come through as clear as a bell to the other person. You won't have to put on a phony false face and butter him up to make it work.

With this new approach you can stop looking for gimmicks to make the other person feel important. You won't need any, for you'll have put your dealings with other people on a firm, sound, sincere, and honest basis.

Sincerity and honesty are better than a gimmick every day of the week, for you can't make the other person important and feel like somebody if deep down inside you really feel that he or she is a worthless nobody. The beauty of this technique is that you no longer have to engage in the games people play to impress each other. All you have to do to make it work is just to *think* that the other person is important. Pretend that it is so—and it will be.

LEARN TO LISTEN WITH EVERYTHING YOU'VE GOT

If you want to learn everything you can about the other person and her problems, you must listen carefully to what she says. Above all, don't interrupt or cut her off. I know of no faster way in the world to insult a person or to hurt her feelings than to brush her off or turn away when she's trying to tell you something.

How many times have you been right in the middle of a good story only to have one of your listeners turn away or interrupt you and start talking about something else? You'd have loved to strangle that individual with your bare hands, right? Even children feel the same way when their parents brush them aside, ignore them, or pay no attention to them and their problems. And if children feel that way, what reason do you have to believe that grownups don't react in the same manner?

Learning to listen to the other person with everything you have means putting aside your own interests, your own pleasures, and your own preoccupations, at least temporarily. For those few moments, it means you must concentrate 100 percent on what the other person is saying. You must focus all your attention on her. You must listen to her with all the intensity and awareness that you can command.

A good way to do this is to face the person squarely, lean forward, and concentrate totally on what she is saying, without mental wandering or interruption. Pause before you reply. This indicates that you are giving careful consideration to what she is saying. If a person has made a point that is not clear to you, say, "What I understand you're saying is this," and feed it back to her. Then ask if your assumption is correct. Always ask open-ended questions to help the person express herself more fully.

What Total Listening Will Do for You

When you listen with everything you've got, it means you are paying complete attention to the other person. And the more attention you pay to other people, the more you convey to them that you consider them to be valuable and important.

You pay attention to others primarily by listening to them. In listening you will find that three things happen. First of all, listening builds trust between two people. Listening also builds strength of character in the listener because active, concentrated listening takes tremendous self-discipline. And listening also builds a better self-image and more self-esteem in the person being listened to.

Learn to Listen Between the Lines

You can often learn more from what the other person doesn't say than from what he does. So learn to listen between the lines. Just because he didn't say that he doesn't want to do it your way is no sign that he does.

The speaker doesn't always put everything he's thinking into words for you. Watch for the changing tone and volume of his voice. Sometimes you will find a meaning that's in direct contrast to his spoken words. And watch his facial expression, his mannerisms, his gestures, the movements of his body. To be a good listener and to listen with everything you've got means using your eyes as well as your ears.

How Listening Can Turn an Angry Employee into a Satisfied One

"My job is to help maintain a harmonious relationship between labor and management," says George Watson, industrial relations manager for an automobile assembly plant.

> And I do that primarily just by listening to what the other fellow has to say. For instance, if I happen to have an angry employee come to see me, here's how I handle him.
>
> First of all, I listen to his story from beginning to end without ever saying a single word. I don't interrupt him—not even once. I let him get it all off his chest. That's the first thing he wants. He wants someone who'll listen patiently to him; someone who'll lend him a sympathetic ear.
>
> Next, when he's through talking, I'll agree with him, even if I don't. I'll tell him I understand exactly how he feels about this, and that if I were in his place, I'd no doubt look at it just as he does.
>
> Now I've taken a lot of the fire out of him already by first listening to him, and then by agreeing with him. You know he wasn't at all prepared for that kind of reception. Now I add the finishing touch by asking him what he wants me to do about his problem.
>
> You know he wasn't prepared for that either. Ninety-nine times out of a hundred, an industrial relations manager will tell an employee what he's going to do for him. A lot of customer service departments handle complaints the same way. Not me; I can't win his support that way.

So I don't tell him what I'm going to do for him. I ask him what he wants me to do.

And that's a completely new twist to most people. I've had people look at me in astonishment and say, "Gee, Mr. Watson, I really don't know. Nothing, I guess. I just wanted someone to listen to my side of the story and see it from my point of view for a change. You've done that so I guess that's all that needs to be done. I'm satisfied; you've helped me."

So they leave, completely happy with the answer I never gave them. You see, they supplied their own answer. All they wanted was some attention and someone to listen to their story. I gave them what they wanted.

So George made people important just by listening to them. He increased their self-esteem and self-respect by paying attention to them. You can establish superior relationships with people when you do the same thing: Just listen. Years ago it used to be said that many a doctor earned his fee by furnishing a sympathetic ear to a patient who wanted nothing more than a little attention. Of course, with the price of health care what it is today, that adage is probably no longer true.

THE FASTEST WAY TO DESTROY A RELATIONSHIP: TAKE IT FOR GRANTED

One of the fastest ways to lose friends or customers is to take the other person for granted. Many people don't realize that it takes as much work to hang on to a customer as it does to get her in the first place. There's an old expression in the retail business that is ever so true: "Take care of the old customers and pay attention to them. They'll bring you the new ones."

Although some of the details in the following example have been outmoded by self-service stations, the principles are still the same, and it illustrates the point well.

I traded at a particular filling station for several years and then I suddenly stopped. But before I took my business to another service station, I told the owner quite frankly and honestly why he was losing me as a customer.

> Before I became a regular customer of yours, Wendall, you bent over backward to give me good service. But once you thought you had me hooked for good, you took me for granted, and from then on, you concentrated only on getting more new customers.
>
> You stopped checking my tires and my battery. You even forgot to clean my windshield several times because you were so anxious to get to the other fellow. You left my gas tank cap sitting on the pump at least three times, and when I got upset and complained about it, you tried to laugh it off. But it wasn't so funny to me, especially when I didn't know it was missing until I was two hundred miles away in Kansas City and had to buy a new one!
>
> And more than once I've left my car in the morning to be lubed and have the oil changed, I've come back in the afternoon when you said it would be ready only to find you'd done nothing at all because you were too busy putting other customers' cars up on the grease rack ahead of mine, even though I was there first.
>
> And perhaps you remember the time I mentioned it to you and you tried to slough it off by saying, "Oh, I didn't think you'd mind coming back tomorrow, Jim. After all, you don't have a real job. You just sit at home all day and write."

And so that ended our conversation. I changed gas stations. You see, Wendall forgot that maxim: "The best way to get new customers is to pay attention to the old ones." Then the old ones will bring the new ones in. In fact, there's really no other way to do it, and you ought to remember that, I think.

TRUE CONCERN: THE HEART OF ALL RELATIONSHIPS

You know, you can't make the techniques I've given you in this chapter work for you unless you really do care about people. You must be deeply concerned about them if you want to establish superior relationships with them. Your heart must be filled with compassion toward others.

The devil pays a lot of attention to people. He's deeply interested in them. But he has no love, no compassion, and no deep concern for them. That's why in the long run he will fail, as did Genghis Khan, Napoleon, Hitler, Mussolini, Stalin, and a host of others. Dictators always do.

There just isn't any use for you to pay attention to the other person unless you honestly care about her, unless you are really willing to share her pain, and to help her solve her problems.

To be concerned about the other person is the basic foundation for all deep and lasting human relationships. It is the heart of all friendship and a real key to a superior relationship with everyone.

15

How to Use the Power Within to Improve Your Family Relationships

Some people work overtime to get along with everyone outside the home—their friends, neighbors, coworkers, business associates, boss, church members, and so on—but they do absolutely nothing to create a happy and joyous atmosphere in their own home.

"People who treat their family worse than they do their friends and neighbors, and business associates figure that they have a captive audience at home who can do nothing at all about the situation," says Doctor Curtis Springer, a clinical psychologist who specializes in marriage counseling. "They fail to realize how really happy their lives could be if they would only use as much courtesy, tact, and diplomacy with their own families as they do with outsiders."

Do you have this problem in your own home? Do you take your frustrations from your business or your work out on your family? If you do, then this chapter will be most helpful to you. Or if your family life just seems to lack something, if you feel it isn't what it could or should be, then you can use this chapter to your advantage, too. In it you will learn how you can use the power within to improve your family relationships.

In the last chapter, I gave you many techniques that are also useful here. For example, I told you that you should always make a person feel more important, use praise instead of criticism, listen and pay close attention to what a person says, build up an individual's self-esteem and pride in himself, do not take people for granted, and be concerned.

In this chapter, I not only amplify and expand upon that vital information but I also give you some additional powerful techniques more suited to a family relationship. You can use these techniques to program your subconscious mind so that you can make your marriage and home life much happier.

As I have told you, unless you give your subconscious mind a specific goal to shoot for, it will not work for you. Your goal here is to establish a more harmonious and happy atmosphere for your entire family. You can achieve that goal when you use the specific techniques I give you here.

BENEFITS YOU WILL GAIN

- A peaceful and pleasant, happy and joyful atmosphere will pervade your home.
- A spirit of cheerful cooperation and helpfulness will be evident in every member of your family.
- Everyone will show a willingness to work together to solve common family problems.
- You'll be loved and respected by each member of your family.
- Arguments and disagreements will be virtually non-existent.
- Your life will be so happy and filled with so much joy that you'll wonder why you stayed single for as long as you did.

TWELVE SECRETS OF LASTING LOVE

I'm now going to give you twelve specific techniques that happy couples use to create a successful marriage. To gain this information, I talked to nearly one hundred couples ranging in age from their early twenties to their mid eighties. From these interviews I gleaned twelve secrets of lasting love that when practiced faithfully will give you a happy and joyful marriage, too.

1. Happy Couples Choose the Kind of Life They Want

Each and every one of us possesses a power that we often fail to use properly. That power is the *freedom of choice.* Many people choose poverty when they need only to choose riches. Some choose failure instead of success. Others choose to be afraid of life when all they need do is step out with courage and take what is rightfully theirs.

What you do about your family life is exactly the same. You have the power to choose the kind of home life you want. You can choose one that is fun: one that is filled with excitement, joy, and happiness. Or you can choose a home life that is constantly filled with resentment, anger, arguments, and bickering. It's all up to you.

Two specific examples will illustrate this. The first one is extremely short. A husband took verbal abuse from his wife year after year until he finally gave up and hanged himself in the barn one morning. He lived across the road from my family. I was only fourteen when this happened, but I will always remember it, for I am the one who found his body hanging from a rafter in the barn.

The second example is that of my beloved sister, Marjorie, and her husband, Ted. Both had disastrous first marriages. In my sister's case, her husband both verbally and physically abused her. I do not know all the details of Ted's previous marriage; I never asked him about it and I never will.

No doubt because of very bad first marriages, my sister and Ted both made the decision to choose to be happy together. And that they are. I have visited them many times, and I have never seen two people more in love than they are.

You can be happy in your marriage, too, if you choose to be. If you make that choice, then you will automatically program your subconscious mind to say kind and courteous, happy and cheerful things to the members of your family. You just cannot choose to be happy and then growl and bark at your family or argue with them. That choice and those actions are completely incompatible.

Remember the rule that if you want to get, you must first give of yourself. If you use courtesy and tender loving care in your family relationships, that is what you will receive in return. You cannot expect to give nothing to your family and get something back just because it's your family. It won't work that way. You must make the first move yourself.

All you need do is choose to have a happy and joyous home life, and the right words will come to you. You won't have to agonize over what to say or how to say it.

Even if you've been married a long time and things don't seem to be going too well, it's never too late to make the decision to be happy with your spouse. When you choose with your conscious mind to be happy, you program your subconscious mind properly so that kindness and courtesy will flow from you with every word you speak. No matter how bad things seem to be at times, they will get better when you make that one simple decision: *Choose to be happy.*

2. Happy Couples Are Completely Comfortable with Each Other

One couple I met impressed me deeply with how comfortable they were together. Each one was deeply in love with the other. That was clearly evident in the way they looked at each other and the way they touched each other. They always walked hand in hand or with arms linked. When they ate in a restaurant, they held hands across the table while waiting for their food to be served.

When I talked with them, I asked them if they held hands when they were in the car. "Sometimes we do if it's safe," he said. "But a lot of times, she just places her hand on my knee or she'll rub the back of my neck."

When you watched them and the way they looked at each other, you would have sworn they were in their early twenties, but in fact they are in their mid seventies.

He told me that he had fallen in love with her almost immediately when they first met. They were both twenty-three. It took her a little longer, but her love for him was just as deep as his for her.

When I asked for the secret of their successful marriage, she said,

> Oh, there are a lot of reasons that I could give you. But one of the main reasons is that we are completely comfortable with each other. And we laugh together a lot.
>
> There are a lot of other reasons why we've been so happy over the years, but one of the biggest is that we are completely comfortable with each other. Neither one of us is a phony. We say what we mean and we mean what we say. There's never any hidden meaning in our words. We know what to expect from the other person and we're never disappointed.

3. Happy Couples Accept Each Other Exactly as They Are

Our church had a program every Wednesday for eight weeks to help husbands and wives better relate to each other. You didn't have to have a marital problem to go to the meetings, so almost every married couple in the church attended.

The person conducting the meetings was a professional marriage counselor. Here is just some of what he told us: "One of the deepest cravings of human nature is to be accepted unconditionally without criticism," he said.

> So if you want to have a happy marriage, then you must accept your wife or husband totally without judgment. In other words, don't try to change your partner and make

him or her over. Don't nag or criticize. You'll never change a person by doing that.

Take your own husband for instance. Have you ever been able to change him very much through all your years of marriage? I know you probably started out to re-make him into the kind of person you thought he ought to be, but did you ever really succeed? I doubt it; I know my own wife never did.

Or if you're thinking of remaking your wife over to fit your own specifications, forget it. I failed at that one, too. I haven't been able to change her one little bit through all these years. She's still the same as when I married her. But now I'm happy that I failed. I realize now I couldn't have improved on her at all.

Out of everything he said, I think this is one of the most valuable points to remember: *The only person you can ever really change or control in your life is you, yourself, and you alone, no one else.* So accept your partner just as he or she is. You'll be much happier when you do that.

My wife's sister husband—my brother-in-law—had a severe problem with alcohol. His father had been an alcoholic, too. He tried to stay sober by joining Alcoholics Anonymous, and he would not take a drink for many months, sometimes even years.

But then for some unknown reason, he would slip and get drunk again. Then it would take several months of hard drinking before he would get back on the AA program again. He was a long-distance trucker whose trips would take him from one coast to the other, and he would often be gone for weeks at a time.

During those weeks, his wife, Dorothy, would sit at home worrying and immersed in self-pity. Then one day Dorothy made an important discovery. "There is absolutely nothing I can do to change my husband's drinking problem," she told herself.

But that is his problem—not mine. I'm as powerless to change him or to solve his drinking problem as he is—in fact, even more so. I cannot live his life for him. So from now on I am not going to torture myself with him or his problem any more. I am going to accept things the way they are.

I will not leave him. He is my husband and I still love him in spite of everything. But I am going to quit trying to change him. I am going to accept him as he is and do what I can to make my own life and the lives of our children as happy as possible under these circumstances.

So Dorothy decided to make a life for herself. She was an excellent pianist and played the piano and organ every Sunday in her church. She began giving piano lessons in her home, and since she was an excellent teacher, she was soon swamped with students.

She then branched out, bought an organ on the installment plan, and gave lessons to some of her students on the organ as well as on the piano. Her life had changed completely. Although it was not ideal, she had gained serenity and peace of mind by accepting the things that she could not change.

Realizing that you cannot possibly change your wife or husband can help you too. Hopefully, your partner's problem will not be as great as Dorothy's was, but regardless, you'll never to able to achieve total joy and happiness in your marriage until you accept your spouse exactly as she or he is.

4. Happy Couples Always Look for the Best in Each Other

Learning to accept your mate exactly as he or she is will help you with this technique. There is an old adage that says, "If you can find nothing good to say about the other person, then do exactly that: say nothing."

For some reason, our perverse human nature leads us to always look for the worst in the other person. We tend to look for an individual's faults and weaknesses rather than for his strengths and good points.

Do that, and I guarantee you'll never be able to enjoy a marriage filled with love and happiness. Happy couples always focus on what is good and true in each other. They always expect the best from their mates.

The basic rule in husband/wife relationships is always to expect the utmost from the other person. From the law of expectations, we know that our expectations tend to be fulfilled. Encourage your partner to expect the best from him- or herself, and tell him or her that you expect that, too.

Your positive expectations exert a tremendous influence on your spouse's actions. When you expect the utmost from your partner, that is usually what you will get, for your attitude is transmitted to the other person even if you never say a word.

When you love someone, you do so in part because you see your best self in his or her eyes. This is what happy partners do for each other. They reflect a real approval of and admiration for their mate.

I asked one couple in their sixties if they expected the best. The wife answered with a twinkle in her eye, "No. Why should I? I already have the best," and she looked lovingly at her husband as she reached for his hand. He took her hand and as he did, he said, "Me, too!"

5. Happy Couples Work and Play Together

It's important that you spend part of your free time with your spouse doing the things she or he likes to do. Don't let her become a golf widow as so many men do. That's no way to keep your marriage happy and intact. If she's athletic, find sports you both enjoy. If sports aren't your mate's thing, if she'd rather eat out, if he'd rather see a movie or go dancing, then do those things, too, taking both partner's needs into consideration.

By the same token, you're each entitled to free time for your preferred activities. If he likes to play cards one night a month or she likes to get together with friends after work, that's fine. You're entitled to time away from one another. Just be reasonable with your demands on each other's free time.

The same thing holds true when it comes to working around the house. Do it together. One of you can make the morning coffee while the other walks the dog, for example. The next day reverse those duties.

At least, don't be like Ed K., a fellow who used to live next door to us. Ed would come home from work, plop down in his easy chair, and yell for his wife, Arline, to bring him the evening paper, his slippers, and a beer.

Ed never lifted a finger to help Arline, after supper or at any other time either, for that matter. He refused to watch their two small sons while she did the supper dishes. His attitude was that he'd worked hard at the office all day and he had a right to relax and take it easy. He simply didn't want his family to bother him in *his* free time.

If you treat your wife like this, it's a good way to end up living all alone. That's exactly what happened to Ed.

6. Happy Couples Show Each Other Gratitude and Appreciation

When you show appreciation and gratitude for what the other person does for you, that person feels that what he or she is doing is of value and consequence to you.

For example, I know a couple who has been married for more than thirty-five years now and very happily, too. I asked Morgan what their secret was.

"Very simple, Jim," he said. "I always show my wife my appreciation for what she does for me by what I say and do. I still say *please* and *thank you* even after all these years together. And she still thanks me, too, for what I do for her. No matter what I do for her, she always shows her appreciation."

So if you want to have a harmonious and pleasant atmosphere in your home, if you want to fill your home life with excitement, joy, and real happiness, then give thanks and honest appreciation to your spouse all the time. You'll both benefit by doing so.

7. Happy Couples Communicate with Each Other

Robert Louis Stevenson wrote that marriage is one long conversation, checkered by disputes. Good communication is so essential for a happy marriage, but unfortunately, it is often missing.

Women and men are different in the way they communicate with each other. A man talks to his wife so he can express ideas and transmit information. A woman wants to talk about feelings and emotions. For instance, when was the last time you asked your husband, "Do you love me?" You know he loves you. He's told you so many times, perhaps, but you have an emotional need to hear it again and again and over again.

A woman expresses her love by words and touching. A man expresses his love by actions—giving her things. She wants love and tenderness; he gives her things. No wonder some couples have trouble and end up arguing with each other.

My mate and I know how important it is to hear the other person say "I love you," and so we tell each other that many, many times throughout the day. At night in bed, if either of us goes to the bathroom, when we come back, we will bend over, kiss the other on the cheek or shoulder, and gently whisper "I love you."

In the morning when we get up, the first words we say to each other are "I love you." Then we say "Good morning, dear." How old are we? We're in our mid seventies. Surprised?

Communication also requires both persons to use the fine art of listening. I sometimes can go for a long time without saying anything, but my mind is always whirling, thinking about ideas for writing. And then I sometimes go off on a tangent, and talk up a storm. When I do that, I'm like a broken record that keeps right on spinning stuck in the same groove.

But my mate, God bless her, is ever so patient. She listens attentively to everything I say. But when her patience is finally exhausted, she might gently and lovingly say, "May I say something?" or "You've told me that before," and I know it's time for me to stop talking and start listening.

Let me conclude by saying that an understanding mate is always in great demand. And understanding the one you love and live with is one of the best ways to communicate. Not all communication is spoken. A lot of it is showing you understand your spouse and how he or she feels and getting in sync with his or her moods.

8. Happy Couples Don't Try to Dominate Each Other

In some marriages the man insists on being the boss. In others, the woman wants to have the final word on everything. I can tell you this much for sure. Marriages in which each person wants to rule the other and make all the decisions are not successful or happy.

Therefore, don't give each other unsolicited advice. As Shakespeare wrote, "Those who school others, often should school themselves." All too often one partner will say, "Well, if I were you, I think you should consider this . . . " When you give advice like this, your partner feels that you're criticizing him or her. Even though your intentions might be good, he or she feels like a child who's being scolded by a parent.

Money often creates a problem when one or the other person wants to have the final say. If both people are working, they tend to consider each one's salary as his or her own. But in happy marriages the couple looks at the money that comes in as *theirs*, not his or hers.

I know a couple where the wife makes much more than the husband. They are happily married and have no power struggles over their financial matters. She doesn't feel superior to him just because she earns more money. As she says, "Who cares? Tomorrow it may be the other way around."

About the closest my mate and I come to an impasse about something is when she says, "Where would you like to eat tonight? O'Charley's? Sweetwaters? Gentleman Jim's? The Casbah?"

My usual response is that wherever she'd like to go, that's where we'll eat. And then she'll respond with, "Would you please pick the restaurant for a change? Just once I'd like to go where you want to eat." That's about as close to an argument as we ever get, thank heavens.

9. Happy Couples Don't Stay Angry at Each Other

Of course, most happy couples don't fight. But over the years, especially in the beginning, when they are adjusting to each other, there may be conflicts here and there. However, happy couples learn not to hold grudges. They storm a bit, perhaps, but then they get it out of their systems, which is much better than holding it inside and nursing it in silence.

Silence is stubborn. The silent treatment does not resolve the conflict; it only intensifies it. The price of silence is too high to pay. It cuts off all communication. If it lasts until bedtime, the unhappy couple goes to bed making sure not to touch each other. If they do accidentally touch, they jerk back as if they had placed their hand on a hot stove.

In Ephesians 4:26, the Bible says not to let the sun go down on your wrath. That is excellent advice. As one happy couple told me, "On those rare occasions when we've had a real knockdown drag-out argument, we make sure that our differences are resolved before we go to bed. Never once has either of us exiled the other to another bedroom. No fight in the world is worth that price. Moving to another bedroom for the night is the first step toward divorce, and can too easily lead to moving out of the house, which is the second and final step."

10. Happy Couples Grow and Mature in Their Relationship

Couples change a great deal throughout the course of their marriage. If they are happy together, that change is usually for the better, and if the change is for the better, then they are happy together. Like the chicken/egg proposition, it's hard to know which comes first.

Let me quickly point out that changes that benefit the marriage are those each individual makes without pressure or suggestion from the other. In other words, each partner still has to accept the other just as he or she is without criticism or finding fault.

It is not a wise idea to go into a marriage believing that the other person has a great many character defects, hoping that those defects can be corrected by marriage. It rarely, if ever, happens. One man I know did that. The woman he married was extremely jealous of everyone. She did not want him to associate with any of his former acquaintances, even including members of his own family, his father and mother, a brother, and a sister. The marriage ended in divorce after a few years. She was unable to change, and the two were completely incompatible.

Of course people do change. Everyone changes, some for better, others for worse. A happy marriage will help the couple change for the better. I hope that has happened or will happen to you.

11. Happy Couples Understand the Importance of Sex

People are often told that sex is not what makes a good marriage. I've often heard that a good marriage depends upon friendship, dignity, respect, commitment, and qualities that remain after passion and sexual abilities die.

That may be true for some, but I do know that if a couple is not sexually compatible, if their sexual enjoyment is not complete, if they are not being fulfilled, then an unhappy marriage and possibly a divorce is almost certain.

As A. P. Herbert said in his book *Holy Deadlock*, "If the bedroom is not right, then every room in the house is wrong." In other words, if there is sexual unhappiness and maladjustment, there can be no complete happiness of any sort. By the same token, if the bedroom is right, then chances are that every other room in the house will be right, too.

Admittedly, sexual love alone won't solve all marital problems, but it will definitely keep them to a minimum and make them more easily solvable. If a woman considers her man to be the world's greatest lover, she's not about to let him escape or file for divorce. Or if she is the ultimate woman sexually to her husband, he isn't going to be looking for another woman, either.

One of the husbands I interviewed told me that his wife was the most beautiful woman he had ever met. This couple was in their early seventies and had just celebrated their golden wedding anniversary the year before. To describe one's wife that way after fifty years of marriage means that he still sees her first and always as a woman. Their love is basically sexual no matter how often or how passionate their lovemaking happens to be.

Now I am not going to turn this section into a sex manual, but I do want to give you a few helpful tips that will be valuable whether or not you're having problems with sex.

Remember that preparation for making love begins in the morning at the breakfast table, so that your spouse can hardly wait to get home from work to make love with you. One of your partner's most basic needs is for you to remain physically attractive; so always try to look your best for one another.

You can also arouse your mate's interest if you call him or her in the middle of the afternoon and say, "Honey, I'm eagerly waiting for you to come home. Please don't be late; I just crave your body." I guarantee you that with a call like that, wild horses couldn't keep someone away from you.

When you do call the office, be sure you've got your spouse on the phone, no one else. Then keep it short, just long enough to let him or her know that you're ready, willing, and waiting. It may be the best news he or she has heard all day.

One husband told me that he and his wife always prepared for sexual intercourse as though it were some sort of festive occasion to be celebrated. They always spent plenty of time in the bathroom bathing together, shaving, powdering, perfuming, and so on. He said that they had a large Japanese-style bath that both of them could use at the same time. "We always soap and rinse each other all over to stimulate our sexual desire," he told me.

Then when they went to bed he said they would massage each other all over with a light and fragrant disappearing body oil. "By the time we finish doing that, nothing could keep us apart," he said. "We've kept our marriage intact and alive for nearly fifty years now by loving each other this way," he said, "and that's a lot more than a great many other couples can say for their marriages."

I would like to give you two final tips that will help turn you from a selfish sexual partner who's interested only in yourself and your self-satisfaction into one whose primary aim is to fulfill the needs and desires of your mate.

1. Make love *with*—not *to*—your partner.
2. After you make love, always show your appreciation by saying "Thank you" to your mate.

12. Happy Couples Make Their Children Happy

To guide, direct, and control your children without effort so they will always do what you know is best for them to do, *make them happy.* When they are happy, they'll be only too glad to do as you desire them to do.

How do you make a child happy? It takes a lot more than money and material possessions. You can start off by telling your children that you love them and then proving that you do by giving them your full and undivided attention.

This is something that every child needs the most of and usually gets the least of—*attention.* As a result, children often feel left out. Lack of attention makes them feel unwanted. You can give them a real sense of being wanted and fulfill their deep need for emotional security when you make a conscious effort to listen to them and to what they want to tell you.

If you have been having disciplinary problems with your children, paying attention to them will go a long way toward solving those problems. I know that for sure—I raised three of my own.

Unfortunately, too many parents make the mistake of not listening attentively to their children. They don't want to be bothered with them or with their problems. But children need and want attention just as much as grownups do, sometimes even more.

Now it doesn't take a lot of extra effort to give your children that extra consideration they need. It just takes time. Ask them to play with you. Don't wait for them to ask you. On many a stormy winter night, when we lived in the north, my youngest son and I used to battle it out in front of the fireplace with a cribbage board. In the summer, you had to get in line to play table tennis in the garage.

Learn to play with your children; pay attention to them— it will improve all your family relationships. Your kids will learn to like you as well as love you. You'll not only be their parents but you'll also become their friends, and that's ever so important. A good game of table tennis in the garage with your teenage son or daughter will do more to reduce the generation gap than all the lectures you can give them in the back bedroom.

Praise is one of the best ways to give your children attention. Children respond to praise just as much as adults do. If you want your children to get better grades in school, then praise them for their efforts. When you do that, you are programming their subconscious minds for successful achievement. If you criticize them for poor grades, those low grades will go even lower, for you are then programming their subconscious minds with negative ideas and failure concepts.

I do know that sometimes you must discipline your children. But good discipline does not include criticism. Discipline should be reasonable and firm, yet kind and friendly.

Parents in unhappy families don't realize this, but in a happy family there is seldom any reason for discipline. People usually discipline themselves in happy families.

So give your children a happy, pleasant atmosphere, encourage their efforts with kind words of praise, work with them, play with them, make them feel they belong by letting them take part in family projects and family decisions, and you'll find that the necessity for discipline seldom exists. Your children will want to do what you ask them to do.

If you really want to enjoy your children and make your home life happier, drop that parent role as often as you can so you can be a friend as well. This approach will bring you wonderful new relationships with them.

Index

Dress for success, 102
Drinking to excess, 10, 12, *See also* Bad habits
  benefits of stopping, 213–14
  breaking habit of, 213–15
Drive, lack of, 10

E

Economic plan, and financial
  success, 58–61
Edison, Thomas Alva, 24, 45
Efficiency, 11
Einstein, Albert, 120
Emotionally-induced illness (EII)
  and allergy, 253–54
  and asthma, 254–55
  and colon problems, 249–50
  and constipation, 252–53
  definition of, 243–44
  deprogramming subconscious
    mind of, 243–56
  and neurodermatitis, 254
  as physical disease, 244–45
  programming subconscious
    mind and, 256–58
  and stomach problems, 249
  stress and, 250–52, 257
  treatment example, 246–47
Emotions, and self-image, 10
Enjoyment, financial success and,
  56–57
Enthusiasm
  and negative self-image, 10
  low self-esteem and, 10
  overcoming fear through,
    192–94
  and promotion, 107–8
  and rapport with top executives,
    107–8
  winners and, 139–40
Entrepreneur, benefits of being an,
  74–75

Examples
  of benefits of attaining goal,
    50–52
  of breaking bad habit, 209–11
  of building credit rating, 59–61
  of building successful business,
    63–65
  of conquering worry, 192–94
  of creative ideas, 126–28
  of creative imagination, 134–36
  of creative thinking, 71
  of customer service, 63–68,
    84–86
  of delegating authority, 162–64
  of developing talents, 41–42
  of EII treatment, 246–47, 251,
    253
  of finding customer's needs,
    79–83
  of goal of excellence, 69–70
  of honest dealing, 87–88
  of importance of remembering
    names, 178–79
  of making people feel important,
    264–66
  of negative programming, 1–2
  of overcoming fears, 29–31
  of perseverance, 24–27
  of playing upon people's fears,
    32–33
  of procrastination, 222–24
  of psychological success, 21–22
  of relaxation in solving
    problems, 123–24
  of self-motivation, 150–52
  of setting goals, 44–45
  of sound economic plan, 58–61
  of sound judgment, 155–57
  of subconscious mind
    susceptibility, 7–8
  of success
    as author and speaker, 134–36
    as auto mechanic, 87–88

in department store business,
63–64
as entrepreneur, 83–86
in plumbing business, 67–68
in real estate, 79–83
in restaurant business, 65
of success in small town, 61–62
of taking responsibility, 144–45
of total listening, 275–76
of visualizing specific goal,
47–48
Executive pitfalls, 108–9, *See also*
Pitfall avoidance
Executives, *See also* Chief
executive officer; Corporate
executive qualities; Executive
pitfalls
benefits of being, 96
essential qualities of, 97–101
knowledge necessary for, 114–18
and knowledge of business, 97,
103–5
looking part of, 102
preparing self for becoming, 104
and relationships with superiors,
106–8

F

Failure, *See also* Failure attitude
abnormal fear and, 205
avoiding fear of, 27–28, 92
deactivating concepts of, 20
definition of, 20–22
don't make excuses for, 105
expectation of, 69–70
fear of, 92, 190
lack of goals and, 38–39
negative self-image and, 9
refusing to accept, 24–27
Failure attitude, 39
benefits of deactivating, 22–23
deprogramming mind of, 23–27

Failure concepts, 20, *See also*
Negative concepts
Failure ideas, 23, *See also* Negative
ideas
Family relationships, *See also*
Happy couples; Successful
marriage
improvement of, 279–95
Fear, *See also* Abnormal fears;
Psychological fears
and breaking smoking habit,
218–19
confronting, 28–31
of criticism, 190, 196
of death, 189, 191
of failure, 27–28, 92
of the future, 14
General George Patton and,
189
getting rid of, 195–99
imaginary, 189–90
of loneliness, 191
of making wrong decisions, 191
of old age, 191
of poverty, 191
psychological, 190–91
of public speaking, 199–203
of rejection, 224
ridding self of, 188–205
ridding subconscious mind of,
189–90
Financial rewards, 23
Financial success
benefits of, 56–58
community service and, 57
economic plan and, 58–61
and freedom, 58
goals and, 38–39
self-achievement psychology
and, 55–73
Freedom, financial success and,
58
Future, fears of the, 14